BULLS, BEARS
& a croupier

First published in 2012 by John Wiley & Sons Australia, Ltd
42 McDougall St, Milton Qld 4064
Office also in Melbourne

Typeset in Bembo 11.5/14 pt

© Matthew Kidman 2012

The moral rights of the author have been asserted

National Library of Australia Cataloguing-in-Publication data:

Author:	Kidman, Matthew, 1968–
Title:	Bulls, bears and a croupier: the insider's guide to profiting from the Australian stockmarket / Matthew Kidman.
ISBN:	9780730377559 (pbk.)
Notes:	Includes index.
Subjects:	Stock exchanges. Bear markets.
Dewey Number:	332.6322

Cover design by Xou Creative

Cover image: © iStockphoto.com/id-work

The McMillan Shakespeare Preliminary Financial Report material on pages 113–115 is included with permission.

Printed in Australia by Ligare Book Printer

10 9 8 7 6 5 4 3

Disclaimer

The material in this publication is of the nature of general comment only, and does not represent professional advice. It is not intended to provide specific guidance for particular circumstances and it should not be relied on as the basis for any decision to take action or not take action on any matter which it covers. Readers should obtain professional advice where appropriate, before making any such decision. To the maximum extent permitted by law, the author and publisher disclaim all responsibility and liability to any person, arising directly or indirectly from any person taking or not taking action based on the information in this publication.

CONTENTS

ABOUT THE AUTHOR

Matthew Kidman worked as a journalist at *The Sydney Morning Herald* covering media, telecommunications and commercial property. In 1997 he was appointed investment editor of the newspaper, with responsibility for all company coverage. He joined funds management outfit Wilson Asset Management in 1998 and over a 13-year period served as an analyst and portfolio manager. In 2003 he was appointed to the role of chief executive officer of the group. Wilson Asset Management specialises in small capitalisation companies and its flagship fund—WAM Capital—over a 12-year period delivered a return of more than 18 per cent per year, compared with the benchmark 8 per cent of the All Ordinaries index. Matthew is also the co-author of two bestselling books: *Masters of the Market* and *Master CEOs*.

ACKNOWLEDGEMENTS

This book was 17 years in the making and many people who contributed along the way deserve thanks. Every successful investor requires the support of a hard-working and productive stockbroking network. I would like to thank Chris Walker, Danny Goldberg, James Gordon, Jonathon Scales, Hugh Robertson, Tony Mitchell, John Zemek, Preston Hamersley, Michael Carmody, Phil Zammit, Jason Bailey, Adam Brandwood, Peter Hollick, Dominic Hoare, Andrew Fincher, Richard Wolff, Adam Weir, David Johns, Danny Dreyfuss, Mark and David Pittman, Peter Argyrides, Tony Bonello, Hamish Nairn and the other brokers who helped along the way. Special thanks to Ben Silluzio and Brett Dawson for their efforts while this book was being written.

In addition, I would like to acknowledge a long list of fellow investors who gave up their time over the years to teach me some tremendous investment lessons. Thanks go to Peter Morgan, David Paradice, Greg Perry, Alex Waislitz, Alan Crozier, David Smith, Karl Siegling, Erik Metanomski, John Abernethy, Mark Hancock, Justin Braitling and Ben Griffiths. Even though he is not a fellow fund manager or broker I would like to pay tribute to Ashley Owen for the research and insights he was able to provide.

As I mentioned in the text, sharemarket investors depend heavily on the people who run the companies they invest in. At

Wilson Asset Management we profited from the efforts of people such as Clive Rabie, Tony Robinson, Glenn Goddard, Jim Minto, Miles Hampton, John Rubino, Greg Shaw, Theo Hnarakis, Martin Ward, Roger Brown and Ron Hancock, to name just a few.

This book would not have been possible without the unquestioning support of the team at Wilson Asset Management. The team was not only fabulous to work with over more than a decade but also supported the concept of the book from the outset. I would like to thank Kate Thorley, Mary Ann Baldock, Mark Tobin, Chris Stott, Matt Haupt and Lilly Johnson. Martin Hickson went above and beyond what was required to help me research many of the facts that I had forgotten over the years. I will miss the company of the whole team and I believe that all are assured of bright futures.

Special thanks must go to Geoff Wilson. Geoff hired me in 1998, based on a hunch that I could make it as an investor. Without this kind of faith I might never have discovered the stimulating world of the sharemarket. Hopefully I was able to repay Geoff over the years for his faith in me. Geoff also deserves praise for providing so much fruitful information for the book and the freely given guidance on a range of subjects over 13 years. As a mentor I could not have asked for more.

I would like to thank Kristen Hammond from John Wiley & Sons for her support from the moment I suggested writing a book about the sharemarket.

Before writing this book I did not know former croupier Peter Proksa. Peter provided a fabulous story willingly and with flair. He trusted me with the information provided and I would like to thank him for being so giving and so colourful. I look forward to hearing about Peter's successes for some time to come.

Finally, I would like to thank my family for allowing me to indulge in my hobby of writing. To my three kids — Bella, Will and Max — I say thanks, and I look forward to spending time with all of you in the coming months. This book would not be possible without my wife, Suzy, who volunteered to edit the book, giving up hours patiently reading and re-reading the manuscript. Suzy is my life-long partner who I have walked hand in hand with for the past 24 years. I long for her company at all times and gain strength from her support. My future is in good hands with Suzy by my side.

INTRODUCTION

A veteran fund manager who took a nine-month sabbatical back in the early 1990s said to me recently that it took him only a few weeks to realise how much he missed the day-to-day cut and thrust of the sharemarket. He said, 'I've never tried heroin but if it's anywhere near as addictive as the sharemarket then it must be a powerful drug'. That same fund manager is now a 30-year veteran of the industry and says that he intends to stay in the game for another 30 years.

The sharemarket is addictive. It is a dynamic beast that presents a raft of new and intriguing opportunities every day as millions of shares in thousands of companies change hands. Human beings from all over the country transact with each other in the belief that they can make money. The market also offers the magnetic grip of competition, with every participant striving to outdo not only the market but everyone else as well.

Despite all of this, the sharemarket has lost its appeal for many people since the onset of the global financial crisis (GFC) in 2008. Despite a nice rally through 2009 and into 2010, most members of the general public have opted out, preferring to take the safe option of putting their money into cash, earning a risk-free yield of around 6 per cent a year. In more recent times this has proven a wise move, with share prices struggling to move higher. We are in a secular bear market that is proving hard to shrug. But as we move into 2012 investors would be advised to prise open their wallets and take a serious look at the sharemarket as it moves towards the next great bull market.

The purpose of this book is to encourage people to start investing in the sharemarket. It is not a prescriptive document that will unveil a secret formula to success—mainly because there is no secret. Books that claim to being anything more than a guide to success should be summarily dismissed. As Italian philosopher Galileo said, 'You cannot teach a man anything, you can only help him find it within himself'. The sharemarket, for the most part, is a kind place that invites anyone who has some excess capital to participate and try their hand at the greatest game on Earth. It does not discriminate based on intelligence, training or style. Just as importantly, it is forgiving, letting individuals make mistakes regularly but still allowing them to eke out an acceptable return if they use some rudimentary working habits. If there is a key to the whole process of investing in the sharemarket it is coming to grips with your own abilities and working within that sphere of talent.

Some time during 2010, due to withering energy and the heavy legacy of experience, I came to the conclusion that, after 13 years, my time as a professional investor was drawing to a close. After the initial shock of the decision subsided, panic set in, with the stark realisation that I needed to work out how I could squeeze out a return from the sharemarket with my own capital that would be sufficient to survive on. The gravy train of fees was coming to a close. Just as ominously, my life of being spoon fed information from a vast channel of research was also nearing an abrupt end. Facing this predicament I needed to formulate a plan to attack the market as if I was the average person on the street—the exact person I had been preaching to for more than a decade. I realised that, as a professional, I had at times been guilty of being dismissive to many mum and dad investors, whom I saw as being overly tentative and nervous about their investments. With my own retirement from the professional ranks looming, I now understood that I should have displayed more empathy. Those retail investors had their life savings on the line, and they had been thrown around like a piece of clothing in a washing machine, experiencing extreme volatility during the tech wreck and later the GFC.

As we swung into 2011, I began to make mental notes about what plan I should put into place. What exactly was the best way to make the sharemarket deliver a return that would keep me off the streets while I wrestled with the possibility of a new career?

In 1997, while working as a business journalist on *The Sydney Morning Herald*, I made the decision to change careers and become a professional sharemarket investor. The only problem was that I had no qualifications. Why would anyone pay me to manage other people's money when I had no track record to speak of and no personal experience? To break into this mysterious field I would have to rely on who I knew, and not what I knew. For three years I had been talking to the best fund managers in the country, discussing the market and individual stocks, and generally forming relationships that would last for many years to come. I snared a job interview at one of the nation's leading investment houses, Perpetual Trustees, and was questioned by its rising star Peter Morgan. The role was for a mining analyst. I had known Morgan for a few years and always found his conversations engaging and his approach to the market quite liberating. I did not get the job but during the interview Morgan asked me if had ever read a book called *One Up On Wall Street*, by US fund manager Peter Lynch. I replied that I hadn't. Morgan said it would be worth my while to go and buy it, declaring that if I was stimulated by the book, like he was, I would love the market and I should keep on searching for a job. With that I went out and bought the book, and over a weekend consumed it from cover to cover. It automatically lit my fires. Surely investing in the sharemarket could not be as easy as Lynch suggested, but if it was, I had to have a piece of it.

The basic premise of Lynch's book was that the average amateur investor could beat the returns being claimed by the professionals on Wall Street. I make no apologies in saying this book is aimed at trying to recapture some of the optimism Lynch espoused way back in 1990.

Fast forward to 2011 and I'm still yet to read a book that laid out how simple sharemarket investing should be. Sure, the American money manager was spinning a yarn for his many readers and the pages were littered with motherhood statements, but at its core *One Up On Wall Street* captured many of the key elements to successful stock picking. After 13 years in the game I am in full agreement with his claims that sharemarket investing, if tackled with the right technique, is one of the easiest games on Earth. There are so many opportunities swirling around every day of the week, that even if you get half of your decisions wrong you still have a genuine chance of generating returns like those of your professional contemporaries. It is imperative that anyone remotely interested in the sharemarket understand that the market doesn't discriminate against any individual and everyone is welcome to join in the game. I can't agree with Lynch that the man on the street can trounce the professionals every time, but I fervently believe that anyone can make a go of the equity game and generate substantial wealth if they are prepared to persist. After spending five years as a journalist, I am also more pragmatic and less serenely optimistic than Lynch, but that is all just a state of mind and you shouldn't let it stop you diving into the market.

> There are so many opportunities swirling around every day of the week, that even if you get half of your decisions wrong you still have a genuine chance of generating returns like those of your professional contemporaries.

At the end of 2005, while preparing to take a few weeks off over Christmas and the new year, I made the decision to stop wasting my spare time reading books about the sharemarket. In a bid to unlock the secret to superior returns, I had possibly read hundreds of books over the years and even co–authored a book of interviews with the best investors in Australia. Ironically I found that, instead of achieving clarity of thought, I was increasingly confused about the right way to attack the market. By 2005 I came to the conclusion that I had to invest in my own way, and copying the likes of Warren Buffett was not the universal remedy to underperforming in the sharemarket. From that point onwards my reading was restricted for the most part to quality fiction, which proved a fabulous way to unclutter my mind and help me think clearly about investing. In fact, in 2008 when the GFC was raging and talk of a second Great

Depression was swelling, I read John Steinbeck's classic *The Grapes of Wrath*. A slow-paced, grinding novel centred on the struggles of a farming family in the United States during the Great Depression, it was as instructive as any investment book I had ever read. The novel showed how severe life had become in the 1930s and talk of a similar environment in 2008 was way off the mark. This gave me the courage to believe the sharemarket would rebound with a spring in its step and not disappear down a dark well. No investment book was prepared to give me such insight.

If you are seriously considering becoming a sharemarket investor I would recommend that you read four and only four books besides this one. The first is Benjamin Graham and David Dodd's *Security Analysis*, which is dry and tough going, but explains the fundamentals of looking for value among stocks in the market. Next I would closely analyse Jim Collins's *Good to Great*, which unlocks the mystery of superior company management, a part of the investing process that professionals just don't seem to have come to grips with. Next I would turn my attention to Trevor Sykes's book *The Bold Riders*, which surgically unpicks the reasons behind some of the greatest corporate collapses in Australia's history. Read this book as a warning that at the end of a bull market the high flyers will not only crash but also disappear into corporate history, and history will repeat itself. Finally, I would read Lynch's *One Up On Wall Street,* to discover that investing doesn't have to be a stuffy profession dominated by pretentious professionals whose decision to enter the money management game has proven far more profitable than their stock picking.

Reading anything more about how others invest will only serve to confuse most people. Instead, sharemarket participants should get on with the job of seeking out information that might actually help them pick winners, such as newspapers, magazines, company annual reports and virtually anything that is related to the all-pervading sharemarket. The sharemarket and stock picking may be measured in numbers, but in its purest form it is about ideas, and you should be ravenous in your consumption of information to generate those profitable ideas. Finally, I would vehemently urge readers to consume any material written on the history of sharemarkets—it can be highly instructive.

This may not be a great way to encourage you to read on. However, I would encourage anyone who is interested in joining the sharemarket game to do so, because it has the unique ability to deliver a rare combination of wealth and enjoyment. I have deliberately structured this book to help people not so much to win but to avoid failure. An early disappointment may not only lose you money but also destroy your confidence into the future. As stated earlier, this book is not a guide to success. It is critical that you lay the correct foundations before you even start and, when you are ready to push the go button, follow a methodical pattern that serves you best. While you work your way through the book I would urge you to keep in mind the prologue and the story of our Melbourne-based croupier. His journey captures the essence of the struggle and inevitable peril an individual can experience when rolling the dice on the market.

PROLOGUE:
THE CROUPIER'S STORY

It was 1999 and the Australian sharemarket, inspired by the internet technology explosion, had entered its sixth year of a surging bull market. Its big brother, the US stockmarket, was leading the charge as it careered into the seventeenth year of the greatest bull run in history. The tech-laden Nasdaq had risen 485 per cent from 1991 to 1998 and was on its way to posting an 85.6 per cent gain in 1999, its largest 12-month appreciation in history. The boom that had begun with the emergence of the personal computer in the 1980s had spread like a virus from the tech heads in Silicon Valley to the insatiably greedy financial players on Wall Street. With the internet adding the icing on the technology cake, stockbrokers, corporate bankers and professional investors made more money from investing, staging (participating in an initial public offering and then selling the shares almost immediately) and flogging (selling aggressively) fly-by-night companies, than at any other time since the Roaring 1920s. The last people on board the financial *Titanic* were the mums and dads. For a brief period the sharemarket, and in particular the tech and tech-related stocks, were like ATMs: put your prospectus application into the mail and a multiple of funds were spat back at you. Australian mums and dads had been slow to embark, but by 1999 the internet miracle had travelled to our shores and there was no time to waste.

Peter Proksa had never bought a share in his life. His parents, migrants from Croatia and the Ukraine, had come to Melbourne in search of a simpler life. They made it clear that they despised the sharemarket, believing it was a mug's game that always ended in tears. A young Proksa had heeded their advice and gone to university, studying to be a health inspector, attempting to carve out a respectable, low-risk lifestyle. However, his idea of a sedentary occupation was spoiled by the practical need to inspect restaurants throughout the city of Melbourne. He didn't like what he saw. Behind the facade of the city restaurant scene were some of the most shocking health and hygiene problems one could possibly imagine, and he faced a life of wading knee deep in it.

Desperate to jump ship, Proksa quit his first vocation and before long found himself working in a gaming venue with responsibility for the poker machines. One thing led to another and it wasn't long before he had landed a job at the biggest game in town — working as a croupier at Crown Casino. This was a vast improvement on his original profession and he quickly established himself as a mainstay on the floors. He had no desire to gamble, but loved the hive of activity at Crown, which symbolised the re-emergence of Melbourne's vibrant economy after the severe recession of the early 1990s. He was promoted to the high rollers room where he saw players from around the globe place bets of up to $300 000 for each hand of baccarat. He watched with amazement as some of the clientele blew on their cards in the belief it would bring them good luck and deliver a second fortune in their lives. This kind of gambling seemed like nothing more than hocus-pocus to the level-headed croupier. Life couldn't have been better—he had a young family and a job that not only did he enjoy but had also provided the source of a nest-egg his parents had dreamed of. He also was stimulated by the variety of people he met over the gaming tables.

Three years into the job, Proksa's abstinence from punting was being severely tested. The tech boom had snaked its way through the casino doors and conversations across the blackjack table were being hijacked by tales of enormous wins on the sharemarket. No matter where he turned, whether to the punters across the table, his fellow croupiers, the doormen or the taxi drivers who took him home at all hours of the morning, Proksa was being bombarded with stock tips. Casinos are places of temptation at the best of times and with his bank balance building slowly from savings over the years, it was becoming too hard to resist. People all around him were getting wealthy without doing anything but ringing their broker and placing the order to buy whatever sounded good on the day.

The latest tip from a regular client was a little known company called Telco Australia. Proksa's research consisted of the tip and the fact the company was in the hot spot—telecommunications and technology. He capitulated and decided to roll the dice, ploughing his life savings of $150 000 into the minnow of a company at 20 cents a share. The stock started to move higher and within months it had doubled in price. The hook was now well and truly taken. Proksa started to look around for similar companies that would deliver a guaranteed quick return, and it wasn't long before he was being told about names that had the right mix of telecommunications and the internet, such as Davnet and Voicenet. They were all thumping along and Proksa, who had worked for close to four years to accumulate $150 000, had managed to multiply his net worth in just a matter of months. Telco Australia pushed higher, hitting 60 cents, a 200 per cent return on the initial investment. As we entered the new millennium Proksa could claim that he was rich—worth close to half a million dollars.

Without warning or catalyst the Nasdaq slumped, giving up close to 10 per cent in just one day in April 2000. As the tech boom had grown mature, extreme volatility wasn't unusual, and the mums and dads around the globe who had enjoyed the cruise had no inkling that the ship was about to sink. While it had taken the Australian retail investing market a long time to catch onto the boom, their professional colleagues were anything but slow coaches when it came to jumping off at the nearest port. Companies with fancy business plans but no profits fell to lows that didn't seem possible. Investors who had been liberal with their capital for the past five years, closed up shop, and many tech companies, which had built large cost bases on the promise of future revenue, were rapidly forced to wind back operations or, in some cases, fold.

Proksa went into shock. The stocks he had cheered on from the floors of the casino with his fellow punters started to melt like ice cream in the Sahara Desert. His flagship play, Telco Australia, sank relentlessly, hitting 1 cent a share before eventually disappearing altogether a few years later. Davnet and Voicenet experienced similar dramatic declines. The speed of the fall had caught many experienced investors off guard—let alone a novice like Proksa. In total his losses amounted to $200 000, an amount inflated by a decision in 2001 to borrow extra funds to save his vanishing portfolio. Not wanting to believe the boom was finished he kept buying shares as they fell, hoping to average down and make a killing when things bounced back. By the end of 2001 it became obvious that no bounce was coming—a realisation that hit late and hard. He vowed never to play the sharemarket again under any circumstances. His private life was also changing: he separated from his wife and was forced to divvy up his only remaining asset—the family home.

Four years passed as Proksa worked diligently to rebuild his lost fortune and care for his two kids, who had moved in with him. While the job of a croupier can be a fruitful occupation, it was no easy path to recoup his lost fortune of $200 000. He relied heavily on the booty from the house sale. As the memories of the demise of the tech sector faded, the Australian sharemarket forged higher as low inflation, rocketing corporate earnings and an emerging resources boom took hold. With the market's revival came the re-emergence of the tips across the casino gaming tables. Still gullible about new technologies, Proksa started to listen to the chatter about smart electricity meter company Intermoco. Time had healed his wounds and his pledge to abstain from the market was set aside as he decided to roll the dice again, parlaying his share of the house sale into the company, buying $150 000 worth of stock at 5 cents a share. At the same time, talk of a mining boom had been carried across the Yarra River and into Crown Casino by the professional punters on Collins Street. Proksa, with his last $15 000, plunged into Flinders Diamonds.

As the boom unfolded, the croupier spent most of his time playing the sharemarket and counting his winnings. Within two years he was back bigger than ever, amassing a fortune of $700 000, with Flinders the star of the portfolio, multiplying in value by 10 times. Even though he was still sitting on paper profits, he was now in a position to seriously consider giving up his day job to concentrate on the real game — investing in the sharemarket.

The Australian sharemarket, in lock-step with the United States, hit a peak in November 2007. Unlike the tech boom, the overall market drifted lower for two months before a wave of selling struck in the first half of January 2008, while most investors relaxed over the summer holidays, blissfully unaware. In the space of just 12 days in January, the market had sunk a soul-destroying 21 per cent — the boom was over once again. Keen not to let go of his new fortune, Proksa chased Intermoco down as it slumped towards 1 cent on the back of a change of state government legislation that undermined its business model. The theory of averaging down on his original cost price, by continually buying stock on the way down, proved to be foolhardy. After a short, sharp bounce in March 2008, the market resumed its decline, accelerating into the fateful GFC that engulfed global markets in August and September 2008. By the time the Australian market had found a bottom after 16 months of tumbling, 54 per cent had been sliced off the value of the overall market — the second largest decline in the nation's history. Proksa was not spared. His $700 000 fortune had withered and when the dust had settled it was worth a paltry $20 000. His total loss in Intermoco alone, which he eventually sold at 1 cent a share, was a confidence-sapping $250 000. Today Intermoco trades at just 0.003 of a cent.

Time had healed his wounds and his pledge to abstain from the market was set aside as he decided to roll the dice again.

With his sharemarket fortune lost for a second time, the capital from his family home incinerated and two children to care for, Proksa had to make some hard and fast decisions. As for the vast majority of the sharemarket participants, his confidence was decimated, and very few players were suggesting it was time to head back into the market in such uncertain times. Should he do the right thing and show some responsibility by pulling in his horns, as he had attempted to do following the tech wreck? It was a torturous decision, but

Proksa could not help himself. Following weeks of reflection he convinced himself that his white-knuckle ride had taught him some profound, although expensive, lessons about playing the sharemarket. Not for the first time, he decided to give it one more shot. He took all of his remaining capital, a trifling $20 000, and placed it into the electrifying but exceedingly risky biotech sector, believing it provided the best possible leverage to get him out of the deep pit he had dug for himself. He was on a financial precipice and he was heading back into the war zone that had inflicted near fatal wounds twice already.

He allocated his modest capital to three securities, all trading at 1 cent or less. Proksa reasoned that the mistake he had previously made was buying companies whose share prices traded at much higher levels, allowing much greater falls. In his mind a company trading at a fraction of a cent could only fall so far, but if it went up, the percentage gains would be gargantuan. He was infatuated with the concept of leverage that low-priced shares offered an investor and was convinced he had struck the perfect formula for playing the sharemarket despite having taken such a roller-coaster ride in previous years.

The largest of his three new investments was a $15 000 foray into the listed options of biotech company Prima Biomed. The options had been left for dead, trading at 0.001 of a cent, the lowest possible price for a listed security. Proksa closed his eyes and piled in, buying around 6 million options at close to an average at 0.002 of a cent. Prima Biomed had been through the ringer during the GFC, rendered totally friendless by shell-shocked investors. Its operations were in disarray and the board had experienced a major upheaval. In late 2007, a relative unknown, Martin Rogers, was appointed to the board as executive director in a desperate bid to stave off collapse. At the time Prima's shares were trading between 2 cents and 3 cents and the options had nearly disappeared, with hardly a soul the least bit interested. Rogers had little if any experience in the biotech industry, spending most of his short career promoting mining stocks in the boom that had started back in 2003, before hitting a hurdle with the GFC in 2008. Rogers took the approach that he needed to start talking, and quickly, to convince shareholders, his board and a future management team that Prima had a bright future. Just as he was starting to get some confidence in 2008, the GFC unfolded, crushing stocks across the exchange, with special attention given to the weak such as Prima. The stock slumped to 1 cent per share and the options started trading at 0.001 cents.

Proksa was lured to the stock because of its penny-dreadful nature and the hint that its product to treat ovarian cancer might just be approved by the authorities one day. (Penny dreadfuls are shares in a company that have dropped to an extremely low level and are struggling to rise again.) The fact that the company had minimal cash on its balance sheet, virtually no revenue and was burning just under $2 million a year did not sit front and centre in Proksa's mind. After taking the plunge and hoovering up the options in late 2008, he decided to give the company a call, first talking to the company secretary before receiving a call from Rogers the next day. Proksa remembers the conversation clearly, and he put the phone down believing the young entrepreneur would somehow pull a rabbit out of the hat. At around this time Rogers was working overtime trying to avert disaster, and he was eventually forced to accept high cost funding. The outfit lent Prima debt at incredibly high interest rates. As part of the deal the lender also received shares in Prima at a significant discount to the prevailing price, allowing the lender to trade them out at a nice profit. This kept a lid on the share price and Rogers new that it was not sustainable. He needed to find a way forward or face oblivion.

The grim situation was upgraded to hopeless by the beginning of 2009, as markets plummeted to new lows. Just as things looked perilous, some good fortune appeared. During March 2009, with investor pessimism at its climax, the market started to rise, notching a gain of 15 per cent in just two months to the disbelief of most punters. Without waiting for an invitation, Prima shares joined the party. It was as though someone had put the shares in a sling shot and fired away, with the company stock hitting 5 cents, a gain of 400 per cent from its lows. Following close behind were the options that Proksa had bought, rising from his average price of 0.002 cents. His gain was closer to 2500 per cent and his original investment of $15 000 had turned into $360 000. By the end of 2009, as investor confidence stormed back into the market, Prima shares and options rose another three times to 15 cents. Within the space of just 18 months Proksa had gone from a Struggle Street croupier down to his last few thousand dollars to a millionaire.

Learning from his earlier mistakes, Proksa decided to cash in some of his enormous profits. He started to sell Prima options as they were heading higher. In fact he offloaded 50 per cent of what he owned, pocketing close to $1 million profit as the ordinary shares and the options rallied towards 30 cent. He made the conscious decision to keep half his holding, because he still believed in the Prima story, but he redeployed the other half of his winnings into a diversified range of other stocks. For the first time in more than a decade Proksa had deliberately taken steps to preserve some of his capital rather than keep it at risk.

As best as he can calculate, Proksa believes his original $15 000 investment in Prima has harvested close to $2 million. The proceeds from the half that he sold have been redistributed into a range of other stocks that were trading at 1 cent or below at the time of the purchase. He has enjoyed significant success with some of these as well, and his wealth continues to increase. Proksa no longer needs to work as a croupier at Crown, having made enough money to give up his day job and become a home dad to his three kids. Even though he still lives in the modest western suburbs of Melbourne, he has taken his children on several overseas trips, staying at five star hotels to celebrate his good fortune. His life has turned full circle, and he can lay claim to being a multimillionaire who doesn't need a regular job any more.

In 2011 Rogers continues to work hard for Prima, revamping the management, reconstructing the board and introducing new shareholders to the register that understand biotechs, including several large US-based funds. He has also mended the balance sheet and the company has sufficient funds to survive until it hopefully gains approval for its ovarian cancer treatment. The days of borrowing money from loan sharks are well and truly over for Prima. Proksa, who now has more than $1 million at risk in Prima, is confident that the company will list on the Nasdaq and then snare the all important regulatory approvals for its cancer drug.

After a long and painful journey, Proksa has also worked out how he would like to invest into the future. He has taken the time to understand his own personality and has mentally drafted a list of guidelines that he has diligently stuck by in recent times. These guidelines are:

- He will only buy stocks that are trading at 1 cent or below, believing they can only decline a small amount, but that they have the ability to rise multiple times if things turn out for the better.
- He deliberately tries to identify stocks that have a product, whether it is a cancer treatment like Prima, or an ore deposit in the case of a mining company.
- He no longer puts all his eggs in one basket, preferring to own a portfolio of around 10 shares or options at any one time, in the belief that only two have to be winners for him to enjoy significant gains. The rest can all fall to zero, as long as he has two stocks that rise from the ashes and post significant gains.
- These days, with more capital at stake, his risk tolerance has fallen, and if a stock rises he will start to sell his shares until he has recouped his original investment. He then lets the rest of the investment run, knowing he can't lose.
- If you can believe it, he is even wary of the next downturn in the market. As we sit here in the middle of 2011, he is intending to cash up, waiting for the day the market falls, rather than having his heart torn out with another collapse. He says 'the only thing that can beat me these days is a meltdown like 2008'.
- From a research point of view, Proksa constantly calls on companies to chat about prospects with the managing director or another senior executive. He is never shy, and loves to hear what management has planned and how they might deliver the next 1000 per cent winner for investors.
- In addition, he has strung together a group of like-minded investors that he talks to every day, sharing ideas and chewing the fat. He also blogs, but tries to avoid spruiking his stories, saying he doesn't like rampers—people who publicly promote the shares they own to encourage others to buy in.

The rest of us can learn many lessons from Peter Proksa. There is no doubting he is his own man, sporting foot-long dreadlocks and bright yellow sandshoes. He has always done things his own special way, but in recent times he has realised that his technique needs guidelines and boundaries to protect his assets from a third meltdown. He has no intentions of returning to the baccarat tables at Crown. Proksa has been on a ride that has almost destroyed him financially, only to end up on top of the heap again with a broad smile on his face.

I do not advocate that anyone invest in such risky stocks as Proksa; however, the lessons he has learned, especially after attaining wealth, are worth taking note of. His diversification, his contact with companies, his willingness to understand himself and his creation of a network of fellow investors are crucial factors that will no doubt hold him in good stead in the years to come. While the sharemarket does not offer any guarantees he no longer invests to fail. Instead, after more than his fair share of good fortune, he has formulated an approach that gives him a very good chance of winning on the sharemarket.

As you read the rest of this book it is very important that you keep Proksa's investment journey fresh in your memory to give you a real life example of why people can fail and why people can succeed when it comes to investing in shares.

Part I
The wonderful sharemarket

Australian retail investors have fallen out of love with the sharemarket since the energy-sapping GFC-inspired collapse of 2008. Seemingly, only the brave have come out of their protective shells to try their hand at the great game. This first section of the book is dedicated to reminding people why they should consider the sharemarket, especially when no-one is talking about it.

Chapter 1

The pitch

Many people say they don't like the sharemarket. In 2002 I was pitching our funds management services to one of Australia's wealthiest individuals, who I had mistakenly believed was interested in allocating part of his vast wealth towards us, when he blurted out that he didn't understand shares. His logic was that shares weren't tangible. He preferred property any day of the week because he could see it, touch it and, above all, he could use it as security to borrow more money from his banks.

He went on to explain how he thought shares were risky and volatile, played by people who punt the market during the day, the casino at night and horse races on the weekend: 'It's not an investment, it is a gamble!' He rounded out the discussion by declaring that all stockbrokers were confidence men—not bad coming from a guy who had earned his first fortune selling cars.

At the time I wanted to take on the challenge and twist this guy's arm until he conceded the sharemarket was a worthwhile investment, but I refrained. These days I think it is fantastic that there is still a squadron of people out there yet to discover the wonderland that is the sharemarket. This leaves more for the people who do want to participate, who can see the benefits of playing the game every day.

In reality it is virtually impossible to convince the doubting Thomases of the sharemarket's merits. However, I have learned from many other discussions over the years that there is also a large group of people out there who would like to be in the market but for some reason or another have not taken the leap: some people have never had the confidence to get started; others just don't have the excess money to start with; and then there are those who think it is a mystery they would enjoy solving, but just don't know where to begin. These are all reasonable excuses, but they are not insurmountable.

Let's get rid of the negatives and focus on the positives.

The easiest game on earth

The consensus view among professional investors is that they operate in a highly competitive and tough industry; that as an individual, you must be careful because there are landmines buried around every corner, waiting to rip an arm or leg off if you take a wrong step—a view trumpeted every day across all forms of media since the GFC stamped itself into the history books back in 2008. The reality, though, is completely different. There might be some hidden landmines, but the fact is, if approached the right way, the sharemarket is one of the easiest games on earth. You can afford to step on the odd landmine, feel mortally wounded and still have a genuine chance of finishing on top of the pile. This is particularly so for an individual investor, who is not shackled by the mandate restrictions that institutional investors regularly complain about. Peter Proksa believes he needs only two of his high-risk investments to work for him to live the life of a millionaire.

So why is the market so easy? The first reality is that markets go up. On average the US and Australian sharemarkets have risen in value in seven out of every ten years, dating back over more than the last 100 years (see figure 1.1). Sharemarket historian Ashley Owen has calculated that, over 1200 separate 10-year periods, the Australian sharemarket has yet to deliver a negative absolute return.

Figure 1.1: Australian sharemarket performance 1883–2010: up seven out of 10 years

<-30	-30 to -20	-20 to -10	-10 to 0	0 to 10	10 to 20	20 to -30	30 to -40	>-40
					2007			
					2003			
					2001			
					1999			
					1998			
					1997			
					1996			
					1989			
					1988			
					1977			
					1969			
					1961			
					1958			
					1957			
					1955			
					1954			
					1953			
					1947			
					1946			
				2000	1945			
				1976	1942			
				1966	1936			
				1964	1935			
				1962	1931			
				1956	1928			
				1949	1927			
				1948	1926			
			2010	1944	1925			
			2002	1943	1924			
			1994	1940	1923			
			1992	1939	1921	2006		
			1987	1937	1919	2005		
			1984	1920	1917	2004		
			1971	1918	1914	1995		
			1965	1913	1911	1978		
			1960	1912	1909	1963		
			1951	1910	1908	1934		
			1941	1907	1906	1933		1993
			1938	1904	1905	1932		1986
		1990	1929	1897	1902	1922	2009	1985
		1882	1916	1896	1900	1903	1991	1983
		1981	1915	1892	1899	1895	1979	1980
	1974	1970	1901	1890	1898	1888	1972	1975
	1973	1952	1893	1886	1894	1887	1968	1967
2008	1930	1891	1889	1884	1885	1883	1950	1959

Total market returns (%)

Source: IRESS

What does this mean exactly? If you measure from January 1911 to January 1921 and then February 1911 to February 1921 and so on, you would get more than 1200 ten-year periods to measure over the last century. A dollar invested at the beginning of any of these 1200 periods would have still been worth at least a dollar 10 years later, not including dividends. That is a major comfort for any Australian investor. There is no guarantee that this will be the case in the future, but it is strong evidence that things won't go too wrong over a 10-year period. Critically, though, a lot of pain can be avoided if you can enter the market when it looks cheap and not after a stellar multi-year upward move. It will be intriguing to observe if the historical 100 per cent strike rate continues for people who bought shares in the Australian market in November 2007. Since that month, the bears have been in charge of the market and they will be doing their utmost to create history and deliver the first decade-long negative return. At this point in time I am willing to bet against them. The US market has had several periods of negative 10-year returns, but at the same time it has enjoyed much longer periods of prosperity.

> Critically, though, a lot of pain can be avoided if you can enter the market when it looks cheap and not after a stellar multi-year upward move.

Equally, I would not like to dispel the myth of the importance of market timing, but with the local sharemarket peaking in late 2007 we may well have avoided the worst time to start investing. If you can make that leap of faith and believe the bulls can recapture the high ground then you are on your way to realising the spoils that are potentially on offer in the sharemarket.

On average, over the last 127 years the sharemarket has delivered an annual return of approximately 10.5 per cent (when capital gains and dividends are taken into account). This is a real return of between 7 and 8 per cent, taking into account a long term inflation rate of about 3 per cent. To put it another way, if you had invested $100 000 and reinvested all your gains into the market, your money would have grown to $271 408.09 over 10 years and $736 623.49 over 20 years. If you got started in the investment game early, then after 40 years your total would be slightly more than $5.4 million — not a bad retirement fund. These figures assume that you only stay level with the market, but if you managed to do 2 per cent better than the market each year and reinvested all your winnings back into the market then your $100 000 would turn into $324 732.10 over 10 years, and more than $12.10 million over 40 years.

Equity reflects many things, but primarily it measures human endeavour. The majority of people go to work all over the world striving to advance themselves, do their jobs more efficiently and generally improve their standard of living. This overall attitude to life and work feeds into equity prices of companies listed on stock exchanges around the globe, as productivity manages to gradually creep higher as time passes. Shares acutely reflect the effort of humans and their ability to continually become more productive. While there are ups and downs over time, as a whole, people have proven remarkably resilient and resourceful. When you think of the sharemarket in this way, as representing the value of human endeavour, it seems short-sighted to claim that it is a risky adventure that needs to be handled with care by seasoned professionals.

Don't leave your common sense at home

That said, the sharemarket, like every other part of life, has the ability to singe your fingers if you forget to bring your common sense and judgement to the game. For example, if a market has been going higher for five years straight, clocking up 20 per cent gains each year, you should tread warily. The sharemarket has a great ability to mean revert. In other words, following those five bullish years, market returns will slip back to the market's long-term average of 10.5 per cent returns per year—which is another way of saying one or more negative years could follow. We will examine the behaviour of overall markets in the final section of the book but, rest assured, taking out a large margin loan and throwing it at the sharemarket following a series of stellar years is a sure way to incur serious financial injury. I do not advocate investors take out margin loans to buy shares at any time, but I cannot state strongly enough my opposition to leveraging when the bull has been parading in the corral for some time.

Conversely, retail investors who have become gun shy since the mauling of the GFC should not turn their backs on what is unfolding. Once the bear goes back into hibernation, there will be a multi-year rally that will deliver enormous returns. You can never predict the exact moment a market turns, because you will only be able to declare it in hindsight, but it is crucial that you start your research when events look hopeless and totally unattractive. Events will turn — they always have.

As easy as kissing

Once you accept that the sharemarket does go up over time and delivers real returns to investors, you can then start to delve into shares and discover why the market is set up for most people to win. Some investors want a peaceful life and so should not concern themselves with trying to pick winners and losers. The better option for these people is to choose the lowest cost managed fund that has a portfolio representing the market. They can then just sit back and collect the 10.5 per cent returns a year.

For those of us who think they have the ability and the risk appetite to pick stocks (shares) the game is completely different. The key is to do some homework on shares that you think are winners and then place a series of bets. Don't throw all your money into one or two stocks and hope they go up like Peter Proksa did in his first decade of investing. Rather, look at investing in 10 or maybe 12 firms across a variety of companies operating in various parts of the economy rather than choosing one concentrated bet. If you have a reasonable amount of spare capital you should think about spreading it further, buying 20 to 25 stocks. Sure, this will cap your potential upside, but it allows you to be wrong regularly, and still have a genuine chance of generating great returns. Buying shares in more companies also takes out a lot of risk that goes with putting all your money on red instead of having the luxury of some of your money on red and some on black at the same time. At Wilson Asset Management, our best estimate was that we got about 50 per cent of our investment decisions right, still managing to get an annual return of more than 20 per cent over 13 years. If you can regularly pick six winners out of ten, you are running with the best in the world, including Buffett. You are a superstar! Is there another profession in the world where you are allowed to get so many things wrong? If you are an engineer and your design is wrong, a building or bridge might collapse. If you are a surgeon and you get half your decisions wrong, people may die. A lawyer who delivers the wrong advice to his clients half the time will be out of business in quick time.

Everyone gets it wrong

Perhaps it is the fact that everyone gets at least one or more investment decisions wrong that spooks people into abstinence. They watch their first investment plummet and, like rabbits frozen in the headlights, just sit and gaze wondering what went wrong. It put Peter Proksa on the sidelines for more than three years. Alternatively, virgin investors see the prices of shares they have not bought move higher and higher, and become agitated that they were not on board the rocket ship. As my former colleague Geoff Wilson liked to say, 'You can't kiss all the pretty girls'.

The key to getting it wrong is admitting you are wrong and making sure you don't hang onto stocks that are heading down over extended periods. Cut your losses and move on. There are more than 2000 companies listed on the Australian Securities Exchange (ASX) and there are thousands more on foreign exchanges, so it's not like you are struggling for choice. At Wilson Asset Management we operated with a trading stop loss rule, which meant that if a stock fell 10 per cent or more we would sell it. This did not close the door on the company, but it meant we needed to sell, walk away and then reassess when and if there was a reason to look at the stock at another time. On the other side of the coin, let your winners run, until they either hit your valuation or if the facts change to alter your view. For now, though, I will just try to sell you on the market.

It is so much better than horse racing

Recently I asked Geoff Wilson why he liked the sharemarket so much. Surprisingly, even though I had known and worked with

Geoff for 17 years, he gave me an answer that I had never heard before, and believe me I heard many of his stories multiple times. This was a thoughtful answer and revealed why someone like him, who loves to place a bet, would be so attracted to the market.

Geoff had always had a weakness for horseracing. Horseracing, like other forms of games of chance, is an industry where most of the punters lose their money to the industry body. For some reason this does not stop most of them from making further bets. In contrast, the sharemarket is set up entirely differently, and it works strongly in favour of the people placing the bets. Geoff said to me, 'What I like about the sharemarket is that you can put a bet on at the start of the race. If your share is going well then you can double your bet. If things are not working out, you remove your bet before the race has ended. It's like you get so many chances to revise your bet before the final outcome is known. You are not locked in from the outset like you are at the horseraces'. Or as sharemarket analysts and investors like to say these days, investing in the market should not be binary, like a horserace, where you are either right or wrong from the outset of the race.

In reality you can expand on Geoff's thoughts. An investor can actually back a series of horses in the one race and, as the race goes on, he can increase his bet on a horse running well and remove all the other bets. The flexibility is quite amazing.

The market can take you around the world

Unlike any other business I can think of, the sharemarket has the wonderful ability to take you to multiple destinations in the economy and to any place on the globe. For most people, investing in or buying a business is a commitment to one part of the economy. For example, if you buy a restaurant in downtown Melbourne, you are basically stuck in that business until you are able to sell it. You ride the ups and downs of the city economy and have to face any competition that might turn up three doors down. If you decide to invest your money in a rental property on the Gold Coast, you are permanently attached to the ups and downs of the beach strip in south-east Queensland. This could be a profitable decision if the property market prospers, but it could be a lobster pot if the market turns down and liquidity dries up—a lobster pot is easy to get into but impossible to escape from.

The magic of the sharemarket is that you can go anywhere you want. In one week I can be in Kalgoorlie digging for gold, selling expensive handbags in Hong Kong, stocking milk on supermarket shelves in Townsville, providing insurance to a company in fast-growing China or building a residential property in Adelaide. The companies are cut into little bits called shares and even if you haven't got a large amount of ready cash, you can still jump on board a company that may be doing well somewhere in the economy. The opportunities are endless and you have maximum flexibility. The value of this advantage is almost immeasurable.

During recent years the place to be has been in the fast-growing mining industry. The returns, especially those of the smaller listed companies, have been astounding. But if you are worried that China's economic miracle might take a breather and demand for Australian resources will therefore stall, you can opt out and sell your mining shares. You might decide to go back to cash or, if you believe that technology services shares or stocks exposed to a recovering US economy have a better short- to medium-term outlook, you can move into those areas as well. No other investment class can give you the flexibility to travel the world trying to work out what looks promising and what looks depressing.

The sharemarket is clean

Compared with other asset classes the sharemarket is clean. You call a broker or place an order online and buy shares in a company. A small amount of commission is paid to the broker for buying the shares for you. Money is then deducted from your designated account and you are electronically allocated your shares. In a short space of time you will receive a statement from the company's share registry showing how many shares you have bought in the company. From that point onwards you wait and see what happens. If you have picked the right company, you receive dividends every six months and the share price starts to rise. There are no maintenance costs, no tenants to look after and very little tax to pay until after you sell the stock. The return you receive from the company is not diluted by the multitude of add-on costs that are associated with owning property. And if the investment does not turn out well, then you can sell it, as long as you have taken care to calculate the liquidity of the stock.

Liquidity

The sharemarket is always open. From 10 am to 4 pm, Monday to Friday, the market is open to all its participants to trade. The prices are printed for everyone to see, with all the bids on one side of the screen and the offers on the other. Depending on the size of the company you should be able to sell your shares or buy more. This is what market participants call liquidity, and it is a tremendous advantage the sharemarket has over most other asset classes. You don't have to wait months to offload the asset, go through a marketing campaign or pay large amounts of stamp duty. If you need money for another part of your life, then you can sell your shares, or some of your shares, that day and the money will be in your account within three days. The only cost is a small brokerage fee on the way out.

When you are buying, you don't have to wait years for the only house you like in the street to come up for sale. If you want to buy a certain stock that you like, then you can buy it then and there. If it is too expensive, then you go to the next company you fancy and, if the price is right, you tell your broker to buy. As a mum and dad investor a lack of liquidity should never be too much of a problem—you should always be able to sell small parcels of shares compared with the millions a professional fund manager might own. However, if you like to buy shares in companies that are smaller and have fewer shares on issue you will need to gauge carefully how many shares have traded in the company in recent history. If the stock trades in the market only every fourth day, or as brokers like to say, by appointment, then you may not want to take too big a position (buy a large number of shares) just in case you end up in your own lobster pot.

Compounding returns

The argument most sharemarket evangelists like to put forward as the clincher to playing the market is the joys of compounding returns. This means that if you buy shares in a company and you stick with that company for an extended period you can achieve enormous returns. For example, if you bought $1000 worth of shares in a bank and it delivered a total return, made up of capital appreciation and dividends, of 15 per cent per year for 10 years, your initial investment would turn into $4045.55. That is a total return of 304.55 per cent. The example assumes that you hold the shares for the whole period and you reinvest your dividends into the stock, rather than take the cash.

For certain investment vehicles, such as superannuation funds, the returns are even higher when you take into account the benefits of franking credits. Superannuation funds in Australia generally only pay 15 per cent tax, while the companies they have invested in pay 30 per cent tax. This means that each dividend, whether accepted in cash or reinvested, will have that 30 per cent tax credit attached to it. As a result, the superannuation fund will get a tax refund.

While there is little doubt about the miracle of compounding, I am not a major fan of the concept. It requires one of two things to take place. First, the riches of compounding normally rely heavily on the existence of a bull market, which is fine most of the time, but is foolhardy when the market is grinding its way through a protracted bear market, as we have experienced in recent times. Second, you must have a knack of foreseeing the long-term future of specific companies. As for perfect line of sight of a company's long-term future, that is a giant leap of faith. As discussed above, the market does go up over time, but this is no guarantee that an individual stock will be invited to the party.

If, however, you do enjoy a major long-term compounding return then watch the miracle unfold.

Shares are not the be all and end all

So far in this chapter I have given you the pitch for why shares are a superior asset class to invest in. The reality is that we can put forth an argument for any asset class. In his book *One Up On Wall Street* Peter Lynch recommends that individuals should always try to buy their own home before investing in the sharemarket. I couldn't agree more with this argument. Everyone needs somewhere to live, and if you have a family, the desire to have the stability of owning the property rather than renting it escalates. In addition, a bank will normally lend you the lion's share of the property's purchase price and won't send you a margin call letter saying they will sell the property by 11 am tomorrow if you do not pump some funds into your account immediately. Finally, in Australia any capital gains on your principal place of residence are tax-free. That makes your home a compelling place to start building your wealth. Once the home has been bought and there is a little spare cash, the sharemarket must be the first place you think about heading.

Chapter 2

The gun investor

The last time I checked no Australian university offered a degree in sharemarket investing. Schoolkids who shoot the lights out in their final year exams might want to be professional investors, but they have to line up with everyone else because there simply isn't a beaten path to managing other people's money in the sharemarket. Some established investors have studied accounting or mathematics, others engineering, some medicine, and then there will be people like me, who studied economics and law. I have found over the years that no single tertiary discipline gives an individual an edge over another when it comes to making money out of shares. Peter Proksa studied to become a health inspector before eventually finding his way to becoming a full-time investor and millionaire. In fact I have found many fantastic investors do not have a tertiary education at all. Without a recognised formal filtering process, it is not easy to identify the innate qualities that determine whether you will be a gun investor or a chump.

There are certain personality traits that will serve a sharemarket investor well. Most people will naturally have some of these qualities, while others will have to garner them through real-life experiences. Rarely, if at all, will one person have the full range in his or her kit bag. If you are fortunate enough to have the complete artillery at your disposal, then my guess would be that you are not just a gun but probably close to the greatest investor on earth. Decisively, I have not found room in my list of qualities for old chestnuts, such as smart, clever, wily or cunning. In fact, my experience tells me that being too smart is a handbrake when it comes to investing: the high IQ set is unable to comprehend how the general market can behave the way it does. One only has to look at the mess caused by the bevy of geniuses at Long Term Capital Management in the late 1990s, which nearly brought Wall Street to its knees, to understand what I mean. (Long Term Capital Management was a highly credentialled hedge fund formed in 1994 by some of the smartest people in financial markets, including two Nobel Prize winners. In 1998 it required a $US3.6 billion bailout orchestrated by the Federal Reserve after it lost $US4.5 billion in just four months.)

So what makes a savvy sharemarket investor?

Confidence

American writer Mark Twain once remarked, 'All you need is ignorance and confidence and the success is sure'. While Twain may have been exaggerating to get his point across, investors should take on board the essence of the comment. A sharemarket investor must always stay confident. The reality is that you will never get all your sharemarket calls right, and over the course of your investment life you will make hundreds of mistakes. The key to survival is not to lose faith in your own ability to pick stocks, otherwise you will become too cautious, which will result in substandard decision making. Even worse, a savage loss could rock you so badly that you walk away from the game altogether. One only has to recall the trauma croupier Peter Proksa felt when he temporarily quit after suffering a near-death investing experience. This sounds a lot like many other activities in life, where a bad experience can slant your thinking for the foreseeable future. In my 13 years of full-time investing, I believe I made a mistake virtually every day. Some were only minor and easy to overcome, while others were major blunders that made me question what I was doing playing this game. After so many body blows I eventually realised that I must accept the mistake and not dwell on it, but move on to seek out the next opportunity — and there always is one. It was also important for me to acknowledge that each trade, on its own, was meaningful, but not the be all and end all. The big picture of trying to accumulate wealth had to be the overriding concern.

> The key to survival is not to lose faith in your own ability to pick stocks.

There will even be periods when your confidence is seemingly shattered by a bad patch, where you get not just one wrong call, but a series of them. Sometimes it is worth cashing up and walking away to get your head clear before coming back, refreshed and confident that you can recapture your self-confidence.

Crucially, you should not be over-confident, displaying arrogance and hubris. The sharemarket eats up investors who are arrogant. The confidence I am talking about is an inner belief that you are good enough to keep up with the market and should be a player in the game. No-one needs to know that you are hitting century after century.

Judgement

Throughout the rest of this book I will mention the need at all times to exercise sound judgement, with a heavy dose of common sense when dealing in shares. You need judgement to choose your stockbrokers; you need judgement to identify quality company management; and you need judgement to realise that you may be being ripped off. You need judgment simply because investing is about making decisions every day.

For example, why would you decide to invest in a company that is trading on a price to earnings ratio (PE) of 25 — an indicator that its current price is 25 times next year's estimated earnings for the company — when it is well above the company's historical multiple average of just 12 times earnings? In simple terms, you would have to wait 25 years before you got back the money you had invested, when history shows people on average will have to wait only 12 years. Sure, you might miss out on the final 10 per cent of a meteoric rise in the share price, but the chances are heavily weighed towards the share eventually trading back to its long-term average. By the time the stock has actually hit a PE of 25, a swarm of people will be following the company and extolling its virtues to all and sundry. The magnetism of the stock will become overwhelming to some people, while those who keep their heads and make a sound judgement call rather than join the stampede will come out in front.

Why would you take on a margin loan to increase your exposure to the sharemarket when it has risen more than 20 per cent for the past four years, as was the case in the years leading up to 2007. Once again you might miss out on the last 20 or 30 per cent of the rally, but a move to the sidelines would have saved you from torching a large pile of money. (A margin loan is the name given to a bank loan given to a sharemarket investor to purchase shares.)

The quality of your judgement will be most sorely tested when you have to make a decision in a hurry, with your broker urging you to buy or sell. I have always thought it was best not to make a decision under undue pressure and simply let the opportunity pass.

It is unrealistic to think you will exercise sound judgement all of the time. I will never forget eagerly buying shares in Brisbane-based property developer Watpac in 2006, after the property market in that city had been flourishing for several years (see figure 2.1).

Figure 2.1: the price to earnings multiple for Watpac 2006–09

Source: IRESS

Watpac was trading on a PE of around 12, compared with its long-term average of something less than 10. When I went to visit the company, I knew that the company's great run would inevitably falter because of the cyclical nature of property, but because the story sounded so good at the time, I just dived in. Sure enough, I picked up the last bit of the upward share price run, only to also experience the heart attack ride down in 2008.

Competitiveness

Just like the professionals, retail investors have to be competitive to make a fist of the sharemarket. To truly succeed over an extended period, you have to want to do well, and attack the market as if you want to beat it. The sharemarket is a game, where the score is kept every minute of the day, ensuring you cannot hide behind a bunch of excuses. In addition, other sharemarket players that you talk to consistently will invariably remind you of how well they are doing, pushing you to perform at a higher level. If you are competitive in other parts of your life, then there is a reasonable chance you will dedicate enough time and approach the sharemarket with the right amount of enthusiasm to make a return, equal to or better than the overall market. If you are not the competitive type, then the market should still provide a satisfactory return, but it might be better to find a professional manager to run your money.

Curiosity

It is not imperative that you are curious to make a decent return from the sharemarket, but I have never met a person who has outperformed the market who is not inquisitive about an assortment of subjects. Whether you are a short-term trader or long-term investor, or you fall somewhere in between, you need to be hungry for information at all times. Effectively, investing in the sharemarket is about coming across ideas that lead to the investigation of companies and finally deciding to make an investment—or not. These ideas will be generated from reading newspapers and magazines, scanning sharemarket tables, talking to your stockbroker, chatting to friends, watching television and observing the business environment around you. The economy is omnipresent and, if you keep your mind and eyes open, you will unearth some fabulous ideas that many others will miss. Some of my best ideas have come, not from sitting at my desk staring at a watch list of stocks or reading a company research report, but wandering around asking people simple questions, or reading what seems to be the most innocuous information, such as a general news story hidden deep inside a newspaper. Importantly, your curiosity must be genuine or it will run out of steam. Just remember, always ask questions and never take what you are told at face value.

I will never forgive myself for closing my mind off to mining stocks during the years from 2003 to 2007, believing the Chinese economic miracle was just a passing phase. My anti-commodity zeal was fuelled by prejudices formed in my formative years in the 1990s. All of this ignorance undoubtedly cost me and Wilson Asset Management investors significant amounts of money during the boom that unfolded a decade later.

Independent thinking

People who happily follow the pack will enjoy some good times in the sharemarket, especially when the bull is bellowing. However, the people who will outperform over extended periods are those who can think independently — even though it is also virtually impossible for an individual to succeed on the sharemarket if they isolate themselves from others. Investors need to collect as much information and formulate as many ideas as they can by communicating with as broad a range of people as possible. Once the information and views are collected, however, the independent thinker will process the information and use it astutely to make money.

If I think back to some of the greatest investors that I have met over the years, they have all been slightly quirky and off-centre. Some could even be regarded as being idiosyncratic and eccentric. They have their own style, not just as investors but also in their personality, including the way they talk, dress and think. In this category I would include Greg Perry, David Paradice, Peter Morgan, John Sevior, Phil Mathews, Ian Harding and Wilson Asset Management's Geoff Wilson. They always shock me when I ask them a question about the market. None gives the sort of formulated answer that sounds good at the end of a marketing document. All have an enormous ability to absorb information in various forms and then uniquely process this to come up with their own conclusions. This independent thinking does not mean they get every investment call right, but they have the ability to see opportunities that others ignore because they want to parrot what they have read or heard from their brokers or the mainstream media. Ian Harding from Colonial First State understood the value of infrastructure assets in the early to mid 1990s, though it took others years to catch on. Colonial First State's Greg Perry pioneered growth investing in this country in the 1990s, while former stockbroker turned hedge fund manager Phil Mathews has the ability to predict trends years in advance and take advantage of them today.

Being an independent thinker, though, does not mean you always run against the crowd. To be a contrarian for the sake of it is a sure way to blow up. If a stock is heading down and you stubbornly hang onto your shares, then you are not doing your job as an investor. You need to think independently and freely, but not shackle your ideas with obstinacy and arrogance. You need to be able to see things that others might be missing. Just look at Peter Proksa's foray into Prima Biomed. He saw the company had a product and a young executive who had the ability to get the company out of a dire financial situation. The share price told us that not many other people saw this as an opportunity.

Modesty

I tend to roll my eyes when people suggest a great quality of an individual is his or her humbleness or modesty. I prefer people who have an ego that instils a self-belief that they can achieve. I also prefer a person who doesn't even stop to acknowledge their own modesty. I think that a distinguished sharemarket investor cannot allow themselves to become vainglorious and unwilling to accept they can ever be wrong. Some people naturally have inflated egos, while others are susceptible to falling into this trap if they are lucky enough to go on a winning streak. If vanity is part of your make-up, I don't think you can change and your sharemarket performance will suffer as a consequence. Those of you who start punching out fantastic performance numbers and become absorbed by your own ability will become complacent — a prerequisite for a major fall.

The sharemarket will always humble you. Essentially the market is a microcosm of human activity and no-one wins all the time, no matter how lucky or how smart you are. The larger your wins now, the greater your potential losses in the future, so do not get carried away with your own self-importance.

Patience

If you are performing at your best in the sharemarket, you will have very little to do. This is unlike virtually any other vocation in life, whether it be medical, political, legal, business, sporting or educational, where the harder you work the better you should perform. If you have done your homework and chosen your stocks carefully, there can be extended periods where you do very little actual investing. You won't need to work, because the stocks you have chosen can outperform the overall market for some time. This doesn't give you the green light to clock off, but it means you will not need to actually invest. In these circumstances, stay alert and assiduously keep on mining for new ideas. Don't become anxious about not doing anything but ongoing research and investigating. Sometimes you just don't need to buy and sell to make money.

Just as importantly, you should never rush a decision to make up for a previous loss. In a case of fright or flight, some people will incur a major loss and be consumed by a lack of confidence and walk away from the whole game. Others will act impatiently, determined to make good in a rush, taking the next trade on offer rather than methodically going through their usual process of investing. It should never be forgotten that the sharemarket keeps throwing up profitable situations every day and if you can snare a small percentage of these opportunities you will end up winning. The sharemarket is more forgiving than any religion I have stumbled across. Equally, people who avoid regular losses by not acting hastily will also find they are ahead of the pack.

Numeracy

You don't need more than primary school mathematics to navigate the sharemarket successfully. However the market is heavily populated with numbers. The market is about ideas, but it is measured every day with numbers, in terms of profits, market capitalisations, share prices and percentages. If you are not stimulated by the simple maths of adding, subtracting, multiplying and dividing, then you will probably find the market mundane. Under these circumstances I would avoid trying to directly invest in the market, opting instead to seek out a professional who has a sound track record and that you are comfortable with. If you lack interest in any pursuit in life, you usually end up failing.

Greed

The first seven personality traits I outlined all have a virtuous component to them, while this trait is one of the seven deadly sins. When broken down to its most pure form, the sharemarket exists to make money for people. Sure, capitalists and academics bang on about the sharemarket being at the heart of capitalism and the most productive way people have found to allocate capital. That is all well and good, and yes it may well be true, but the fact remains that sharemarket participants invest in shares only to get richer. There is no greater cause when investing in the sharemarket and I have never met anyone who thinks about appropriate allocations of capital when they are buying a new share or participating in a float. To make more and more money for yourself, you have to be greedy. You have to arm wrestle with your stockbroker for a hefty allocation in a good float, and you need to have a voracious appetite for picking winners. You cannot be satisfied with just matching the market performance. Our croupier showed a streak of greed in aiming to generate quantum gains and not just your average household 10.5 per cent per year.

It is dangerous, however, to be excessively greedy. To want more and more, and not see the danger signs when a stock or market has enjoyed a magnificent run, will lead to ruin. In bull markets there is plenty of food laid out on the table every day, but if you eat too much, then you will become overweight and the consequences of your actions will haunt you for many years to come. It is vital that you read the rules set out in chapter 6 and moderate your greed with these. It is also essential that you mix your greed with a heavy dose of judgement.

Conclusion

To fully understand yourself and your investing capabilities, it is worth looking at these nine qualities and working out how many you possess. If you can't place a tick next to all nine, don't panic, but it is worthwhile studying each one carefully and attempting to broaden your range of skills.

Chapter 3

No training and no idea

If truth be known, when I started life as a professional investor in 1998 I had no idea of how to invest. I had never bought a share for myself. The closest I had ever come to a tipple in the market was registering my wife's name for the Telstra float in 1997. She received a small number of shares which, under my advice, she sold in the first few days of listing at around $2.60 each, a gain of about 30 per cent. We couldn't believe someone could make such easy money by simply filling out a prospectus form, attaching a cheque and posting it off. It was a real eye opener. Had the smart guys been making such easy money for years and keeping it a secret from the rest of us? Just like that, Suzy had made enough money to buy a return plane ticket for a European holiday: it sure beat slaving away in her café from 6 am each morning. Suzy said her Telstra share profit was equal to selling 2000 cups of coffee. History shows that Telstra's shares climbed strongly for the next few years, peaking at around $9.00 ($7.65 adjusted for the partly paid shares). If we hadn't been so impatient to cash in, we could have sat on our investment and been rewarded for being idle, earning ourselves enough money to put down a deposit on our first home.

Don't be fooled, you can do it

In 1998 I joined Wilson Asset Management as full-time employee number one. I had spent the previous five years of my life as a journalist and had been recruited by Geoff Wilson for two reasons—to help him fulfil a long-held ambition to write an investment book, and to ensure that he got out of the office and visited companies. He had found that, as a one-man-band, he was chained to his desk fielding calls from stockbrokers and finding little time to get out into the world and visit companies.

On my first day at work, after discovering where the toilets were, I sat in my little windowless office pondering what to do. The long desk had a phone and nothing else. There was no computer screen, no pen, no pad and no instruction guide on how to start investing. Geoff sat in the office next door talking loudly on the phone, discussing companies in a language that I didn't really understand. He talked about PEs, returns on equity, cash flows—and what seemed like incredibly serious conversations always ended with roaring laughter. As a finance journalist, I had spent hours talking to stockbrokers, fund managers and company management teams, so I foolishly assumed that I could just carry on and everything would fall into place. But now I didn't know who was the right person to call or even how to address them. I pulled out a pen and paper from my bag and feigned busyness, showing I was a worthwhile guy to have hired.

After about half an hour I called some of my old colleagues at the newspaper to see what was going on, but it was becoming increasingly obvious to me that I was utterly clueless. I couldn't adjust from talking about what would make a good news story to how we could make money by buying and selling shares. By 10.30 am I was so tense about the situation I almost gave Geoff a hug when he came into my room and told me that a company was coming in to discuss a possible listing on the sharemarket. At last I had something to do. The company was clothing retailer Noni B, and its managing director and founder, Alan Kindl, was generous in answering my dim-witted questions about his retail chain. The learning had begun and it has never really stopped.

Of this I am certain—if I could eke out a living from investing with no training and no knowledge to start with, there is nothing stopping the vast majority of the general public achieving the same outcome. Many investment houses refuse to hire someone who has not bought and sold shares for themselves before. If that was the case I would never have got a start in the industry. Not only had I never bought

The learning had begun and it has never really stopped.

or sold a share before I started as a professional investor, I cannot recall at any stage in my childhood, teenage years or early adult life discussing the sharemarket with anyone. The discussions around the dinner table at home with my parents and brother on the farm were generally heated debates about politics, farming and sport. The reality was that my parents did not have excess capital to invest in the sharemarket and the subject was never broached.

The first time I can recall hearing about the sharemarket was from a guy called Paul whom I met at university. He constantly reminded my friends and me about the amount of money he was making playing the market, while the rest of us worked for $8 an hour at various fast food chains. Paul was the only guy I knew at university who carried a business briefcase to class each day, obviously filled with sharemarket paraphernalia. He also spent an inordinate amount of time on the public phone between classes (no mobile phones then), instructing his broker to buy and sell his shares. Come October, Paul lost all his winnings in the crash of 1987 and he seemed to go remarkably quiet. For me the sharemarket seemed a game of chance that resembled horse racing and I had no interest in trying to discover how it actually worked. After making a poor cameo performance, the sharemarket disappeared from my life for another seven years, when I was lucky to get a job on the business section of *The Sydney Morning Herald*.

The market does not discriminate

My understanding is that many investment houses will not take the type of risk Geoff did when he employed me. They usually require a certain level of education as a prerequisite to winning employment, and personal experience is seen as a desirable quality. This rigid approach to hiring people fails to understand how the sharemarket and investing actually work. The sharemarket does not discriminate. There is no absolute right or wrong way to attack investing and, from my experience, the vast range of courses that teach you about investing can be helpful but are certainly no guarantee you will be a success. Over the years, I have come into contact with many people who have successfully studied for the much fabled US investment course for the Chartered Financial Analyst (CFA) qualification. The course requires a serious amount of work, but completing it reflects more the person's ability to apply themselves to a task than his or her ability to invest. Nothing seems to compensate for common sense and good judgement. Most people will lose these qualities in long bull markets and severe bear markets, but it is those who can reclaim them quickly and hold them at the core of their investment philosophy who will eventually win the day.

Part II
Building the foundations

For those of you who are now eager to investigate or rediscover the sharemarket, it is critical that you enter the game with a plan that prevents you from failing. Part of that plan is to prepare properly. So before you even contemplate buying shares in a company you must lay the right foundations—a step that all of us have to take regardless of our pedigree. The following chapters provide the key steps in building those foundations.

Chapter 4

Who are you? The road to discovery

Benjamin Graham, the father of value investing, observed: 'The investor's chief problem—and even his worst enemy—is likely to be himself'. Just ask Peter Proksa or anyone else who has dabbled and lost money on the market, and they will tell you they could have avoided the damage if they had stuck to their original plan and acted within their own capabilities. One of Australia's great traders, Stephen Rabin, lives by the mantra, 'An investor must know his limitations'. Rabin's success has come from his unbreakable discipline. He sticks religiously to what works after identifying early in his career the approach he should take to making money from the market. He was trained as a mergers and acquisitions lawyer and he has used this skill base to extract the best returns he can from the sharemarket by concentrating on complex events. Another highly successful futures trader turned sharemarket investor, Daniel Droga, has managed to notch up quarter after quarter of positive returns because he has discovered his strengths and set a disciplined approach to the market that he rarely tampers with. Conversely, Peter Proksa spent the best part of a decade searching for his sharemarket personality, resulting in a distinct method that might just work for him in the long haul.

To explain what I mean by getting to know yourself better it is worthwhile giving you a real-life example of the road to discovery.

A game of roulette

In 1995 I attended the opening of Sydney's temporary casino at Pyrmont, just west of the CBD. Even though it was the first casino I had ever visited the event was slightly underwhelming, given that the casino was housed in a long tin shed. My then girlfriend and now wife, Suzy, and I had never really been gamblers. We had operated a small business and understood some vague financial fundamentals, but games of chance were foreign concepts. Playing a friendly game of cards for some housekeeping money seemed silly, and going to the races ruined a potentially enjoyable day. Besides being strong-armed into the office sweep, I hadn't even bothered to place a wager on the Melbourne Cup.

At the casino that night I felt embarrassed. I didn't know how to play any of the games and to simply roll up and ask a professionally dressed croupier how to play a certain game in front of an expectant audience was outside my comfort zone. As the night laboured on, I eventually clawed together enough courage to buy $20 worth of chips to play on the roulette wheel, a game where I could bet on red or black. My ability to comprehend anything more than a 50/50 outcome was marginal. The $20 worth of chips was eaten into by each failed $2 bet, before I finally hit the last chip. Suddenly my luck turned and I went on a winning streak with my $2 multiplying before my eyes, all the way back to the original $20. At that stage I looked at Suzy and, without a word, we took our small pile of chips and headed to the cashier. I had no interest in making any money, but I knew that I did not want to lose it. A break-even outcome suited me fine.

When it came to dealing with money, that night probably gave me the greatest insight into my psyche. In fact, I remember walking away from the long tin shed that night thinking I just didn't have the mentality to make a decent amount of money from investing. I had no stomach for risk and there was zero excitement or adrenalin rush when my bet on black came up three times in a row. As a financial journalist at the time, I had already started contemplating whether I could cut it as a stockbroker or fund manager. I had built up a rapport with several high-profile money managers, and found the conversations with them stimulating, and relished debates about various businesses and why some worked while others didn't. I particularly prized our discussions of who were the stand-out managing directors in the market and why they continually outperformed other managers. However, I decided that, unless you got a buzz from guessing right, whether it's the right horse, the right colour or the right stock, then you just didn't belong in the game of investing.

Luckily, I didn't close the door on the sharemarket following that night. I subsequently learned the sharemarket is available to everyone and caters for all types. It does not discriminate against anyone. It embodies a cross section of businesses around the globe and just because the adrenalin does not pump through your veins every time a stock price ticks up a cent, that does not mean you should pack your bags and walk away. Ironically, if you are one of those people who get a thrill from calling heads or tails correctly, the market is probably going to be a slight let down. It doesn't mean you can't join the party but there are other pursuits that provide win–lose outcomes, like the casino or horse racing, that can feed your addiction.

The fact I had no capacity to suffer any significant losses stayed with me for years to come. When I entered the sharemarket as a fund manager about three years later, I found myself investing in a style similar to the way I had bet at the casino that night. But unlike roulette, the stockmarket is much more forgiving and you can work hard at mitigating your losses. At no stage in 13 years of professional investing did I look at a stock's upside before working out where it could go wrong. My first question was always: does it have any downside? Once I secured a degree of comfort that the downside was slight, then I could start buying the shares. This method did not ensure immunity from poor stock choices, but if a stock happened to climb higher I would be genuinely surprised. On the odd occasion that I contemplated the blue sky, or upside, of a stock, I would invariably end up with a loss that would make your eyes water.

Genetic make-up

I also quickly realised that, when one of my stock picks headed south, I didn't have the punter's gene that willed me to hang on or even double up in the hope that fortunes would turn and I would recoup and, possibly, still make money out of my investment. Instead, I would cut and run, and try not to dwell on the poor decision that I had just made. This approach in part explains why our main fund, WAM Capital, has held an average of 29 per cent cash since it listed on the ASX back in August 1999. Most fund managers, because of restrictions imposed by their investor mandates, can hold only a maximum of 10 per cent cash, but both Geoff and I felt extremely uncomfortable about embracing so much risk and preferred to revert to the low-risk play of cash if we couldn't identify a reason to buy a stock. I can say confidently I would have failed to deliver acceptable returns if I had been forced to be fully invested—it just didn't suit my or Geoff's personality.

We were emboldened when we were lucky enough to talk to super-star investor, Colonial First State's Greg Perry, who told us, 'Avoid the losers and you end up a mile in front—the winners will take care of themselves'. The greatest thing about this realisation was that I could still participate in the market, even though I had a low tolerance for risk. It skewed my investment style to picking stocks that were relatively cheap rather than those whose share price was relatively expensive and susceptible to the slightest negative news. And everyone needs to go through this journey. Without doubt, you can only be successful in your pursuit as an investor if you have a clear view of your own personality and what it means for the future. If you don't bring yourself to the game you will be found wanting.

What type of investor are you?

If you are of the view the sharemarket is all about finance and numbers you are mistaken. The market is a dynamic beast that represents a large slice of society and a vast range of personalities. There are buyers and sellers of every stock, every day of the week, every month of the year. So to perform successfully in this environment you must get to know yourself and work out where you can fit in. It is no different from any other aspect of life, such as deciding what career best suits you and which partner is your ideal match.

> You can only be successful ... as an investor if you have a clear view of your own personality and what it means for the future.

At Wilson Asset Management we learned the importance of this lesson the hard way when, in 2003, we started a fund that bought shares in companies with the intention of holding them forever. This decision was based upon a tax benefit introduced by the federal government at the time. We were chock full of confidence at the time, following a successful first five years of managing money for other people—but we discovered that it was hard to simply buy and own stocks forever. Previously, we had bought and sold shares frequently and we found we could not stray too far from this process. Taking on a long-term fund meant that we left our personalities behind and tried to be someone else. It also delivered a lesson that you should never, under any circumstances, make a sharemarket decision based on a tax benefit. The fund's performance was patchy and eventually we decided to convert it into a stock pickers fund, an approach that was more aligned to our way of thinking. To date the performance of the fund has improved. But the experience probably gave me the most crucial lesson that I learned in the 13 years of managing money professionally.

People start with the wrong question

The most common question I have fielded as a fund manager is: 'Do you have a hot tip that might make me a couple of thousand dollars quickly?' Besides rarely having a hot tip, I would look at the person and wonder why they would ask such a question. Sure, we all want to make easy money, but I don't recall seeing many of these people rushing out to the casino or the racetrack trying to pick up a hot tip. In both of these venues the punter has a history of winning about 15 per cent to 20 per cent of the time. These odds mean you won't make money. Most of the time, something described as a sure thing in the market has no more street credibility than a hot tip at the racetrack. I presume these people think that just because I work in the sharemarket I must have a long list of stock tips that are certainties, almost as if I have some form of superior knowledge of future events. This also means that I am aware of a few thousand dollars idly sitting around that is waiting to be picked up every day of the year. For the majority of these people I try to change the conversation or simply say, 'Would you be happy to lose a few thousand dollars if the hot tip doesn't work out?' To a person they respond, 'No way, but I know that is unlikely to happen.' Unfortunately, hot tips have an extremely poor strike rate.

These people should not simply turn away from the market. Instead, they should carefully think about their personality and how they deal with money in the rest of their lives. If they have no tolerance for the loss of a few thousand dollars, then they shouldn't be investing on flimsy tips. They should leave that game to individuals who love to risk money to hopefully make money. Once they have cracked the mystery of who they are they can take their few thousand dollars and start investing on the market with a real chance of making a decent return.

Now we will consider some of the categories that I have discovered that people fit into. Sometimes an individual will fit into one of these categories and others will fit into two, but very few have the skill base to traverse the whole spectrum.

The punter

The punter is someone who is spellbound by the market. They see the buying and selling of shares as another game of chance that can deliver fantastic returns just like a horse race or a game of roulette. These people should not attempt to alter their personality. No doubt they will make profits in bull markets, where all prices trend up, but they will also be stripped of significant portions of their gains when the bets go wrong. The sharemarket does not have to be turned into a casino for most investors, but for the punter that is exactly what it is. These people love risk, and they should never buy a conservative portfolio of shares that promises to deliver gradual capital gain and a steady stream of dividends. If they head down this path they will lose interest; they won't understand the reason they have bought the shares; and, over time, the portfolio will look like a neglected garden with weeds engulfing the flowers and the lawn. Even a conservative portfolio needs some love and care.

For the punter, the key should be to maximise the thrill of the ride. They should actively seek out the highest beta stocks. Beta is a Greek word used by market analysts to describe how much stocks move compared with the market. For example, the overall market might increase in value by 5 per cent, while a high beta stock might jump 20 per cent higher in the same time frame. Unsurprisingly, these stocks will also fall 20 per cent when the overall market experiences a mild 5 per cent decline. In Australia the highest beta stocks tend to be found in the smaller end of the mining industry or in the biotech sector. The punter should roam in this area of the market and try to concentrate his or her bets on just a handful of stocks. In bull markets the punter will also clamber over the slew of new floats that all seem to rise on day one of listing.

For most investors, I would strongly discourage borrowing to invest (gearing) in the sharemarket, but for the punter I would make an exception. For the punter, taking on debt in the form of a margin loan might enhance the experience.

On many occasions the sharemarket will be a slight let down for the genuine punter. The thrill of the sharemarket does not match other games of chance, even when some form of debt is introduced to increase your returns. An alternative is to consider buying options, which allows you to put a fraction of the total share price down up front, or contracts for difference (CFDs), which involve your borrowing up to 90 per cent of your investment. These products will increase the risk involved and feed your enormous appetite.

You will only truly know if you are an authentic punter when you lose your whole sum wagered, plus your loan, and still go back for more.

Many people who are not punters for some reason approach the sharemarket like it is a casino. They are inclined to get burnt early on with a substantial loss and spend the rest of their lives grizzling about the market being a trap that only mugs and thieves play. Consistently they resurface years later when the next bull market is at full steam, only to pick the top and lose all their money again. These people do not understand themselves. The authentic punters love the roller coaster ride and wouldn't have it any other way.

The trader

In recent years the trader's name has been besmirched by the arrival of the day trader on the back of online systems. Day traders attempt to buy stocks in the morning and sell them by the afternoon, locking in a profit. The decision to buy will be made on the back of a rumour, stock momentum or, in some instances, a positive announcement by the actual company. A traditional trader is a completely different creature, who sits at the other end of the risk spectrum.

Traders try to find the lowest risk plays that will provide a definite profit. They look for anomalies in the pricing of individual stocks and work hard each day scouring the massive list of stocks where the market has got the price wrong—and that's where they buy. Typically a successful trader takes a small profit and moves on. Traders have no faith in the overall market, and they do not like to entertain nebulous concepts, such as economic cycles, future earnings growth of shares or the quality of company management. They like to reduce the investment opportunity to pure numbers and specific events where the odds are in their favour. The best trader I have met over the years is Stephen Rabin, who stays firmly within the parameters he set himself many years ago. His plan has worked a treat and now he manages his money on his own, without the need for any outside help.

Many traders use short selling to further reduce their risk. Even though shorting gets plenty of newspaper space, it is generally not understood, and for good reason, given that it is totally back to front to a normal trade, in that you sell first and buy second. To summarise, short selling is taking a view that a share price will fall by selling a share you do not own. I know it sounds complicated, but I'll try to explain it. Because you do not hold the shares in your portfolio, you call your stockbroker and ask him or her to borrow them from someone who does own them. Borrowing shares is a completely legal activity and takes place every day on the sharemarket. You borrow the shares, paying the lender a small fee, and then sell those shares into the market, say at $1 each. If your bet is right, the share price falls and then you buy back the shares in the market, say at 80 cents each. Then you return the shares you have bought to the person you borrowed them from. You have profited from the fall because you have locked in your sale price of $1 a share before you decide to buy the stock at 80 cents, a profit of 20 cents. Of course, if the price happens to go up, you lose money, because you have to repay the lender more than you borrowed.

A classic opportunity for a trader is a takeover bid. When a takeover for a company is announced, the target company may for some reason (frequently to do with the terms of the takeover) trade at a discount to the announced takeover price. A trader will assess all the information at hand and then buy shares in the target company. If the trader can borrow the stock, they can short the company making the takeover bid. The trader aims to arbitrage this pricing anomaly for a small but definite profit. (An arbitrage is when investors aim to take advantage of a pricing difference in a market when in theory the difference should not exist.) This is not always a foolproof method, because the takeover may hit a road block at any stage in the process, but careful reading and many phone calls to the participants involved in the corporate activity should mitigate the chances of a bad trade eventuating. The trade is completed when the takeover is finalised and the pricing anomaly disappears. The trader will then move onto the next low-risk profitable play. Great traders have no emotional attachment to particular companies or shares and are also able to move on when a trade turns sour.

Another fertile province for traders is secondary capital raisings. When a company is raising capital by issuing new shares into the market, the shares are usually offered at a slight discount to the prevailing share price in a bid to entice investors to take the new stock. A trader will look at the discount and decide whether the risk is on his or her side and, if so, will take some of the stock being offered. Because most capital raisings take some time to settle, most traders will, at the same time, madly scramble to borrow shares in the company and sell them straight away, locking in the small profit. Once they receive the stock from the capital raising, they deliver this new stock back to the person they borrowed it from to short sell.

There are literally hundreds of trades going on in the market each day. The people who prosper most from this style of investment are those who love to deal in numbers and probably excelled at mathematics at school. They must work hard to find the opportunities and they always try to mitigate the risk. Geoff Wilson of Wilson Asset Management definitely possesses a trading gene. His comment was always, 'If I see $10 in the corner of the room, I'm going to try to pick it up'.

Traders loses their way when they start trying to pick market directions or individual stocks based on fundamentals, or if they become too emotional.

The helicopter pilot

The sharemarket can also cater for the people who love to follow the big economic events around the world. In sharemarket phraseology these people are seen as top down investors or helicopter pilots, who look at the major economic and political events of the world and then determine how these will affect various sectors of the market and individual stocks. The market is a derivative of the world's major economies and virtually anything can affect it, from interest rates and fiscal policy to natural disasters, such as the 2011 earthquake and tsunami in Japan. Many fund managers around the world love to play the macro-economic trends or at least have an overlay of macro policy in what they are doing. The most prominent of these in Australia would be the highly successful Platinum Asset Management, run by Kerr Neilson. These funds have a cocktail of investments that include taking bets on currencies, fixed interest and equities in various parts of the globe.

Retail investors who are simply too small to play big global markets, such as currencies and bonds, shouldn't feel inadequate. A small helicopter pilot can be accommodated within the realms of the local sharemarket. For example, a helicopter pilot may have read avidly about the Chinese economy back in the early part of the new millennium. His or her conclusion may have been that China was growing at a phenomenal clip and it was now big enough to have an impact on the global economy. The natural conclusion for the helicopter pilot might have been that, for China to achieve its ambitious growth plans, it would need to industrialise its economy, which would result in strong demand for raw materials (commodities) from Australia. This would have led the helicopter pilot to buy a bunch of commodity-based stocks, such as BHP and Rio Tinto, on the ASX in the early years of the new millennium, at a good time. This trade would have been highly profitable, given these stocks have increased in value by some 400 per cent and their dividends have more than tripled.

There are countless trades driven by macro-economic data, and people who love to follow big events should take advantage of this and apply the appropriate investment style. Individuals who are adept at this approach to investing should not be found trading stocks for a small percentage game during a takeover.

The stock picker

Most Australian fund managers describe themselves as stock pickers. They believe they can outperform the overall sharemarket by investing in the right stocks. This allows them to be paid well by marketing a skill base that seems rare, especially to people who do not operate in the market.

The stock picker trawls through the market looking for opportunities. They consider a range of company fundamentals, such as revenue growth, costs, cash flow, valuations and management. They mix this all together and decide to buy a stock or leave it alone. Some stock pickers short individual companies, but this is uncommon in the Australian market. Most of these professional investors, like traders, will concentrate heavily on the numbers available. However, they will differ in two distinct ways — for stock pickers, a company's forecast earnings will be paramount and they will also use discretion to make their choices. At Wilson Asset Management we were stock pickers who concentrated on fundamentals and the identification of a catalyst that would re-rate the stock in the market's eyes. At the end of the day it was the portfolio manager's innate judgement on an investment that usually delivered outperformance of the market. Not surprisingly, using this methodology underperformance could also be tracked directly back to some wayward decision making by the individual rather than miscalculations of the numbers.

There are hundreds of varieties of stock pickers, which is more to do with marketing to investors than stark differences in practice. These varieties are generally grouped into two distinct areas—growth and value. Growth stocks are those that have the ability to generate higher profit growth rates, but they are generally more expensive to buy. Value is at the other end of the spectrum: these stocks have less robust growth but they are more attractively priced. Over the years it has been proven that value investors tend to outperform growth investors, except in years of strong gains by the overall market. Among Australian value investors, it is those who have focused on the volatile small companies end of the sharemarket that have managed to produce the best results for their investors. Alex Waislitz from the Thorney Group is a prime example of a value investor focusing on smaller companies and generating fabulous returns over more than a decade.

Some of Australia's great stock pickers include Colonial First State growth investor Greg Perry, small cap maestro David Paradice, legendary value investor Robert Maple-Brown and Perpetual Trustees' John Sevior. A range of up and comers could also, in time, join this group, such as Justin Braitling, Ben Griffiths, Phil King and Karl Siegling, all of whom have enjoyed enormous success in recent years. Consistent performance over an extended period will be their ultimate test.

The visionary

Some people can see into the future. Many investors claim to be in this category, but very few succeed. Those who can regularly predict economic trends probably accumulate more wealth than virtually anyone else in the market. These people love to take on risk and put their views on the line by taking concentrated bets on events that may unfold in the future.

One of Australia's most successful and wealthiest hedge fund managers, Phil Mathews, is a visionary. He reads everything that he can get his hands on; spends most nights gawking at overseas markets; interviews hundreds of company managers; and keeps a close ear to Australia's market. He takes all this accumulated knowledge and makes his investment decisions based on themes that he believes will unfold into the future. Mathews classifies himself as a thematic investor rather than as a visionary, but the reality is that a theme unfurls slowly, and to make great returns you must see what is happening before the rest of the market. By the time you and I can see what is happening, the chance to make a significant return on our investment would be very short. In the 1990s Mathews latched onto the theme of wealth management and how it would explode in Australia on the back of compulsory superannuation. He tipped a significant portion of his fund, predominantly his own money, into Lend Lease, which owned the highly successful wealth manager MLC. He made a significant profit from this trade. The next decade he turned his attention to energy stocks and made millions of dollars from riding them higher on the back of a rocketing oil price. His biggest position for much of this time was North West Shelf gas giant Woodside Petroleum, which clocked up enormous returns and easily outstripped the overall market (see figure 4.1). The visionary, just like the trader, can make a very nice living by knowing what they are good at and sticking to it.

Figure 4.1: price chart for Woodside Petroleum 2004–08

Source: IRESS

The believer

A range of investors out there love to buy and hold stocks. They usually pick large companies that pay solid dividends, and then just hold them. Their intention is to enjoy the magic of compounding returns and building wealth over a long time. The believer has a spiritual attachment to the market, living by the creed, 'It is time in the market and not timing that matters'. They have an appetite for fully franked dividends, which are distributed to investors with a 30 per cent tax rate already paid by the company.

For the believer to be successful, the market must move higher over time. In this way they don't have to be fussed with regular trading, trying to pick the best times to move in and out of stocks. A secular bear market tends not to suit the believers, because they are always exposed to the market. In a secular bear market, the best a fully invested general sharemarket investor like the believer can hope for is a gain of a few per cent each year. When inflation is taken into account, that could result in the destruction in value of the believer's funds. However, secular bear markets have proven to be the exception over the past century, with the market on average, recording up years 70 per cent of the time. Possibly the greatest buy and hold investors in Australia are the highly successful listed investment companies AFIC, Argo and Milton. They gradually accumulate stocks whenever cash is available, and then sit and wait for the returns to roll in. The long-term investors in these funds have grown gradually wealthier as the years have rolled by.

The believer method also nicely suits individual investors who just can't handle the stress of trading stocks regularly — my father is a prime example. Many investors, like me, do not have the patience for this approach and feel uneasy just sitting and waiting.

Conclusion

This list of types of investors is just the tip of the iceberg. There are many others, such as chartists, and qualitative and quantitative investors, who rely heavily on computing programs, to name just a few. As mentioned earlier, the market does not discriminate against anyone, and everyone is welcome to take part in the game and ply their wares. The key, though, is trying to understand yourself and your distinctive personality traits that affect the way you will invest. This may take a few trial runs and many mistakes before you hit upon the jackpot, but if you keep competing in the 100 metres sprint when you should be in the marathon, you are never going to win this game — a lesson that Peter Proksa garnered from hard won experience.

Chapter 5

Creating your own Wall Street

Professor John Cacioppo of the University of Chicago has pioneered research into loneliness and the detrimental effect it has on the health of individuals. His work has led the academic world into believing lonely people not only suffer higher levels of depression but also experience higher stress levels in their lives, putting enormous pressure on their physical health. It stands to reason that humans need contact with other humans as much as they need food, oxygen and water. Loneliness might take longer to take grip, but the slow burn can mete out similar harm. At some stage in the not too distant future you can imagine that a coroner might diagnose a person's cause of death as loneliness.

Very few vocational pursuits can be achieved in splendid isolation, and to be a lonely investor in the market place is a sure way to underperform. It is fashionable for professional investors and fund managers to declare there is too much market noise, and true enlightenment comes only when you can distance yourself from the blustering crowd. This comment is short-sighted and has a whiff of arrogance about it. For the vast majority of investors, including many professionals, isolation can cause death in rapid time.

Professionals need shoulders to lean on

Professional investors operate in a market place where people interact every day, trading on bits of information. They go to that market place to read, talk, analyse and trade, before they head home to contemplate what they have learned. At the heart of all interaction is communication of various forms. Conversations are held every day with work colleagues, stockbrokers, other professional investors, company management teams, stock analysts and investors, and from this the professionals generate ideas that result in investments. Sure, there is a lot of information to dissect, of which a high percentage is absolutely useless, but without it most professional investors would flounder and eventually walk away from the whole game thinking they are not up to the task in hand. It is essential that investors are independent thinkers, but anyone who believes they come up with all their own ideas will spend most of their time tripping over their own ego. Does anyone honestly believe that Warren Buffett sits in his office all day and just reads annual reports? I'm not privy to Buffett's daily routine, but from all the interviews he gives, a large portion of his time is spent talking to informed people, gathering vast tracts of information that he can disseminate and put to good use.

Without doubt you must find time to withdraw from the noisy crowd and think, read and ultimately make decisions in isolation, but this can be applied to virtually any part of your life, whether it be your job or your personal relationships. Investors will succeed only if they have great information flows and then be able to use that information to make investment decisions. Judgement is also crucial.

What is the name of your street?

Just like professional investors, individuals must create their own market place. You need your own Wall Street, and if you search hard enough it is there for the taking. It is not feasible to consider sitting in your study or kitchen wading through annual reports, broker research and newspapers day after day without the contact with the rest of the community. Besides the fact that most financial reports are written as if designed to put you to sleep, humans are social creatures who are stimulated by interaction with other people. Peter Proksa has realised this and is energetically growing his own crowd of sharemarket contacts.

A much underestimated concept among investors, both full-time professionals and part-timers, is the need for ideas. The sharemarket is distinct from other businesses, in that it is not part of the real world. It is a reflection of the real world where people go to work and do things like make cars, sell clothes, prepare food, market software, give tax advice, police the law, teach classes and dig coal out of the ground. The sharemarket sits on top of this, feasting like a parasite on the back of an elephant. As mentioned in chapter 2, there is no specific university course or apprenticeship that gives you a sharemarket qualification. The most common route to becoming a professional investor is to study numbers-related courses, such as accounting, finance, business or economics. These are all valuable and helpful, and I would never dissuade anyone from studying these disciplines, but none of these courses delivers the golden ticket to success on the sharemarket. Don't be fooled into thinking that investing is about numbers or financial ratios: it is primarily about generating ideas and acting on them. Without a constant stream of new ideas you might as well pack up and find another vocation to pursue. Ideas are the heart of the sharemarket body and, as Professor Cacioppo has discovered, this heart needs to be nourished with human interaction. Everyone hankers to tell others about their winners and be consoled when things turn to mud.

Going for broke

So how do you create your own Wall Street?

The first step is to find a good stockbroker. Once you have found one go out and find another, and then try to seek out a third. To talk to only one stockbroker, or even worse, trade online, is simply too limiting. Even the best stockbrokers might only discover one or possibly two interesting ideas each month, and interesting doesn't necessarily mean you will invest in them, but at least you will have something to follow up on. It is not easy to unearth a high-quality stockbroker, especially one who suits your style of investing. It could well be that you start with one person and have to change a few times before finding the person who is wired into your way of thinking about shares.

This process may take some time and involve several investing mistakes along the way. Once again, your judgement about who you hire as a broker is paramount. If time permits you should always go and meet your broker face to face and see if you feel comfortable with them. While the majority of stock brokers are decent and trustworthy people, it would be gullible to believe that everyone is above board and working in your best interests. If you are only a small investor, there is always a chance that a broker will use you to help out their bigger and more profitable clients. For example, if one of their bigger clients is looking to offload a stock and there are no buyers in sight, you need to be careful that your broker doesn't try to stuff their smaller clients with the stock just to resolve the matter.

You should also be careful that your broker doesn't try to churn your account. While technically this is illegal, it can be done with subtlety. Most stockbrokers get paid to transact, not according to how much money they make you from their ideas. Quality brokers will always try to talk you out of an investment if they believe it is the wrong action to take, instead of simply being happy to take the order and the commission. Over time you should try to measure the strike rate of the investment calls that your broker makes. If this study reveals a bare cupboard then you need to find another broker.

In addition, you should be wary of brokers who continually push the flavour of the month. For years many brokers gladly put their clients into the multitude of listed property trusts that appeared on the market following the unlisted property crashes of the early 1990s. During the decade leading up to the GFC, property trusts traded at a premium to the value of their underlying assets, because the income yield was seductive, delivering a better return than cash in the bank. Many promoters would mindlessly preach that all property is as safe as houses.

When the GFC hit, the emperor was found to have no clothes. The trusts were paying such a high yield because the managers of those trusts had gradually taken on larger amounts of debt, which allowed them to increase the real returns paid to investors. When property markets stalled and credit dried up, property prices fell and the banks had to be repaid. Investors were blown out of the water, and the property groups raised capital through deeply discounted share issues, which meant that many investors would never be able to recover the capital losses caused by the debacle. Today, property trust units generally trade at a discount to the underlying assets, providing an opportunity for investors to make a significant return over the years to come. Over the past 18 months, only a handful of the 25 or so stockbrokers that I speak to have suggested listed property trusts as a place to put your money.

In the current environment your antennae should be up if your broker limits their ideas to gold exploration companies and small mining stocks just because of their stunning returns since the middle of 2004. It is fine to have a portion of your stocks in these areas, but common sense and sound judgement will tell you that if a sector has risen by 250 per cent in a very short time, it has the ability to mirror that performance on the downside.

Finally, you should always ask your broker whether his or her company has a corporate relationship with a specific company. There is nothing more annoying than buying shares in a company recommended by your broker only to be hit with a capital raising underwritten by their firm that dilutes the value of your stock soon afterwards. The broking firm collects a healthy corporate fee while you are stuck with a loss-making trade.

Big or small?

Stockbrokers are important not only for buying and selling your shares but also for connecting you to the much broader market place. A stockbroker goes into the city each day and collects information from other brokers, company analysts, other clients and listed companies. In addition, your stockbroker, especially one who works at a big house, will have a wall of company analysts behind him or her. The analysts are crucial because they compile financial data about the companies in the market, and develop decisive forecasts and financial ratios used to make investment decisions.

You should not discount using a stockbroker at a smaller firm that has limited resources. Over the years some of the best ideas I have received have come from stockbrokers at the smaller firms, who tend to rely on their own wits, rather than a flotilla of analysts at a bigger outfit.

All investors should try to employ, as a minimum, several stockbrokers. This will provide a more fertile landscape for ideas and generally improve your performance. The only major hurdle to achieving this structure is generating sufficient brokerage to pay everyone. If you don't pay your brokers a meaningful amount of commission, they will stop contacting you or find some way of avoiding your calls, no matter how well you get on. This means you must meet them half way. It is worthwhile taking on some low-risk trades just to generate brokerage, encouraging your broker to work for you by providing ideas and passing on the house research to you.

Some people will ignore this advice and decide to trade online because it is the cheap option. This is your own choice, and for a limited number of punters it may prove to be the correct avenue, but for the rest of us you cannot talk to your computer. You need human contact.

Are online trading accounts worthless? Definitely not! The internet revolution has not necessarily improved our investment performance over the years, but it has brought the sharemarket into our lounge rooms. With an internet connection you can have a watch list of stocks, ticking up and down in front of you every minute of the trading day. The internet also brings you every company announcement, which is probably the richest source of research information you will find anywhere. The greatest website in Australia for investors has to be the ASX website at <www.asx. com.au>, which provides the information you need about all listed companies. Serious sharemarket investors should scan the ASX company announcements frequently, looking for any updates on their own stocks as well as any interesting announcements from other listed companies. This is a rich source of ideas.

Talk to your next door neighbour

Once you have discovered your posse of stockbrokers the next step is to find other people, like you, who might be interested in shares. While professional investment managers feel like they are deluged with too much conversation and too much information, the average investor does not have enough people to talk to. There is a mountain of information to read about the market every single day, and it is vitally important to read, but this must be supplemented frequently by discussing your ideas with other people who are also hooked on the market.

When my family and I moved house in 2003, within a matter of weeks my new neighbours had discovered I was a fund manager. A few months later at a street party the word had passed around that I worked in the sharemarket and before I knew it I had a small crowd milling around, eager to discuss the shares they owned and how they would perform in the future. In the end a group of us decided to make a regular meeting of it. Since then a gang of five has met one night every second month. We discuss a range of subjects but always dedicate a fair slice of the night to the market and the stocks we have been looking at or have bought. I can honestly say that each person at our gatherings would be more than capable of successfully working full time in the market. All of them are enthusiastic and have insightful ideas, some of which have been worthwhile following up. We don't quite have Wall Street but we do have Warren Road.

For most people it might not be easy to find other people who have a passion for the sharemarket. If that is the case, contact the Australian Shareholders Association (ASA) and ask where your nearest branch is. The ASA branches have monthly meetings and regular guest speakers. You may well find a few soul mates who could be the source of many great investments in the years to come. Another approach is to take out a subscription to a financial newsletter and follow it up by making contact with the authors and keeping in contact with them. This may cost you a fee each year but just one good idea could deliver profits that equal a multiple of the costs of taking out the subscription. There are also many sharemarket blogs online that could be worth looking into, but be careful that people don't just appear on these venues to spruik what they want to sell. If you are really daring, you should seriously contemplate contacting a handful of newspaper journalists who are tapped into the market. They are always a fount of information.

Another means of acquiring information is following a fund manager who you believe is skilful and has the ability to deliver superior returns in the future. Some managers publish their top stock holdings to their unitholders, so it could be worthwhile investing a small percentage of your available funds with this manager to receive information on where they are investing. Investing with a funds manager could also offer an opportunity to speak to the manager in person at an investor presentation. Those with chutzpah might call the manager frequently to talk shop.

Judgement

Once you have cobbled together your own Wall Street you enter an area where no-one can help you—judgement. The vast majority of information written about the sharemarket discusses picking stocks or predicting the direction of the market. This information is crucial and we will eventually get to that, but before you can consider picking stocks you must put the right foundations in place that will allow you to perform. All this groundwork requires supreme judgement—deciding which people you should trust and what information is worth acting on. Only experience will tell you if you have good judgement and no doubt you will make enough mistakes to make you ponder quitting. Whatever you do, don't quit.

All in the conversation

There are many lessons to learn when you are a professional investor, and very few are more important than understanding that the market does not close when you clock off each evening and head home. There is reading to do on the train and offshore markets to gauge on the television and internet overnight. This type of information collection and idea generation is taken as a given by people who make a living from the market. What is less obvious is the fact that everyone you meet in daily life can deliver an insight and, on some occasions, be the catalyst for a fantastically profitable trade.

An investor's primary job is to collect as much information as possible and work out which ideas are worth having a shot at. In his book *One Up On Wall Street*, Peter Lynch talks about the advantages the average person has over the professional on Wall Street. He spends time explaining how you can pick up some great stock tips just by observing what is going on around you in everyday life. He is correct, because ideas can come from the most unorthodox places.

> An investor's primary job is to collect as much information as possible and work out which ideas are worth having a shot at.

In the 1997 Australian film *The Castle*, Darryl Kerrigan, fighting in the courts to save his home from developers, is enjoying a cigarette outside the courtroom. Kerrigan, not the shy and retiring type, spots a lonely looking Lawrence Hammill and strikes up a conversation. Kerrigan had never met Hammill before and had no inkling he was a retired barrister who specialised in constitutional law, exactly the person he needed to fight his long-shot case. As the story goes on to tell, Hammill was attracted to Kerrigan's larger than life personality and decided to fight his case all the way to the High Court of Australia, eventually achieving victory. Kerrigan got to keep his house when only a few months earlier it all seemed lost. The unlikely result would never have happened if Kerrigan hadn't decided to have that pleasant chat outside the courtroom.

Unlike Lynch I have always found it difficult to latch onto possible investment ideas by just walking the corridors of the local shopping centre. For me it has been about conversation rather than observation and I have enjoyed many Darryl Kerrigan moments. It always helps if you like to talk. As long as I can remember I have found it effortless to engage people, including those who I have just met, in conversations about themselves and what they do. Whether at the kids' soccer match, on holidays, in a restaurant, over a coffee or even on the bus heading home, you can talk to people and ask them about what they know. When I am stuck in a shop or a place of business with my wife, instead of suffering from boredom I tend to ask the salesperson how things are travelling and what people are buying and ignoring. Most people like to talk about what they do and are also willing to share information with you. This all might sound a little esoteric, but as an investor you must keep your mind open at all times. Here are some examples of Kerrigan moments.

The not so wild west

I first realised the power of collecting ideas from the strangest places, when I went to a sharemarket conference in Perth in November 2000. I listened to nine companies present on day one, and not one of them was remotely interesting. That night I attended the conference dinner and wished I had skipped the whole event and gone to bed.

At breakfast the next morning, I saw fellow fund manager David Paradice eating breakfast with another gentleman whom I did not recognise. David motioned me to join them and he introduced me to the other gentleman who turned out to be Adelaide-based fund manager Erik Metanomski. After five minutes David excused himself saying he had to meet a company manager, leaving Erik and me uncomfortably alone. It wasn't long, though, before Erik was talking about what he liked in the market, including grocery wholesaler Metcash. Previously known as Davids Holdings, Metcash had nearly collapsed only a year or so before, but was now under new management. 'For the life of me, I can't see what is wrong with the stock. I've looked at it from every angle and it must be worth twice as much as it is today,' Erik said. I had nothing to offer, given I hadn't looked at Metcash, having written it off as a corporate casualty.

That afternoon I flew back to Sydney and next morning at work the first call I made was to the Metcash head office in Silverwater, in Sydney's west, to organise a company visit. Soon afterwards Geoff Wilson and I met with company managing director Andrew Reitzer and his offsider Edwin Jankelowitz, spending close to two hours with them discussing the business. It became apparent the new management team were smart, tough and had a clear plan to restore the company to its former glory. If they could restore the group's long-term profit margin the stock would re-rate dramatically. At best, the company was trading on a price to earnings multiple of around five, about 40 per cent of its long-term average. To top off the story, Reitzer said that hardly any professional investors or stockbrokers had come to visit the company for a long time.

On the way home in the car Geoff and I discussed the company, and we could not believe Metcash was yet to be rediscovered by the market. You beauty! We started buying shares in the company and before long it was one of our biggest holdings. Over the next 18 months, as the management delivered what they outlined in the meeting, the stock generated a return of more than 100 per cent, at a time when the market was going backwards.

I had spent nine hours on a plane from Sydney to Perth and back, to pick up a fabulous idea about a company that did not even present at the conference from a person I didn't know.

A solution in the dark

Ideas don't have to come from people in the market. They can appear from virtually anywhere, so long as you stay alert in all conversations. One night I was walking home along Macquarie Street in Sydney when I ran into a former university colleague. I hadn't seen Craig for several years and after a few minutes asked him where he was working these days. He said he had recently joined software group Solution 6. I knew nothing about the company except that I recognised its name from scanning the share tables in the newspaper. He didn't pass judgement on the company except to say: 'We are flat out at the moment. We could do with a lot more people; the place has got so much work on'. With that, I rang Solution 6 to organise a company visit with the chief financial officer (CFO). When Geoff and I turned up for the visit, we were greeted by the now infamous managing director Chris Tyler, who informed us that the CFO had quit the business that day, to take up a job for a company in Tasmania. The charming Tyler took the meeting and confirmed the company was flat out and there were a lot of tenders for work in the market. We went back to the office trying to work out the group's possible earnings potential. No stockbroking firms covered the stock, so we had to rely on our own numbers and, whichever way we cut it, the stock seemed remarkably cheap. We bought some shares at 80 cents and then they started to rise at a rapid clip. The company took advantage of the rising stock price by issuing new shares in a placement to professional investors. In the heady days of the tech boom of 1999, the stock shot up to $2 a share, hitting the valuation we had put on the company, at which time we sold out. This move proved to be silly, with the share price rocketing higher in the climax of the tech boom, eventually hitting a peak of around $18 a share. As the stock careered towards it peak, the company was followed by a swarm of stockbrokers and fund managers hungry to get exposure to the burgeoning technology market. The company took advantage of this demand by undertaking a share placement, which was six times oversubscribed, making it close to impossible for us to secure any shares in the capital raising.

In May 2000, Tyler left the company under the cloud of a criminal record in his home country of the United States, and the share price headed south at a rapid pace. Eventually, Solution 6 was taken over by accounting software group MYOB for a fraction of the price it had reached at the summit of the tech boom.

Anyone for breakfast?

On another occasion I was invited to a friend's house for brunch one Sunday morning. Among the guests were a husband and wife team who worked at accounting software group Reckon, which was one of the larger shareholdings at Wilson Asset Management. Without pressing them for information and placing them in an uncomfortable position, I simply asked what it was like to work at Reckon. Without hesitation both said it was a fabulous place, with a great culture and a very capable management team. That is where the conversation about Reckon ended. I was already familiar with the financials of the company and went home feeling extremely comfortable with our investment. In the coming weeks we added to our position, making it the largest in our flagship fund. The stock trebled in value over the next three years (see figure 5.1) and I can thank a random conversation with two excited employees, over a casual meal with friends for the substantial profit the investment delivered.

Figure 5.1: the rise and rise of Reckon 2001–11

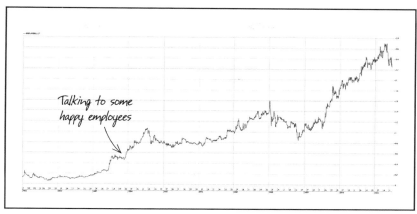

Source: IRESS

I should have my eyes checked

There are instances though where I have failed to pick up an idea that was placed right in my lap. One such occasion was when my wife and I attended the wedding of a colleague. To the groom's immense embarrassment some people were uncomfortable about the seating arrangements, and to resolve the problem he shyly approached us to ask if we would move and remedy the situation. We were relaxed, but if I had been alert I should have been buying him a bottle of expensive champagne. The person I ended up sitting next to was a pleasant lady who happened to be a long-term employee of listed private hospital operator Ramsay Health Care. I had got to know Ramsay's former CEO Pat Grier over the years and was interested to know whether she thought the mantra Grier preached of the Ramsay Way was genuine. She said it was a fantastic company with a superb culture of meritocracy. I was pleasantly surprised by the certainty of her comments. I returned to work on the Monday and looked at the Ramsay numbers again, but could only conclude that it was expensive and the returns were far from attractive. So I ignored the information I had received. I paid for my closed mind: since that day the stock has enjoyed several earnings upgrades and the price has doubled in a period when the market has struggled. I hadn't bought one share.

Conclusion

The market is everywhere and open all hours. The clear message is this: don't be backwards in coming forwards, and make sure you are curious enough to ask people the simple question of 'What do you do?' There could be some ideas lurking. If it worked for Darryl Kerrigan, it can work for you too.

Chapter 6

The nine rules of success

With your ideas now flowing freely, the next step in the investment process is to live by some rules that will keep you from straying into dangerous territory. There will be a large group of investors, primarily the punters, who will not like the idea of having to adhere to a set of rules. They want to roam free and explore all types of risk to ensure they get their fix. My advice to these people is don't obey any rules and go with your natural instincts, allowing you to enjoy the tidal gains and gut-wrenching losses that will follow close behind. For every other type of investor some simple rules will over time enhance your returns and allow you not only to sleep soundly, but also hopefully make some money while you sleep. For Peter Proksa, it took 12 years and some near-death experiences before he fully comprehended the importance of having some strict parameters to make sure he could keep his capital safe and potentially grow it into the future.

> Some simple rules will over time enhance your returns and allow you not only to sleep soundly, but also hopefully make some money while you sleep.

For me the following nine rules are the key to sustainable sharemarket investing. These rules though are not prescriptive and you may decide to draft your own set. The takeaway is that without a set of rules, anarchy reigns and returns start to drift.

Don't fall in love with yourself

An investment rule that I have read about and heard from other market participants for many years has been don't fall in love with a stock. I think there is a grain of truth in this comment, but sometimes to get the full benefit of an investment decision you want to fall in love with a company. Like relationships in your personal life, a lasting love affair can be much more rewarding than a series of one-night stands. Some of you will disagree with this, but from my experience the nirvana of investing is waking up every day and scanning the portfolio to see the same familiar names staring back at you. So long as the fundamentals still add up, based on your vigilant reviewing, then there is no reason to walk away from a stock. After all, a re-rating of a company can go on for many years. In many ways owning a company's shares is like a personal relationship that requires a great degree of monitoring and maintenance, ensuring that things don't go off the rails.

A much less rewarding approach is falling in love with your own ideas. As we have already discussed, picking stocks on the sharemarket is about generating ideas, researching them and finally making a decision to invest in them. For most people, once the decision is made to buy a share a strange event takes place—the value of the share you now own starts to go up in your own head. This phenomenon is not peculiar to shares. Anyone who buys a house, business, car or painting becomes emotionally attached to their decision and they suddenly believe their asset is worth more than it actually is, and definitely worth more than those people who might be interested in buying it would think. This type of value assessment doesn't even need to relate to an investment. People who follow a football team become emotionally involved and start to think their team is better than it actually is. Parents who decide to send their kids to a private school become attached to that school and start to believe it is the best educational institutional available, and invariably tell anyone in earshot their opinion. Objectivity flies out the window, simply because this was your idea.

So rule number one for any sharemarket investor is not to fall in love with your own ideas. Vanity is a powerful force for all of us and there is no room for it in the sharemarket, which has the ability to humble all of us. The malevolence of vanity is nothing new: the ancient Greeks warned us thousands of years ago with the story of the youth Narcissus who fell in love with his own reflection, eventually dying because of his obsession. There is nothing wrong with conviction, but to stare into the mirror each day and think to yourself that you're a brilliant thinker and smarter than most people in the market will be your undoing.

A juicy idea

In 2004 I came across a company called Signature Brands, which was being floated on the market. The business earned its revenue from royalty streams from a grab bag of brands it owned in the wine and clothing industries. Despite its unimpressive business model, the stock burst out of the gates when Signature Brands listed on the market, jumping from its 25 cents issue price to a staggering 80 cents. It wasn't long, though, before the business started to change quite rapidly. Its new plan involved rolling out a series of juice bars under the Pulp Juice brand, with former Virgin and Sony executive, Englishman Ian Duffell, leading the charge. The warped logic put forward by company management was that Pulp was just another brand and the company wasn't really changing directions.

Duffell, along with some business colleagues, had sold Pulp into Signature Brands in return for a chunk of shares and a lucrative option plan that would add to his already substantial wealth if everything worked out well. These radical business and management changes should have sent alarm bells ringing in my head about Signature Brands. Instead, I listened carefully to the juice bar story and was quickly seduced by its potential. I convinced myself that I had discovered a tiny company (known as a micro cap) that would one day become a major retail presence in Australia. My belief grew out of personal experience in retail. My wife had owned and operated a small coffee bar in the Sydney CBD and I had worked closely with her and thought I understood how a retail beverage business worked. The espresso business was just like the average Pulp Juice bar in terms of size and average customer purchase size. I thought Pulp was a fantastic idea that, if managed properly, could work wonders. The concept seemed so attractive I ignored the facts that it was a start-up business that had no track record of profitability and the management team was unproven.

After an initial surge in the number of shops and the Signature Brands share price, things started to stall. A colleague told me he had been speaking to one of the franchisees of the Pulp Bar chain and they made no bones about how badly things were working out. I chose to ignore this view. I retorted that I had also spoken to a franchisee who said operations were tracking along nicely. This was an exaggeration, and the reality was the franchisee whom I had spoken to was less than forthcoming with information. Soon afterwards the numbers released by the company revealed the initial business plan was failing: the cash flow was negative (it was losing money) and the company needed to raise capital just to keep the dream alive (see figure 6.1). I started to make up excuses for why things were starting to unravel and agreed to tip more money into the venture in the hope that some scale in the business through more stores, including some flagship shops in key sites, would magically turn the ship around.

Figure 6.1: the decline of Signature Brands 2004–06

Source: IRESS

In my desperation to will the venture to succeed I found myself going to the nearest Pulp Juice bar and buying one or maybe even two drinks a day, to help boost sales. Every week I would visit head office in Double Bay to see management in anticipation of the business starting to hit its stride. I was becoming delusional. Eventually the Pulp Juice chain failed and Signature Brands fell into administration, and we were forced to write the value of the investment down to zero. The decline was swift. Vanity had beaten me and I had been punished.

A sickness that needs to be cured

The way to cure this illness is to look at your portfolio of stocks every day as if you had never made the decision to buy them in the first place. Instead, you should view your portfolio as if you had inherited it from someone else. This is a sobering approach. How many times have we seen a new managing director appointed to a company who, through a fresh set of eyes, has decided to offload an underperforming business unit or asset, even if it meant taking a major haircut on the purchase price. The previous managing director who had made the decision to buy the asset could not make the follow-up decision to sell the asset when things started to go pear shaped. They had made the choice to buy the asset and had fallen in love with their own idea. The rest of the world could see the idea was failing. The same approach can and should be applied to a share purchase by an investor.

Learn to deal with your mistakes

Many books on sharemarket investing state that you have to learn from mistakes. To me this is a risky strategy to take into the investment market. I say this for two very simple reasons. First, most people who have made mistakes in their lives have a very good chance of being repeat offenders at some time in the future. Second, most of the time when they repeat the mistake, they are totally unaware of what they are doing until after the event, which is far too late. We are not discussing run-of-the-mill day-to-day errors that everyone can make, but the fatal flaws in our investment approach that need to be totally cut out before they become cancerous.

Let's examine a few real-life examples. Many people get married a second time thinking they can learn from the mistakes of the first marriage. Before long, the marriage is failing and the new partner wants a divorce because it's just not working out. The divorce rate among people getting married for the second time is significantly higher than among those marrying for the first time.

A person with a drinking problem gets horribly drunk and ends up in a fight. Initially, they vow never to drink again, but something turns sour at work or in a relationship and the urge to hit the drink grips them again. The person doesn't intend to end up in trouble but as the drinking progresses the chances of getting into strife escalate and inevitably something goes wrong and a mess is created.

A third example would be a person with a gambling addiction. The young man gets his pay packet on a Thursday and to let off a bit of steam he heads to the local club to buy a beer and play the poker machines for half an hour. All good fun! Before he realises, it is closing time and more than half his fortnightly pay has been sucked into the machine, never to be seen again. During his time in front of the poker machine he is always highly optimistic that he will get on a winning streak and walk home with booty. Two weeks later he gets his fortnightly pay and does all the right things, such as pay his bills and shop for the groceries. With the couple of hundred dollars he has left he thinks he needs to treat himself for his discipline and heads to the races with his friends only to win some money in the first race, igniting a taste for the punt again. This is the beginning of the end, and by the final race he has lost everything, and may even owe money to one or more of his friends.

The croupier Peter Proksa kept making the same mistakes before he realised that he needed a more disciplined game plan that would keep him away from his near-death experiences.

These examples are extreme. However, the point is very clear — we all have weaknesses that cannot be cured by self-containment and thinking you can learn from your mistakes is misguided. The first step to beating these vices is to identify them. Once this is achieved you have to make a pact with yourself never to get into a situation where you could be a repeat offender. Once you are an alcoholic, you have a lifetime condition that means you should never pick up a drink again. It is fanciful to believe that when confronted with a situation a second time you will have learned from your previous mistake and be able to handle it with aplomb.

My major weakness has always been stubbornness. I love to publicly announce a view or even a prediction that I am convinced will turn out correctly. Even if the evidence mounts against my view, I find it tough to budge and admit that I was wrong. If you can't admit you are wrong then don't go into investing. I have to keep a lid on my predictions so I don't have to admit to anyone that I could be wrong. Others have a weak gene for fabulous salespeople. Some investors gravitate far too easily towards the current story in vogue just because everyone in the markets is talking about it. And then there are some investors who have a fatal attraction to certain sectors, such as gold, biotechs or technology. All of these companies could be the next big thing, but most end up disappearing with a whimper.

As I write these words I have yielded to another one of my weaknesses. For years I have sworn off biotech companies, especially those awaiting a company-making decision from regulators in the northern hemisphere. Many years ago I suffered a major loss for our investors by believing, along with many others, that regulatory approval would be obtained, only to watch a stock plummet when the opposite actually happened. With that in mind and trying to apply my rules I have steered clear of all biotech companies, including Pharmaxis, a market darling and a bellwether of the Australian biotech community. The company's value had climbed to around $600 million on the back of investor belief that it would eventually gain approval for its key drug, opening the door on a $1 billion a year market. After years of saying no to Pharmaxis, I caved in to temptation in April 2011. The company told the investment community it would get European approval in the next two months and it was hopeful that it would be a green light rather than outright rejection. I took a small position in the stock and, sure enough, two months later the regulators gave the company the thumbs down. Pharmaxis shares fell 70 per cent that day and we had to cut our holding on the spot. I hadn't learned from my mistakes and should have stuck to my rule of never investing other people's money in biotechs.

Say sorry

The first realisation all sharemarket investors must come to terms with is that mistakes will be made, and made consistently. Every wrong decision is still going to be terribly painful, but if you can reconcile in your own mind that you are not immune from making incorrect calls then you can get on with the more enjoyable business of trying to make money from investing.

There is no value in ignoring an error or, worse still, trying to prove that it was not your fault and that circumstances conspired against you. None of this will reverse the loss. A far better option is to say sorry, sell out of the position and move onto the next opportunity. I have found over the years that apologising to my colleagues was liberating, and provided the energy and confidence to push forward.

Practically, it is easier to say sorry when you are working with other people than when you are a private investor sitting alone in your kitchen. This should not make you exempt from following the same rule though. A good habit to force yourself into is to review your portfolio of shares each day, checking the prices, and apologising for any decisions that have not worked out profitably. Once you have mastered the apology then you can follow up with some rules about selling.

Work hard on selling

All investment books and courses concentrate heavily on working out when to buy stocks. Very little time is allocated to the other side of the equation — selling. An army of investors out there have endless stories about how they were sitting on an enormous profit before seeing it all evaporate as the stock headed south. Peter Proksa is a prime example — before he realised that selling can be a profitable activity.

An equal number of people have stayed loyal to a stock that has headed south from the outset in the hope that a magical cure will appear to turn the stock price up. Hope is a forlorn emotion when it comes to the sharemarket and more often than not these investors will ride the investment down to next to nothing. You have to learn how to sell. When you book a plane ticket, you usually book the return flight at the same time. When it comes to investing you must spend a lot of time considering when to sell and then acting upon your plan.

At Wilson Asset Management we reviewed our trading positions every morning at 9 am. For trading positions we would have a 10 per cent stop loss rule. This meant that if a stock fell 10 per cent from the average cost of purchase we would sell the shares. Alternatively, if the price of shares we had just sold (a short position) rose more than 10 per cent, then we would buy the shares back. The only genuine exception to this was when a stock was relatively illiquid and took some time to buy back.

The genius behind this rule was that it took blame out of the game. The natural reaction to a falling share price is to hold onto the share or even try to reduce the average price paid by buying more shares. On many occasions this simply compounded the problem and resulted in a significantly greater loss. Many people have complained to me over the years that this is too cut throat an approach and opportunities will be missed when a stock turns. That's fine, but I can guarantee that we have saved a lot of money, time and effort by following this rule, reassured that there are so many other opportunities out in the market at any one time. It is my firm belief that you will waste enormous amounts of energy and probably miss other opportunities if you become fixated on one falling share price. A cleaner and more efficient option is to sell the stock and start prowling around the market for something that is going to make you money rather than drain the life out of you. The market is such a fertile landscape that there are plenty of other patches of ground that will create prosperity.

On Friday mornings we not only reviewed our trading positions but also carefully looked through our longer term investment positions. At Wilson Asset Management we employed a dual approach to the market. For about half the funds we managed we aggressively traded, while for the other half we heavily researched opportunities to buy well-priced companies that we could hold for a longer period until we believed the shares had became expensive. For these longer term researched positions, we did not apply a 10 per cent stop loss rule. Instead, there was a level of scrutiny from all staff members to make sure we did not hang onto an investment if there was no catalyst that would re-rate the stock. People who did not make the original decision to invest would commonly ask the decision maker, why we were still holding this stock. If there was no real reason to hold, then we would sell.

Making the decision of when to sell is always taxing. The saying 'your first loss is your best loss', carries a lot of weight and should be considered carefully, especially at a time when a bubble is bursting. When the tech bubble popped in April 2000, many people wanted to buy more shares on the initial dip. When stocks did not recover, investors who had fallen in love with technology went into denial. Instead of coming to grips with the reality that most of these stocks had no earnings to speak of, these investors lived in hope that the euphoric emotion created by a surging share price would return. Living in hope normally results in disappointment. They said a correction in prices was healthy and would pave the way for another major bull run into the future. As share prices continued to head south, denial turned into a commitment to hold the stocks until they at least break even again. Finally, as the share prices fell to unimaginable lows and losses were running at 80 per cent or possibly more, these investors finally threw up their hands and sold, unable to bear the sight of the tech names they used to be in love with.

Investors will always be shocked at how far share prices can fall. We have only to reflect on the mindset of Peter Proksa, with his determination to hold onto condemned stories, such as Telco Australia and Davnet, when the tech decline went into overdrive. In hindsight these tech junkies had no selling policy, and the experience of the tech crash proved to be so painful many investors did not return to the market for many years, and they completely missed the bull run from early 2003 to the end of 2007.

Selling a company that has risen sharply can be just as difficult to deal with. When buying a share, most investors are happy to experience a modest gain, hopefully one greater than the overall market. When the stock shoots up, however, the mentality starts to change. People race to grab their calculators to work out how much money they have made and then they start to calculate what kind of profit they would make if the stock rose another 10, 15 or 20 per cent more. Suddenly the exhilaration associated with making money starts to take over from common sense and sound judgement. The share price spike may have sent a stock up to a price to earnings ratio of 25, or 60 per cent higher than the market average. Instead of thinking this makes the stock expensive, fantasy takes over, and justification of why the stock you have bought should trade at an even higher multiple starts to kick in. Talk of an upgrade or an acquisition, or whispers of a takeover mean you don't sell that stock even though there is no concrete reason to stay on the share register. Then, out of a blue sky, bad news of an earnings downgrade comes and the stock falls like a brick all the way back to where you bought it. Once again there has been no discipline or policy on selling.

There is no steadfast rule to selling stocks, but for the most part it is a good habit to be selling something out of a portfolio at all times. If your portfolio is made up of only a handful of stocks, then selling will be far less regular, but anybody who has a selection of 20 or more stocks should be seriously considering that one or possibly more have no reason for staying in the family any longer. If, after rigorous scrutiny and constant reviews the story still adds up, based on sound valuations, then there is no urgency to push the sell button. But when flimsy and easy excuses to hold stocks start to take hold, such as the possibility of a takeover, then act promptly. Individual private investors have a major advantage over professional investors in that they do not have to be invested and can take the liberty to sell when the moment is right and head into cash. Unlike the discipline of buying, selling is significantly easier because you can only sell what you already own, so the universe is captured right in front of you each day. Buying, on the other hand, kills you with choice.

Don't concentrate too hard

A rule that all investors who want to stay in the game for an extended period should take on board is diversification. Peter Proksa was a quick learner. At the start, he thought that the shortest road to becoming rich was putting all his capital in one or possibly two stocks. The speed of his fortune building was surpassed only by the swiftness of its departure when things turned ugly. As Sir Isaac Newton told us, 'For every action there is an equal and opposite reaction'. Eventually, and after much turbulence, Proksa realised that if he was to survive in the sharemarket, he needed a mechanism to protect his capital.

The most obvious way to protect capital is to not concentrate your bets but spread them around. Just how many stocks you own depends on a variety of factors, including how much capital you have spare, how many good ideas are available and if the overall market is providing opportunities. I recommend that people invest money in at least 10 stocks and possibly up to 30, but to suggest an exact number would be too restrictive. Owning more than 30 stocks will become unwieldy for most individuals. Owning one or only a handful of stocks, on the other hand, means you can't afford to be wrong, and that is starting to think unrealistically.

Don't let the bank make decisions for you

In 2004 I decided for the first time in my life to take out a margin loan to buy a stock. I was a director on the board of the company and believed the correct thing to do was own some shares. For the best part of four years I hardly read the monthly notices that were sent to me from the lender. In November 2008, after the market had fallen more than 40 per cent from a year earlier, I was on a work trip that took me away from home for two days. I arrived home late one night and went straight to bed. The next morning I opened my mail, which included a second monthly notice from the lender. It stated that I had breached my limit on my margin loan and that I needed to either buy more shares or place some cash into the account. If I did not act immediately the lender would be forced to sell a percentage of my shares in the company. I was getting a margin call. This was a shock, given I thought that a margin call was a phone call or even an email, and not a two-day-old letter in the mail.

The whole situation was unacceptable given that I was a director of the company and had a personal policy of never selling any shares in a company that I sat on the board of. I set my mind to buying more shares that day, avoiding the embarrassment of having to announce to the market, as a director of the company, that I had sold shares. When I read the notice more carefully I realised that because I had been away for two days the deadline to fix the margin problem had passed. The lender had sold my shares the day before. Flustered, I quickly rang them and the woman at the other end of the phone put me on hold for some time. Eventually she came back to confirm that I had received a margin call, but that, given the overwhelming number of people receiving margin calls at the time, they had not been able to keep up with the deluge and had not got around to dealing with my loan. I could not believe it! I raced out and put $5000 into my loan account to pay down the size of my debt, keeping my shares fully intact.

Three months later I received another notice in the mail from the lender. By now I was closely monitoring every note relating to the margin loan and knew that I was comfortably within my borrowing limit. This time, the letter explained that the lender had reduced the margin limit on my company and that I was once again in breach of the loan. Because of the snail pace of the traditional mail I had been given no warning that the breach had been triggered. I had to buy more shares in the company that day before 11 am. By this stage I called the lender and among other harsh words suggested they rename the margin call as the margin letter! Luckily, by the end of that day the share price jumped up three cents and I was back within the margin limit. The company's share price, along with the overall market, just kept rallying from that day and I have never received another margin letter.

The moral to the story is that borrowing money means that at some stage the decisions about buying or selling a stock will be taken out of your hands. This is an unacceptable situation and should be avoided at all costs.

Watch out for double dipping

There is another reason why share investors should keep their distance from debt. Most companies have some form of bank debt, with the average sitting at around 30 per cent of total assets. There are different ways for companies to measure their levels of debt, but the more conservative approach is to calculate a simple percentage of debt to equity on the balance sheet. A more dangerous measurement is when a company measures its percentage of debt over its equity plus debt level. All this serves to do is seemingly lower the gearing level, but the amount of debt is exactly the same. A third measurement that is also worth following is interest cover, which is how many times a company's earnings cover the annual interest bill from the debt on the balance sheet.

In the lead up to the GFC, balance sheets became pregnant with debt, as lenders around the world scrambled to juice up their profits by pushing money out the door. After the GFC, the average debt level declined rapidly, and companies raised record levels of capital by tapping the sharemarket by issuing more shares.

To explain why taking out a margin loan is dangerous in this situation, let's look at a company that has a long-term average debt level of around 40 per cent of its total assets. As a shareholder, you are buying only into the equity component of the company—in this example that's 60 per cent of the capital. The earnings generated by the company have to be used to pay the interest bill, pay off the debt and pay taxes; whatever is left is there for the equity holders in the form of profits. So shareholders sit right at the bottom of the payments queue.

When you take out a margin loan, worth say 50 per cent of the value of your shares, you are effectively placing borrowing on top of borrowing. The company has 40 per cent gearing of its own debt and then you are adding a further 30 per cent, leaving just 30 per cent of debt-free equity. From your point of view the company is, suddenly, highly geared at around 70 per cent. In figure 6.2, the first bar shows the company's value without a margin loan, while the second bar shows the reduction in equity with the introduction of the margin loan.

There is a possible problem here. If the company falls on difficult times and is forced to write down the value of its assets, then its gearing levels can start to rise. This happened to many companies in the GFC. In our example the company that has 40 per cent gearing might see its gearing rocket to 70 per cent if it is forced to write down the value of its assets by 50 per cent, leaving just 30 per cent equity. If the company is forced to make this write down and you have the added burden of the margin loan, the value of your equity shrinks, not to 30 per cent but to zero. This unenviable position is shown in bar 3 of figure 6.2.

Figure 6.2: The risk to your equity in a company when a margin loan is introduced.

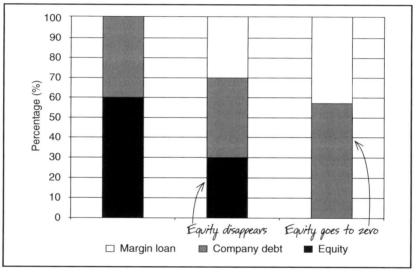

In this example the company's bank may tap the company board on the shoulder and say it would be advisable to try to raise some fresh equity from shareholders to get the gearing level back down to the long-term average. The company has very few options, and it is forced to raise equity through a discounted rights issue. This forces you to tip more money into the company or face your share of the company being heavily diluted. In these circumstances, the share price tends to fall towards the rights issue price. Your margin lender will now write you a letter demanding that more money be deposited into your account or it will sell your shares. This causes a double whack on your investment. First of all you have to stump up the cash for the rights issue, and then top up your margin loan account.

The flip side of gearing on gearing is that it can work fabulously if a company's share price rises and rises. As a passive investor with no control over the company's operations you are living in hope that things will go right. I would rather take a slightly lower, ungeared return where I can make the buy, hold and sell decisions rather than hand this responsibility over to a bank or other financial institution.

In 2008 and early 2009 the levels of margin calls were at historic highs and showed how much debt had built up in the market. We sat at work and watched some of our stocks plummet, just because the faceless investors in various companies we owned had been margined. Suddenly there was more risk in your fellow shareholder than there was in the company you were investing in. These unfortunate people were physically ripped out of their stocks just at a time when the overall market was warming up for a 50 per cent rebound.

Follow the rules of life

A rule that requires little explanation is to approach investing as you would approach any other task in life. Those who stay calm, apply a fair share of common sense and never lose their judgement will eventually rise to the top of the investment tree. These rules work in all walks of life, including managing staff, bringing up your children, driving a car, playing sport and organising events. People who can keep their poise and look at a situation with a clear head tend to come up with the best solution. Despite periods of high volatility, this approach will also normally work in the sharemarket.

For example if a story sounds too good to be true, then it probably is. Use your common sense and steer away from it. If a company is trading on a price to earnings multiple that is double the market average, common sense tells us that it has more downside than upside risk, so maybe it is time to start selling it. If a company does not earn any money and will not for some years to come but is valued at many tens of millions of dollars, then you might want to stay clear of it in the short to medium term. If a managing director gets paid twice the salary of the average managing director, then it's time to ask some questions. If the overall market has risen on average by 20 per cent for five years, then maybe it's time for a pullback, and you should head to the sidelines.

None of these examples requires a rocket scientist to work out, but the person who acts calmly and does not get carried away with the madness of the moment will start to see above-average long-term returns.

Read until you drop

Finally, there is no substitute for reading. I have discussed at length the importance of talking to people from all walks of life to harvest information that might enhance your knowledge of a stock or industry. Just as important, and possibly more so, is the requirement to read anything you can get your hands on. This does not mean performing the arduous task of raking through stockbroker research with a fine tooth comb. It means reading the newspaper, reading about the economy, reading company announcements, reading fiction, reading investment books and, yes, reading some research. The more information you can collect the more ideas you germinate and the more success you should have in the market. I honestly believe you are never wasting time if you are reading. Over the years I have attempted to find between one and two hours a day just to read. At the breakfast table, on the bus, on the train and before I go to sleep. A great place to read is on a plane trip, rather than watch a movie. I always thought I should ride on more transport so I could read more. The more technical stuff has to be absorbed in the morning when I am most alert, and the lighter material was left to last thing at night.

Conclusion

These rules may not resonate with you. You may even be able to construct a fresh set of rules to fit your investment style, just like the ones Peter Proksa laid out for us in the prologue. The essence of this chapter, though, is to stress the importance of having rules that will keep your investment performance healthy.

Part III
Ready, set, go!

Now we have reached the big moment—buying and selling shares. This section is not meant to be prescriptive; instead, it is about explaining the way we approached the market at Wilson Asset Management over the years and some of the key factors we concentrated on. This method served us well, but didn't make us immune from mistakes. As a stock picker I have focused heavily in this part of the book on how I look at stocks. Hopefully it will help you try to discover the best method for yourself.

Chapter 7

Finding stocks that go up

At times I felt like I had mastered the technique of buying high and selling low. This insidious problem was most painful in bull markets when I managed to select the only stock going down in the hottest sector on the market. Whether it is mining, biotechs or software companies, I have managed to jump on the one dog that goes down, despite the remainder of the sector bursting upwards. My best guess is that I'm not the only one who has been struck down by this affliction. Stay in the sharemarket long enough and buying stocks that look fabulous only to see them tumble lower is a phenomenon that cruels the best of us.

To eradicate this bad habit we have to know how to find stocks that go up. Professional investors like to say that they fish where the fish are or they catch the train as it leaves the station, but the facts are that unearthing the gems that actually do rise and deliver great returns is a fine art that needs a great deal of attention. Many investors spend their whole life looking without finding much. Let's make sure you are not part of this army of people.

Too stupid to fail

When word came through to our office in May 2003 that AMP was raising up to $1.2 billion through a placement of shares at a price representing a 40 per cent discount to its previous closing price, I assumed that Australia's largest superannuation group had made the long anticipated decision to split its business in two. I believed the money raised would be funnelled into its UK operations and then it would be listed separately from its Australian operation. Given rumours had been circulating in the market that AMP's UK business needed funding, the whole episode made sense. The broker on the other end of the phone politely said, 'I'm not sure what you are talking about'. He then went on to say that the money being raised was for the overall business and a company split would take place after that. I barked back, 'But how can a business raise money at such a big discount to its previous closing price, especially when it is a placement?' His comment was, 'Yeah, it sounds strange, but that is what is happening'.

By law, a placement of new shares by a company can be offered only to high net worth individuals and institutions. The mum and dad retail investors are excluded. A placement of shares allows a company to increase its share capital by 15 per cent virtually overnight, with no need to provide a prospectus. Usually, a placement would be offered at a discount of 5 to 10 per cent off the previous closing price to encourage investors to participate. This offer was close to a 40 per cent discount, and it would greatly dilute individual shareholdings in the company, especially for those retail investors who were left out in the cold by the offer. As a rule, a company would raise money at such a massive discount through a rights issue which, unlike a placement, is offered to all shareholders on a pro-rata basis, ensuring that shareholders were not fleeced by the dilution.

A rights issue just didn't cut it for the blue chip AMP, because it would have required a prospectus, meaning it would have taken between six and eight weeks for the money to roll in. A few hours later, once the shock had subsided, I commented in the office, 'The authorities in the UK must have told them to raise money quickly, or else'. AMP needed the funds in its account within two days and no reason for the placement was really given to those retail investors, who would see their investments collapse before their eyes. Curiously, shareholders did not question the whole process.

Unfortunately for our investors at Wilson Asset Management, we had started buying AMP shares before the capital raising was announced. Our investment case was straightforward — the company had specifically said some months earlier that there was no need to raise fresh capital. In addition, the stock had been crunched to historical lows in the enormous decline in the UK market following the tech wreck from 2000 to 2002 and the company looked relatively cheap compared with historical prices. With the overall market starting to bounce, it seemed like the ideal time to wade into the company. When the capital raising bombshell exploded, we had no choice but to bid hard for as many shares in the placement as possible to reduce our overall entry cost. But once everything washed through, we were staring at a loss on our investment of around 25 per cent, as the share price slumped to trade just above the heavily discounted placement price. We were fuming, and the lack of disclosure about the group's capital position was unnerving. Surprisingly, we hardly heard a peep from AMP's major shareholders.

The lasting lesson from the whole unsavoury incident was the realisation that many large Australian companies operate with a privileged status. During the banking collapses of the GFC, the US press coined the phrase that some financial companies were 'too big to fail'. In Australia I would go one step further and suggest that the Australian market place has taken the view that many of the top 50 listed companies live in a world where no matter how stupid they are, they simply can't fail.

Fifty stocks that are safer than houses

In the run up to the GFC, a long list of top-ranked companies in Australia took big risks with shareholder funds that verged on stupidity, only to be saved any embarrassment by a forgiving market. These included GPT, Wesfarmers, Westfield, Rio Tinto, Suncorp and all the four major banks, just to name a few. Every one of these companies entered the GFC highly geared with bank debt, and if their lenders decided not to roll over their debts they would have to liquidate their assets or raise new equity just to survive. This segment of corporate Australia took very little responsibility for the pressure this put their shareholders under. The companies were happy to say the GFC was a highly unlikely event that sideswiped just about everyone. However, a closer look at history shows that banking collapses and credit crunches have been frequent in both Australia and the United States.

I believe that there is no reasonable excuse for a company to be in a position where a bank can pull the plug on it under any circumstances. It can be soundly argued that all of these companies would have faced financial ruin if the sharemarket, swelling with superannuation savings, did not ignore incompetent management decisions and happily plough in fresh capital. Capital raisings by all these companies from late 2008 until early 2010 during the GFC were offered at major discounts to the prevailing share price, but few asked questions about why the money had to be raised.

A study of these companies shows management took on unhealthy levels of debt when borrowing was cheap and money was free-flowing. Instead of facing the consequences when conditions changed, they were let off scot-free, with no explanation required. This is akin to an unspoken and unwritten pact that certain companies will be bailed out by the market under any circumstances.

This is a great comfort to shareholders who want to restrict their investing activities to the top 50 Australian companies. Sure, you can take a haircut on your investment, just as we did with AMP, but you can rest assured that these companies will stay solvent.

If you are going to invest in, say, 10 of the top 50 stocks then you don't need to do more than a surface level search for names to put your money into. A possible approach would be to ask one of the brokers you have grown comfortable with, to provide a list of the top 50 stocks, listed in sectors with their price to earnings multiples and income dividend yields. You can diversify your investments by choosing companies from a range of sectors and go with the stocks that have the highest yields. One possible further observation is to check with your broker that the companies you have picked have relatively low levels of debt, which would minimise the need for them to raise capital in a way that will dilute your share holdings.

Turn up the risk dial

For those who have a greater appetite for risk, you need a completely different approach to finding stocks that you believe can make you money. About 2000 companies are listed on the ASX, from a range of sectors, including retail, manufacturing, software, mining, exploration, energy, media, transport, banking, insurance and property, to name just a few. There is a smorgasbord of companies to choose from. The key is to have a method that allows you to narrow this list down to a number of stocks that you want to own and can adequately manage. Everyone has their own technique; Peter Proksa limits his investment universe to stocks that are trading at 1 cent or less, which has proven to be highly effective for him. My guess is that this is too risky for most investors, so we have to look at other techniques.

The role of the broker

A stockbroker's role is to help their clients make money from investing in the sharemarket. So, instead of swallowing whatever he or she force feeds you, turn the tables and make the broker work for you.

Once your broker has spent sufficient time working out what type of investor you are or would like to be, he or she can start running screens for you. A screen is simply plugging a handful of financial criteria into the computer that will take the information and spit out a list of companies that provide what you are looking for. If, for example, you're in search of risk through buying high beta companies, then your stockbroker can run a screen working out the highest beta stocks that have market capitalisation over a certain level. Remember, high beta stocks are those that climb more than the market when it is rising and, conversely, descend further when the market is falling. This screen will deliver the level of risk that you are after, and it will also make sure that you have sufficient liquidity to move in or out of the stock when you want.

Another investor might be eager to generate the highest possible franked income stream and is happy to wander outside the top 50 companies, in a bid to increase that yield. Your broker can then add some other criteria to the screening process, such as the company's debt levels, liquidity and payout ratios. A payout ratio is the percentage of the company's profits represented by the dividend. If a company is yielding a high fully franked dividend, but is paying out 100 per cent of its profits to achieve this payout, then you may not want to include it on your list because the dividend may not be sustainable. Brainstorming with your broker will throw up numerous screens that can be run.

A fantastic screen is charting the long-term price to earnings multiple of the companies that you may be interested in. A broker can graph this and you will easily see from the chart whether a company is trading well above, or below, its historical averages. Either of these situations should be the catalyst for further investigation and possibly trigger a sell or a buy.

One screen that we liked to run over the years was to identify companies whose shares were trading at below the stated value of the assets on the balance sheet or, even better, the net cash level. This technique has proven highly profitable since the GFC decimated stock prices in 2008.

Behind the broker

A stockbroker is a salesperson. Sitting behind the broker are a range of people, including a bevy of analysts who scour the market every day, building financial models. Analysts are not always good stock pickers, but they are excellent at their job of compiling numbers and ferreting out information. It is always worthwhile asking your broker what his analysts have been talking about, and whether they have produced any new reports. Make sure you ask your broker for all of the research reports his or her company produces. Most of them will consist of dry arguments, but you should devour them in a bid to learn about individual stocks. Critically, these reports will provide a financial model of the company you are reading about and deliver key earnings forecasts, along with a range of other financial ratios that we will talk about in the coming chapters. If your broker starts to taper off in telling you what his or her analysts are discussing, think about searching for a new broker with better ideas.

Old news

The role of the newspaper in the sharemarket has been heavily diluted by the advent of a range of new technologies, particularly the internet, which has seen its readership fall and influence reduced. Despite this I still get a lot of value from the newspaper. Each day, usually while riding on the bus to work, I would go straight to the share tables and run my finger along the sectors that interested me. This would provide a gentle reminder of the various stocks that exist in that sector and give me some material to follow up on that day.

Sitting next to the share tables in the paper is a table of the rolling 12-month highs and 12-month lows. Without doubt this is the most valuable table presented to the public every day. Interestingly, you will find that both the stocks hitting the highs and the stocks hitting the lows should unearth some tremendous investment possibilities in the short to medium term.

Higher and higher

I have come across many professional investors who believe it is too late to plunge into a company once it has hit a 12-month high. My experience tells me something quite different. A stock touching a 12-month high can continue to rack up new highs for some time to come, and you ignore them at your own peril. A perfect situation is when a company has hit a 12-month high, and further investigation reveals that it is at the embryonic stage of a major turnaround. Over the years at Wilson Asset Management, we would sell a stock we were invested in when a negative catalyst, such as an earnings downgrade, had been announced. Once soiled by an earnings downgrade, a company can be in the doghouse for an extended period. Sometime later, maybe 18 months down the track, the stock would appear on the 12-month rolling high list. On closer inspection we would discover the company, after a torrid decline, has been the beneficiary of a positive catalyst, such as a change in management or a divestment that was bringing back investors. Sometimes the catalyst could simply be that the market had got so negative on a company that it had become ridiculously cheap and so represented compelling value.

A prime example of this was debt-purchasing group Credit Corp, which after falling 97 per cent from its peak in September 2007, bottomed out at just 39 cents a share in early 2009. Board and management changes, the reduction of debt and an emphasis on increasing collection rates were all catalysts for the stock to move higher. The first time we discovered this was by scanning the 12-month rolling high list. The stock had motored up to around 60 cents from its low and by mid 2011 the stock was trading at around $5 a share. A handy gain of more than 800 per cent in just over two years.

Down but not out

Stocks hitting 12-month lows are normally an uninspiring group of low-profile companies. Many of them will be tiny organisations that desperately need capital to survive and unless you have the ability to behave like a corporate doctor or a vulture fund, I would advise giving them a wide berth. Buried among this group, though, will be an interesting name that has run into hard times and the market has washed its hands of it. After the tech wreck of 2002 this group of stocks proved to be a fertile hunting ground, with a swathe of tech stocks plumbing new lows day after day, with investors absolving themselves of their sins of the late 1990s. By 2002 the tech sector was so unloved that most people sold their stocks out just to brag about the fact they didn't have any tech companies in their portfolio. Ironically it was exactly at this time in the cycle that people should have been getting hungry for a piece of technology.

Two such situations that became incredibly profitable trades for us were accounting software group Reckon and domain registration outfit Melbourne IT. Both companies had been market darlings in early 2000 and both were smart enough to have raised sufficient cash from eager investors to survive the ultimate downturn when it hit. Although we argued among ourselves about who identified Reckon as an investment opportunity, we could easily have discovered it by simply running our finger down the list of 12-month rolling lows.

The stock, after peaking at around $2.00 a share, cratered along with the rest of the sector, hitting a low of just 7 cents a share. This decline took some time, but after closer inspection we discovered that Reckon had been forced by the ASX to release quarterly cash flow updates. These quarterly updates revealed a company that had about 8 cents a share in cash on its balance sheet and a positive operating cash flow. The company had also recently changed its management team. These days Reckon trades at around $2.30 a share and pays regular dividends.

Melbourne IT was a bellwether for the tech sector in Australia. It floated in 1999 and the share price multiplied in a matter of weeks, rocketing up towards $18.00 before the story started to fall apart. The bullish numbers hoped for by investors started to look unobtainable and, with the onset of the tech wreck in the United States, the selling of the stock became fierce. Each day, spooked investors clipped a dollar off the share price. In the end, the stock sunk all the way back to just 30 cents a share. Like Reckon, a closer examination of the company showed a balance sheet with around 33 cents a share in surplus cash. It was also reporting small but growing profits. If you were quick enough to invest at 30 cents, you were getting a company for less than cash and the business for free. I can't think of another place on the globe where such an opportunity can arise. As you can see in figure 7.1, over the next five years Melbourne IT's share price climbed back to more than $4.00 a share.

Figure 7.1: share price of Melbourne IT from January 2001 to June 2007

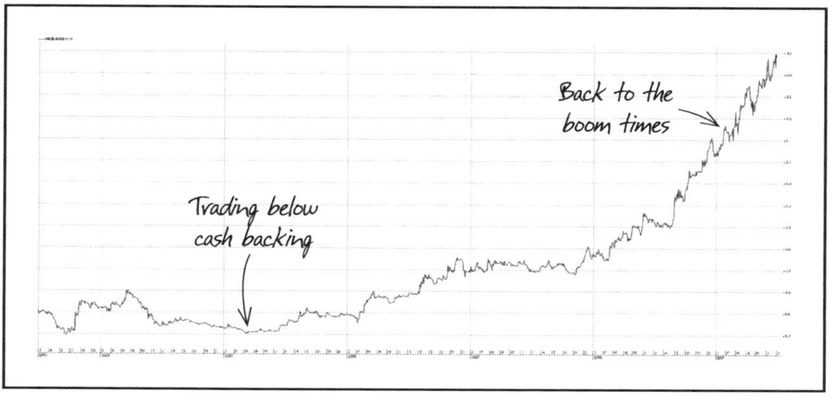

Source: IRESS

The 12-month rolling low list can be next to useless when the market is in the middle of a major bull run. During the back end of the 2003 to 2007 bull market, we were lucky to find more than three or four lonely stocks sitting in the 12-month rolling low table. By contrast, the 12-month rolling high list required more space just to fit them all in. However, when the market goes through a correction, suddenly a stock that has risen for the best part of 12 months can fall sharply, further than the overall market, for no specific reason except investor panic, driving them to a 12-month low. This is another chance to re-load your investments.

Charting a course

Fundamental investors, who concentrate solely on the financial statements of a company, take great pleasure in discrediting the vocation of charting. As its name suggests, charting is the science of predicting the future movement of a stock or overall market by studying the history of the share price or index. The general opinion among fundamentalists is that charting is only one step away from witchcraft, and people who use charting to identify good investments are looking for an easy way to pick stocks and become rich. I won't be so disparaging, because I know several people who have achieved more than respectable returns by using charting as their primary means of picking stocks. I even like to talk to people who study charts because charting analyses human activity and the repeating nature of it. However, after much reflecting, I do not believe that charting is the best way to pick stocks. Usually a chartist will tell you exactly why a stock has behaved in a particular way in the past, and then proceed to say that in the future the same stock will do one of three things. This can normally be summarised as go up, go nowhere or go down. As legendary value investor Robert Maple-Brown has said, charting is like looking in the rear vision mirror.

I strongly recommend, though, that all investors consistently look at charts. Not so much for their predictive value but because they provide a historical snapshot of a company's performance. If you spend an hour a week looking at a range of stock charts, I guarantee you will discover a cluster of companies that are worth following up and doing more research on. It could be that you notice a company has either fallen or risen sharply without any news being announced. Another scenario could be that a company has endured a long and painful decline and has recently started to edge higher after bumping along the bottom for a number of months. This could be telling you that the worst is over, and some general reading and calculation of the financials should be undertaken to see if a turnaround is starting.

> I strongly recommend ... that all investors consistently look at charts.

Another interesting chart is one that shows a company's share price has enjoyed an upward march and is now starting to move higher at an increasing rate. The higher it goes and more expensive it gets, the faster it rises as people get desperate to get on board a runaway train. Usually this type of rise is the forerunner to enormous volatility, which could see a stock move 4 or 5 per cent daily. If you own this stock the alarm bells should be ringing loudly to get out. A stock that surges 100 per cent inside 12 months and is suddenly becoming increasingly volatile will, at some stage, change direction and head down at a pace that will stun the average investor. The example that sticks in my mind is the zinc company Zinifex, the forerunner to Oz Minerals. Riding on the back of the resources boom, the stock was trading at around $1 a share before the price gradually increased during 2004, and then took off through 2005 and 2006 to hit $20 a share in mid 2007. During 2007 Zinifex's shares could be up 4 per cent one day and down 3 per cent the next. This extreme volatility paved the way for a sharp reversal in direction, and the price fell some 60 per cent over the next 12 months (see figure 7.2, overleaf).

In summary, price charts are stock storytellers that an investor worth their salt will take a keen interest in. I am happy to dismiss charts as a mechanism of predicting the future, but investors who refuse to look at charts from a historical perspective are simply ignoring an important source of information. It is so easy to get bogged down in your everyday life and forget to do some simple things, like glancing at a list of company price to earnings multiples, studying price charts or scanning the 12-month rolling highs and lows tables. All this information is readily accessible to investors big or small, and it doesn't take a great deal of effort to check the information. My advice would be that, even if your time is limited, don't ditch your weekly chart investigation.

Figure 7.2: surging Zinifex—share price from April 2004 to December 2006

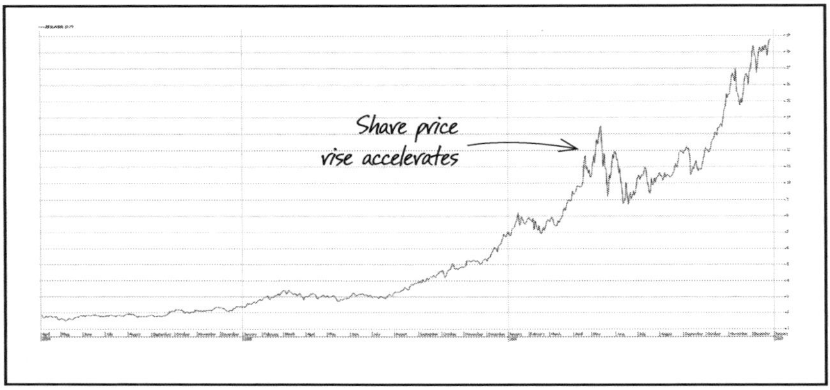

Source: IRESS

Announcements

A brief comment should be made about the need to scan the company announcements made to the ASX each day. All listed companies are required to make announcements to the ASX for public consumption if they believe the event being reported will have an impact on the share price. The ASX website posts all of these announcements, so they are available to the general public. While newspapers and other commentaries will cover a lot of the market news, there will be gaps. These gaps can be filled by reading the company announcements. You may find some opportunities in terms of a capital raisings or a change in management, especially if you are delving into the smaller end of the market. The ASX website is a particularly fertile place to dig in August and February when most companies post their financial results for the previous six months. A glance at the profit and the cash flow statements they provide has been one of the greatest sources of investment ideas for me over the last decade or so.

Curiosity makes you rich

If there has been one technique that has proven the most consistent way of discovering stocks over the years it has been asking questions. You should always be on the look out for stock ideas, no matter what you are doing. This does not mean making the person you are talking to feel uncomfortable. I have found the simplest approach is to simply ask people what they do. The majority of people are happy to wax lyrical about their jobs and how things are travelling in their company and industry. They are usually keen to convey a message about a competitor, especially if a company is struggling. This is not about extracting inside information from people, but finding out things like industry dynamics, company culture and views on what management teams are like. If you take the time to ask people you meet in your wander through life what they do, you will be pleasantly surprised what you can learn.

You can take this approach even further. When you go shopping, you should always try to find out from the person serving you how business has been and whether they like their management team. On several occasions a staff member has offered a positive report on the company they work in and, by coincidence we were already shareholders. It is a nice affirmation for retaining the investment. If, for example, you are doing your weekly shop in the supermarket you might ask one of the staff members which product in various sections tends to be selling the most.

I have met people on the bus, in shops, at other people's homes, on holidays, sitting on chairlifts, watching kids' sport and at school functions that have given me ideas that have led to profitable investments. Some people will find this slightly uncomfortable or confronting, but it is a fruitful arena. At the end of the day you must remember the sharemarket is not just about companies, numbers or profits: it is about collecting information — and it's out there, ready to be snared.

Conclusion

The active investor will always be on the look out for a new idea and possibly a new investment. The ideas are floating all around us — we just have to be alert enough to see them.

Chapter 8

Primary school numbers

The sharemarket is swimming in numbers. There are revenues, profits, costs, dividends, ratios, indexes, salaries, models and forecasts all based on numbers. To the average person on the street this is utterly confusing, thoroughly incomprehensible and possibly the single biggest reason why people throw up their hands and give their money to professionals. They think numbers are nasty and should be avoided at all times. Market insiders thrive in this environment because it opens a window to charging the general public hefty fees. The retail investor looks on in bewilderment and believes that only the smart guys can get their minds around all the numbers.

A closer examination, though, will reveal it is not the numbers that are complex, but the language employed to describe them. It is a form of trickery employed by many professions (such as medicine, law and accounting) to make sure they can keep the general public confused. To professional sharemarket participants, developing an understanding of the field's confusing language is even more important, because there are no prerequisites and no barriers to entry to the sharemarket. Anyone can enter the market if they have some money to play with. In addition, the sharemarket offers a financial reward unparalleled by any other profession just because of the sheer weight of money swirling around.

Maths is not a prerequisite

I tried to avoid doing mathematics in my final year at school. I loved maths as a youngster but when I was introduced to algebra in early high school I lost interest, because I couldn't comprehend what letters were doing in the maths room. In the final wash up I cut a deal with my school to do the easiest maths course available. Then, at university, I charted a wide berth around accounting, preferring to go with general economics. Eight years later I was overjoyed to discover the sharemarket, where I could get back to some simple mathematics. I quickly realised that I needed only primary school maths to keep up with people in the market. All I needed to know was how to add, subtract, multiply, divide and work out percentages. Anything else was superfluous unless I wanted to get into futures or options, but even then most computer models did all the work for you. So the overwhelming message is this: don't be scared of the numbers.

What is not quite as simple as doing the maths is working out what numbers to focus in on. In this chapter we will concentrate on which numbers to look at without getting too confused.

The key financials

Australian listed companies are required to report their financials every six months. It is crucial that all sharemarket investors read these reports from front to back and absorb every word. If you are not in a position to interview company management, in the way that professional investors do, look at the half-yearly financial results, which provide the most accurate update on how a company is performing. Once you have read the words in the report it is essential to read the vital numbers. Given the litany of numbers presented in these reports, you need to be efficient and go straight to the

> Look at the half-yearly financial results, which provide the most accurate update on how a company is performing.

key figures that will provide you with all the information you need to know. What I have found over the years is that if the numbers throw up more questions than answers, then a red flag should be waving in your face. Companies that are functioning well typically have easy-to-read accounts, not ones that confuse you.

The three key pages

With this in mind, what should we look at? The three key pages in each half-yearly (and annual) announcement are:

- *Consolidated statement of comprehensive income (profit and loss)*. This is the one that gets top billing. It used to be known as the profit and loss statement (also called the P&L). Why the authorities believe it necessary to give this statement such an elaborate name is a question that has no sensible answer. Many people continue to refer to it as the profit and loss, so that's the term I will use here.
- *Consolidated statement of financial position (balance sheet)*. This is the second key page, located right after the profit and loss. Historically it has been called the balance sheet, and since many people still use this term, it's the one I will use here.
- *The statement of cash flows*. A few pages after the balance sheet sits the statement of cash flows. Cash flow is a topic that many professional investors love to espouse as crucial, but I have never seen any investment lecture papers or books talk specifically about this part of the financial accounts.

Using the three key pages

When a company releases its half-yearly results to the public in August or February, I have always taken a brief look at the profit and loss statement before moving on to what really matters. More serious analysis will see you work backwards through the accounts—cash flow first followed by the balance sheet and finally the profit and loss. All three are fundamentally related and once you have looked at each one separately you need to check how they are interlinked and make sure they all add up.

Cash flow is the truth

The cash flow statement is the profit and loss statement on truth serum. You can argue with the profit but you can't argue with the cash that a company produces each year. If a company claims a sizeable profit but there is no cash to show for it at the bottom of the cash flow ledger then you need to start asking a few questions. None of this is really surprising to anyone. Individuals who do their own budgeting at home know if they have managed to generate any cash during the course of the year. Individuals tend not to play games with themselves and put certain items aside and not count them as a cost. Money in and money out is what most people live by in their private lives but unfortunately we cannot say the same for many companies. You should be aware that a company can make their accounts look better to the unsuspecting public by making the profit and loss statement look much healthier than it really is. The only foolproof way of checking this is by concentrating heavily on what is happening in the cash flow statement and the end results as depicted by the balance sheet.

Australian accounts split a company's cash flow into three parts — operating activities, investing activities and financing activities.

The first of these is about the company's operation, and here the receipts from all the customers for the period are added up, and then the operating costs, such as staff wages, rent and taxes, are deducted to get a net figure.

Investment activities covers all non-operating costs and revenue, such as capital expenditure, asset purchases and asset sales.

Financing activities represents all the money raised from share issues and debt, minus any dividends paid to shareholders.

The final bit of the cash flow statement adds up all of these three categories and shows whether the company has managed to generate any cash for the year or actually recorded a loss and, as a consequence, reduced its net cash or even added more debt.

The next step in the process is to flick backwards to the balance sheet. This is a snapshot of the company's financial health at a point in time, which is 31 December and 30 June for most Australian companies. The balance sheet became a hot topic during the 2008 GFC when lazy balance sheets were quickly re-badged as overgeared and in desperate need of repair.

The balance sheet is split into four main categories—current assets, non-current assets, current liabilities and non-current liabilities. Assets are obviously a positive and liabilities are the negatives that are owed to other people or companies. At the bottom of the balance sheet are the net assets of the company, which is simply all the assets minus all the liabilities. Other terms for this are total equity or the book value of the company.

Just to clarify the language, the term 'current' refers to assets that can be realised as cash in the next 12 months, and current liabilities are those payments due in the next 12 months. Movements in the cash flow statement over a period will be directly reflected in the balance sheet.

Finally we return to the profit and loss statement. This is the most unreliable of the three pages we are looking at and it should be viewed with a moderate degree of caution. This page states all the revenue earned by the company for the period, and then it deducts all the costs incurred, which will include interest costs from debt, and taxes owed to the government. At the bottom of the page is the net profit attributable to the equity holders of the firm, which is code for what is left for the shareholders. The report then calculates for you what this amounts to in earnings per share.

These are the three crucial pages a sharemarket investor needs to look at when analysing a company. Now that we have identified and explained these three pages we need to work out how to read them so we can start analysing a company. To fully explain why these pages of numbers are important we need to have a look at some examples to highlight the key points. As we go into these examples it is worth keeping in mind two general rules. The first rule is that cash flows should match or at least be close to the profit. Second, the current net assets should always be greater than current net liabilities.

Let's take a look at an example where the accounts should have forewarned an investor that the company was going broke, even though it was seemingly highly profitable.

ION Limited

In this section I will discuss the financial statements of automobile manufacturing group ION Limited, referring to table 8.1, the profit and loss statement (the statement of financial performance); table 8.2 (on p. 102), the balance sheet (statement of financial position); and table 8.3 (on p. 103), the statement of cash flows.

ION had been listed on the ASX since 1985 and struggled to grab shareholder attention. After 15 years the installation of Graeme Salthouse as managing director sparked the dormant operation into action. Under Salthouse's guidance, ION established a position in the tough automobile manufacturing arena. The centerpiece of the operation was a contract to supply wheels to the US motorbike company Harley Davidson. Sales started to gather momentum. This growth story also ignited investor interest.

Not happy with having to rely on Harley Davidson as the primary customer, Salthouse undertook a textbook customer diversification program. This involved making a series of acquisitions, sticking to its niche of manufacturing parts for automobiles. The canny Salthouse seemed to be able to make these purchases with bargain basement prices, winning favour with institutional and retail investors alike. As the accounts will show though, many of these headline prices paid by ION were only part of the price. Each one required enormous amounts of subsequent capital expenditure just to update the plant and prove they could retain many of their major contracts. Salthouse had learned many lessons, including the key to convincing shareholders that he could buy assets cheaply. Unfortunately, time tends to catch up with everyone.

ION Limited went into administration in December 2004, after reporting a profit for the year to 30 June 2004 of $28.75 million (see table 8.1). This was well down on the previous year's net profit of $53.08 million, but at face value there was absolutely no hint that a solvency problem was brewing. At the time of reporting the 2004 yearly accounts, the company stated that its interest cover was 7.8 times. So how could the company be in administration only a couple of months later?

Table 8.1: ION Limited's statement of financial performance (profit and loss), 30 June 2004

ION LIMITED
STATEMENT OF FINANCIAL PERFORMANCE
FOR THE FINANCIAL YEAR ENDED 30 JUNE 2004

	Consolidated	
	2004	2003
	$'000	$'000
Revenue from ordinary activities *Strong revenues*	711,216	678, 971
Raw materials and consumable used	(265,042)	(285,838)
Employee benefits exercise	(214,649)	(191,653)
Depreciation and amortisation expenses	(30,118)	(26,515)
Repairs and maintenance expenses *Non-cash items*	(24,104)	(15,789)
Operating lease costs	(10,963)	(11,232)
Subcontractors' costs	(32,267)	(8,768)
Borrowing costs	(11,280)	(8,364)
Restructuring costs – redundancies	(8,869)	–
Write down asset values to recoverable amount:		
– Property, plant and equipment *Healthy reported profits*	(22,187)	–
– Deferred research and development costs	(15,422)	–
Other expenses from ordinary activities	(71, 287)	(57,663)
Profit from ordinary activities before income tax expense	5,028	73,149
Income tax benefit/(expense) relating to ordinary activities	23,725	(20,068)
Profit from ordinary activities after related income tax expense	28,753	53,081
Adjustment to retained profits at 1 July 2002 as a result of the adoption of AASB 1028 'Employee Benefits'	–	(288)
Increase in asset revaluation reserve arising on revaluation of non-current assets	–	1,422
Increase in foreign currency translation reserve arising on translation of self-sustaining foreign operations	1,670	1,039
Total changes in equity other than those resulting from transactions with owners as owners	30,423	55,254
Earnings per share:		
Basic (cents per share)	12.5¢	24.9¢
Diluted (cents per share)	12.5¢	24.6¢

Table 8.2: ION Limited's statement of financial position (balance sheet), 30 June 2004

ION LIMITED
STATEMENT OF FINANCIAL POSITION AS AT 30 JUNE 2004

		Consolidated	
	Cash levels drop	2004 $'000	2003 $'000
Current assets			
Cash assets		433	39,427
Receivables		81,678	63,785
Inventories		48,202	44,589
Current tax assets		7,551	5,538
Other		9,059	10,896
Total current assets		146,923	164,235
Non-current assets			
Receivables		16,622	18,589
Property, plant and equipment		478,693	406,168
Intangible assets – goodwill		14,604	1,034
Deferred tax assets		24,427	9,390
Deferred research and development costs		14,256	20,945
Other		843	–
Total non-current assets		549,445	456,126
Total assets		696,368	620,361
Current liabilities			
Payables	*Current liabilities*	107,834	111,677
Interest-bearing liabilities	*surpass current assets*	11,390	9,757
Current tax liabilities		8,664	5,311
Provisions		23,169	24,562
Other		3,343	6,975
Total current liabilities		154,400	158,282
Non-current liabilities			
Payables		25,088	4,000
Interest-bearing liabilities		185,352	175,329
Deferred tax liabilities		26,004	47,249
Provisions		8,474	5,107
Total non-current liabilities	*Debt jumps and cash drops,*	244,918	231,685
Total liabilities	*despite company raising*	399,318	389,967
Net assets	*$65m in equity*	297,050	230,394
Equity			
Contributed equity		233,747	169,596
Reserves		9,968	8,298
Retained profits		53,335	52,500
Total equity		297,050	230,394

Table 8.3: ION Limited's statement of cash flows, 30 June 2004

STATEMENT OF CASH FLOWS
FOR THE FINANCIAL YEAR ENDED 30 JUNE 2004

	Consolidated	
	2004 $'000	**2003 $'000**
Cash flows from operating activities		
Receipts from customers	733,534	757,929
Payments to suppliers and employees	(650,297)	(646,306)
Interest received	343	515
Borrowing costs paid	(11,280)	(8,861)
Income tax paid	(11,158)	(22,631)
Net cash provided by operating activities	61,142	80,646
Cash flows from investing activities		
Proceeds from sale of property, plant and equipment	2,968	842
Payment for property, plant and equipment	(121,638)	(116,877)
Payment for businesses	(17,931)	(5,761)
Research and development costs paid	(7,260)	(10,761)
Net cash used in investing activities	(143,861)	(132,557)
Cash flows from financing activities		
Dividends paid	(27,918)	(19,783)
Proceeds from issues of equity securities	65,363	5,126
Payment for share issue costs	(1,212)	–
Proceeds from borrowings	33,140	121,286
Repayment of borrowings	(28,929)	(45,670)
Repayment of employee share plan loans	1,544	899
Net cash provided by financing activities	41,988	61,858
Net increase/(decrease) in cash held	(40,731)	9,947
Cash at the beginning of the financial year	39,427	29,480
Cash at the end of the financial year	(1,304)	39,427

Enormous capital expenditure budgets

Capital raising to survive

Piling on debt in 2003

Capital idea

The answer to the question posed on page 100 lies in the most important of our three pages—the cash flow statement. As can be seen from table 8.3, the first section of the cash flow statement for June 2004 stating the operational cash flow (net cash provided by operating activities) showed an extremely healthy $61.1 million. However, the next section of the statement, covering cash flow from investing activities, show the situation starting to deteriorate rapidly. This discloses that payment for property, plant and equipment was an enormous $121.6 million (see table 8.3). Property, plant and equipment is code for capital expenditure (capex) that a company makes to ensure capital items are replaced and repaired during the reporting period. The company does not have to show capex as an operational expense, instead it can shovel it off into the less examined cash flow statement. The net impact is an improved profit. These capitalised costs will then appear on the balance sheet as an asset that needs to be depreciated over the useful life of the asset. If more costs can be capitalised and added to the balance sheet, not only does this boost short-term profits but it also smooths out future profits.

If you want to boost your profit, the easiest way to do that is to convince your auditors to allow you to put as many costs as possible into capex instead of operational expenses. If a company can sneak some operational costs, such as paying staff, into capital expenditure then to the outside world the picture looks much healthier. Of course, this is difficult given that auditors have to operate under strict rules and guidelines.

A way for investors to check that a company is not capitalising too many costs is to match the capex number against its overall depreciation expense, which can usually be found in the profit and loss statement. If the capex is significantly higher than the depreciation expense then you should query what is going on. Capex may not match depreciation in one year, but over two or more years it is critical that the numbers start to align. If capex runs at a higher rate than depreciation for two or more years, start selling the stock.

In 2004 ION's capital expenditure was $121.6 million, while its depreciation was a paltry $30.1 million (see table 8.1), a gap of $91.5 million. In the previous year the gap was $90.4 million. This represents a concerning trend for any outfit, but it will be terminal for a company that is only managing to produce a profit of $28 million. Over the course of two years, 2003 and 2004, the company managed to report a total profit of $81.8 million, but it actually lost $106.5 million in cash. During these two years, the company also raised $70.4 million in fresh equity, which meant that during the normal course of operations it burned just shy of $177 million. The disparity between cash and profit was a staggering $258.7 million. This difference was exaggerated by the $47.7 million it paid out in dividends to shareholders. It is mind-boggling that the company was still paying out dividends when it was in such a parlous state. The only explanation for the company continuing to pay dividends was that it wanted to say to the investment world that everything was still fine.

Trying to make it balance

Once you have worked out the cash flow of the company you then need to turn your attention to the balance sheet and see if solvency is a looming problem. The balance sheet (see table 8.2) will show you if the company's current assets are greater than its current liabilities. If a company fails this simple test then it can be argued it cannot meet its obligations over the next 12 months. For ION's full year accounts for 2003 and 2004, the current assets minus current liabilities went from a small positive of approximately $6 million in 2003 to a small negative of just under $8 million in 2004. This is not a great result, but it's not frightening. However, if we continue to link the cash flow statement with the balance sheet, we will remember that during the 2004 financial year the company raised $70 million from issuing new shares, as shown in the cash flow statement. I can only imagine the company was strong-armed into raising this money to pay back some of its debt to the bank immediately. Without the fresh equity, the company's net current assets would have been in deficit to the current net liabilities to the tune of $73 million, which would make the company insolvent. More worrying is the fact there were no signs the company's binge on capital expenditure was abating. There is only one conclusion to be drawn from this: *get out* of the stock.

What did investors do?

From January 2001 to October 2002 ION's share price had rocketed 400 per cent as the company went on a buying spree of assets. At this early stage, investors viewed the acquisitions as being executed on low and attractive PE multiples, but most of the assets bought required enormous amounts of follow-up capital expenditure, which was needed just to continue to operate. ION shares peaked at $3.13 in late 2002 and then started to head south. When the capital expenditure binge of 2003–04 became apparent, the share price was still at $2.80 a share and when ION raised $65 million of capital in February 2004 the stock was still above $2.00. By December 2004, the company had gone into administration and never re-listed. The shares traded at 93 cents before they were permanently suspended. In its last throes the company changed management and refinanced its debt, with a facility much larger than the market could have possibly guessed. The final company presentation, in November 2004, to the market was one month before the administrators were called in. The rise was rapid and the decline, breakneck.

It's as easy as ABC

ABC Learning Centres was one of the highest profile corporate collapses from the sharemarket cave-in during the GFC in 2008. The company grew from a micro company listed on the ASX in 2001 to a multibillion dollar global operator in 2007. Heading the company was charismatic poster boy Eddy Groves, who went on a debt-fuelled buying bender that had the market frothing at the mouth at a time when credit was gushing from banks in every corner of the Earth. ABC Learning went into administration in August 2008, but a closer inspection of the accounts showed some significant cracks were emerging all the way back to 2006.

The ABC Learning supernova was a salient reminder that an investor must always be on guard when a company becomes a serial acquirer of other businesses. As we have stated in other parts of the book there is nothing wrong with a well-priced strategic acquisition, but when a company starts to spend most of its time looking at what it can buy, you need to seriously consider if value is being created.

What is most disconcerting for the investor is trying to work out, by viewing the accounts, whether each purchase is a positive or a negative. The revenue line generally explodes and you can be guaranteed the management of the acquirer announces each purchase is earnings per share positive. In bull markets this is typically enough to get analysts and institutional investors excited. However, the only true way to gauge whether a company is buying astutely is a close examination of the operating cash flow. Remember that the cash flow is the profit and loss statement on a truth serum. For some time Eddy Groves deflected criticism of deteriorating cash flows and anaemic returns on equity. Even when many investors started to question the whole model the company managed to find investors around the globe who thought the story was a robust one.

I suspect that many investors are like me, and don't have the financial investigative skills to pinpoint what goes wrong with a company like ABC Learning. However, if the cash flow throws up too many unanswered questions you just have to walk away and let other investors deal with it.

Let's have a look at our three key pages and work out what might have gone wrong with the figures. Table 8.4 (overleaf) is the profit and loss (income statement), table 8.5 (on p. 109) is the balance sheet and table 8.6 (on p. 110) is the cash flow statement.

The last set of accounts were released to the sharemarket in February 2008, for the six months to 31 December 2007. In that period the company reported a profit of $37.1 million (see table 8.4), a number that was hit by a one-off write down in assets of $36.2 million. In other words, the company was saying its operations managed to produce a profit of $73.3 million for the six months, a fact promoted heavily in the company investor presentation.

Table 8.4: ABC Learning Centre's income statement (profit and loss),
31 December 2007

INCOME STATEMENT (ABC LEARNING CENTRES LIMITED)
CONSOLIDATED FOR THE HALF-YEAR ENDED 31 DECEMBER 2007

	Consolidated	
	2007 $'m	2006 $'m
Revenue from operations	**1,023.3**	657.3
Other income	**83.6**	10.5
Total revenue	**1,106.9**	667.8
Changes in inventories of finished goods	**–**	(9.6)
Employee benefits	**(615.90)**	(351.7)
Depreciation and amortisation	**(34.2)**	(14.0)
Impairment	**(1.2)**	(0.5)
Finance costs	**(80.6)**	(22.2)
Rental and other property expenses	**(167.9)**	(106.8)
Children catering and consumables	**(46.1)**	(25.4)
Advertising and promotions	**(8.4)**	(7.6)
Insurances	**(7.7)**	(4.7)
Communication	**(7.5)**	(4.0)
Travel and motor vehicle expenses	**(15.2)**	(7.7)
Change in fair value of financial assets (listed shares)	**(36.2)**	(0.1)
Other expenses	**(36.5)**	(20.0)
Profit before income tax expense	**49.5**	93.5
Income tax (expense)/benefit	**(12.4)**	(29.6)
Profit for the period	**37.1**	63.9
Attributable to:	**37.1**	63.9
Equity holders of the parent	**–**	–
Minority interest	**37.1**	63.9
Earnings per share:		
Basic (cents per share)	**7.9¢**	16.2¢
Diluted (cents per share)	**7.9¢**	16.2¢

Revenues surging

Profit in decline, but positive

Table 8.5: ABC Learning Centre's balance sheet, 31 December 2007

BALANCE SHEET
CONSOLIDATED AS AT 31 DECEMBER 2007 (ABC LEARNING CENTRES LIMITED)

Cash levels dropping despite capital raisings

Current liabilities blow out

Debt levels spike even after capital raising

	Consolidated	
	31 Dec 2007 **$'m**	**30 Jun 2007** **$'m**
Current assets		
Cash and cash equivalents	135.1	227.8
Trade and other receivables	140.7	66.1
Other financial assets	26.0	54.9
Inventories	2.2	0.7
Current tax assets	5.0	–
Other	53.2	30.4
	362.2	379.9
Non-current assets classified as held for sale	179.9	12.0
Total current assets	542.1	391.9
Non-current assets		
Trade and other receivables	4.0	4.3
Other financial assets	120.8	120.2
Property, plant and equipment	657.2	549.6
Deferred tax assets	115.8	110.0
Intangible assets	3,055.2	2,891.1
Other	33.0	–
Total non-current assets	3,968.0	3,675.2
Total assets	4,528.1	4,067.1
Current liabilities		
Trade and other payables	312.5	272.5
Financial liabilities	3.3	–
Borrowings	4.4	1,149.7
Current tax liabilities	–	12.3
Provisions	19.6	19.4
Total current liabilities	339.8	1,453.9
Non-current liabilities		
Other payables	17.3	12.3
Financial liabilities	14.9	–
Borrowings	1,808.1	610.4
Deferred tax liabilities	96.0	87.4
Provisions	28.9	1.5
Total non-current liabilities	1,965.2	711.6
Total liabilities	2,305.0	2,165.5
Net assets	2,223.1	1,901.6
Equity		
Issued capital	2,185.6	1,744.5
Reserves	(129.9)	(15.4)
Retained earnings	167.4	172.5
Parent entity interest	2,223.1	1,901.6
Minority interest	–	–
Total equity	2,223.1	1,901.6

Table 8.6: ABC Learning Centre's cash flow statement, 31 December 2007

CASH FLOW STATEMENT
CONSOLIDATED FOR THE HALF-YEAR ENDED 31 DECEMBER 2007
(ABC LEARNING CENTRES LIMITED)

	Consolidated	
	2007 $'m	2006 $'m
Cash flow from operating activities		
Receipts from customers	**988.3**	611.6
Payment to suppliers and employees	**(907.2)**	(547.4)
Dividends received	**1.2**	1.3
Interest received	**7.0**	4.4
Interest and other costs of finance paid	**(87.0)**	(21.1)
Income tax paid	**(22.1)**	(21.7)
Net cash provided by/(used in) operating activities	**(19.8)**	27.1
Cash flows from investing activities		
Payment for investments	**(33.5)**	(201.2)
Proceeds on sale of investments	**–**	1.7
Proceeds from repayment of loans	**4.4**	–
Amounts advanced for loans	**(19.4)**	(32.7)
Payment for property, plant and equipment	**(202.3)**	(69.4)
Proceeds for sale of property, plant and equipment	**2.3**	0.6
Payment for intangible assets	**(167.5)**	(193.3)
Payment for other non-current assets	**(33.0)**	–
Proceeds from sale of childcare licenses	**–**	9.8
Payment for businesses	**(73.8)**	(262.5)
Net cash used in investing activities	**(522.8)**	(747.0)
Cash flows from financing activities		
Proceeds from issues of equity securities	**443.6**	–
Payment for share issue costs	**(8.7)**	(0.1)
Proceeds from borrowings	**878.5**	876.8
Repayment of borrowings	**(802.9)**	(108.3)
Dividends paid	**42.1**	(20.1)
Net cash provided by financing activities	**468.4**	748.3
Net increase/(decrease) in cash and cash equivalents	**(74.2)**	28.4
Cash and cash equivalents at the beginning of the period	**219.6**	131.7
Effects of exchange rate changes on the balance of cash held in foreign currencies	**(10.6)**	(3.7)
Cash and cash equivalents at the end of the period	**134.8**	156.4
Cash and cash equivalents	**135.1**	156.4
Borrowings (overdraft)	**(0.3)**	–
Cash and cash equivalents at the end of the period	**134.8**	156.4

Handwritten annotations:
Operating cashflow sickly and in decline
Massive jump in capital expenditure
Capital raising staves off administration

Go to the cash flow

If we look at the cash flow statement (see table 8.6) a different picture emerges. Unlike ION, ABC Learning did not even manage to produce any operating cash in 2007, losing $19.8 million (cash flows from operating activities). If we look at cash flows from investing activities, our concerns start to compound with a negative $522.8 million being reported. While this number has ballooned because of a number of purchases of assets, it is a real worry. The capex (payment for property, plant and equipment) is a mammoth $202.3 million, while the depreciation rate is only $34.2 million—a gap of $168.1 million. The capex is stated in the cash flow statement (see table 8.6) and the depreciation charge can be seen in the income statement (see table 8.4). Somehow the company still saw fit to pay a dividend to shareholders for the period, even though it was raising $443.6 million in fresh equity during the period. Despite this enormous capital raising the company still managed to reduce its cash levels.

In reality, you would expect to see numbers like this if a company was about to call in the administrators. However, if we look back to 12 months earlier, when the stock was still trading at elevated levels, signs of the decline were already emerging. For the six months to December 2006, the company reported a profit of $63.9 million. A quick check on the cash flow statement for December 2006 reveals the company only managed to generate operating cash flow of $27.1 million. Compounding the problem, capital expenditure sat at $69.4 million, compared with a depreciation rate of $14 million—a gap of $55.4 million just in one half of the year.

Balancing the numbers

So what does the balance sheet tell us about what was going on? The 30 June 2007 balance sheet (see table 8.5) shows that current assets were dwarfed by current liabilities to the tune of $1.06 billion. The company was surviving at the discretion of its bankers and shareholder willingness to chip in the missing cash. Luckily for ABC Learning both parties came to the party for another 12 months, but as the December 2007 numbers show, the company just tore up that money as it remained on a collision course with administration. The profit numbers reported weren't worth the paper they were printed on.

It is unrealistic for investors to believe they have a firm grasp on the business models of the companies they own shares in. A better and simpler approach is to look carefully at the numbers. If they don't add up, and you start asking questions about what is happening, just leave the company alone. If you do happen to own a company that has gaping holes in the three key pages, then sell it and seek out other companies to invest in. Just remember there are more than 2000 listed companies in Australia alone and choice is not something we have to be overly concerned with. It is imperative that you scrutinise these three pages every six months for all of the companies you own, because this will increase your understanding of what you are searching for. Don't be thrown off by the language—just concentrate on the numbers.

So what looks good?

So far we have concentrated on companies that you should avoid because their accounts don't add up. But what are the signals in the accounts that you should buy a stock? This question is slightly harder to answer, but we do not need to stray too far from our three key pages to find the answers. Two of the things to look out for are that operational cash flows should match or be close to profit levels, and current assets should exceed current liabilities. In addition there are some other elements we should calculate to make sure we are on the right track. Let's look at some examples.

Strange name, great returns

A company that has performed tremendously since listing on the sharemarket back in 2005 has been a salary packaging group with a name that would throw any serious investor off track—McMillan Shakespeare. Until recently the company's core business offering was salary packaging for employees, and a large percentage of these people worked for the various governments around the nation. Employees receive certain income benefits if they structure their pay packets correctly. McMillan Shakespeare is the leading company in Australia for working out this type of structuring, and it receives a fee for delivering enhanced after-tax returns for individuals. Over time the company's share price has sometimes suffered from various regulatory risks revolving around changes to tax legislation, but the company has never had its own financial concerns, as its accounts clearly show.

In the year to 30 June 2008, the profit and loss statement shows that the company reported a profit after tax of $17.3 million, which meant 25.7 cents a share (see table 8.7, overleaf).

The cash flows from operating activities, which can be seen in the cash flow statement (see table 8.9 on p. 116), show that the company produced $20.5 million for the period. This cash being generated is slightly higher than the profit, indicating that the company, despite experiencing 22.2 per cent revenue growth, was able to get its customers to pay more quickly than the company needed to pay its suppliers. This is commonly referred to as positive working capital and it is a lovely problem for a company to have because it means it can grow its business without having to go to the bank or shareholders for more money. The cash flows from investing activities on the cash flow statement (see table 8.9) show that capital expenditure was about $1.3 million, almost the same as depreciation of $1.2 million. The net result was that the company could pay a dividend equivalent to 60 per cent of its net profit and still add more than $8.2 million in cash to the balance sheet.

The balance sheet (see table 8.8 on p. 115) shows that current assets exceed current liabilities by a healthy $11.7 million, meaning the company cannot go broke in the next 12 months. Another look at the balance sheet, under current liabilities, shows the company had no bank debt, which is ideal for a small company that is growing so quickly.

Importantly, this stellar set of accounts are not a one-off for McMillan Shakespeare. The previous year's numbers, the 12 months to June 2007, saw a net profit of $13.2 million and an operating cash flow of $15.8 million. So, once again, the company had positive working capital. In addition, the capital expenditure revealed in the cash flow statement (under cash flows from investing activities) is about the same as the depreciation amount in the profit and loss statement. Finally, the company's balance sheet has positive net assets over net liabilities and no bank debt. What a combination, especially when you are producing 20 per cent revenue growth. A beautiful thing!

This kind of analysis, along with a calculation of the return ratios explored in the following chapter will go a long way to determining whether you are buying a gem or driving down a one way street the wrong way.

Table 8.7: McMillan Shakespeare Limited's income statement (profit and loss), 30 June 2008

APPENDIX 4E – ATTACHMENT A
MCMILLAN SHAKESPEARE LIMITED AND CONTROLLED ENTITIES
ABN 74 107 233 983
INCOME STATEMENT
FOR THE YEAR ENDED 30 JUNE 2008   *Easy to read!*

	Consolidated	
	2008 **$'000**	**2007** **$'000**
Revenue and other income		
Remuneration services	65,778	54,091
Non-operating interest income	842	399
Other	4	46
Total revenue and other income	**66,624**	**54,536**
Expenses		
Employee and director benefits expenses	30,379	24,578
Depreciation of plant and equipment	1,206	1,220
Amortisation of software development	245	123
Technology and communication expenses	2,719	2,907
Property and corporate expenses	1,898	1,793
Finance costs	69	175
Other expenses	5,189	4,661
	41,705	**35,457**
Profit before income tax expense	**24,919**	**19,079**
Income tax expense	7,551	5,842
Profit attributable to members of the parent entity	**17,368**	**13,237**
Earnings per share	**Cents per** **share**	**Cents per** **share**
– basic earnings per share	**25.76**	**19.79**
– diluted earnings per share	**25.46**	**19.51**

Revenue climbing

Moderate non-cash expenses

Robust profit and earnings per share growth

Table 8.8: McMillan Shakespeare Limited's balance sheet, 30 June 2008

MCMILLAN SHAKESPEARE LIMITED AND CONTROLLED ENTITIES
ABN 74 107 233 983
BALANCE SHEET AS AT 30 JUNE 2008

		Consolidated	
		2008 $'000	2007 $'000
Current assets			
Cash on hand	*Cash levels growing*	2	2
Cash at bank		6,697	8,825
Short term deposits		11,270	882
Trade debtors net of provision for doubtful debts		4,606	2,310
Other debtors		2,955	3,914
Prepayments		1,275	1,412
Total current assets		**26,805**	**17,345**
Non-current assets			
Plant and equipment		2,053	2,283
Capitalised software development		563	342
Goodwill on acquisition		33,328	33,328
Future income tax benefits		688	786
Total non-current assets		**36,632**	**36,739**
Total assets	*No bank debt*	**63,437**	**54,084**
Current liabilities			
Trade creditors		4,806	2,107
Amounts due to vendor		–	1,194
Sundry creditors and accruals		4,968	5,767
Tax payable		3,206	2,565
Accrued employee benefits		1,814	1,587
Income in advance		270	432
Total current liabilities		**15,064**	**13,652**
Non-current liabilities			
Accrued employee benefits		166	165
Total non-current liabilities		**166**	**165**
Total liabilities		**15,230**	**13,817**
Net assets		**48,207**	**40,267**
Equity			
Issued capital		22,637	21,734
Option reserve		304	184
Distributable reserve		25,266	18,349
Total equity		**48,207**	**40,267**

Table 8.9: McMillan Shakespeare Limited's cash flow statement,
30 June 2008

APPENDIX 4E – ATTACHMENT A
MCMILLAN SHAKESPEARE LIMITED AND CONTROLLED ENTITIES
ABN 74 107 233 983
CASH FLOW STATEMENT FOR THE YEAR ENDED 30 JUNE 2008

	Consolidated	
	2008	**2007**
	$'000	**$'000**
Cash flows from operating activities:		
Cash receipts from customers	74,432	62,213
Cash payments to suppliers and employees	47,854	42,268
Interest received	779	399
Interest paid	–	(237)
Income taxes paid	6,811	4,308
Net cash from operating activities	**20,546**	**15,799**
Cash flows from investing activities:		
Acquisition of subsidiary, net of cash acquired	(597)	(578)
Payment for capitalised software	(481)	(366)
Acquisition of plant and equipment	(976)	(1,055)
Net cash used by investing activities	**(2,054)**	**(1,999)**
Cash flows from financing activities:		
Equity contribution	219	355
Proceeds from borrowings	–	2,400
Repayment of borrowings	–	(5,715)
Dividends paid by parent entity	(10,451)	(7,697)
Net cash provided used in financing activities	**(10,232)**	**(10,657)**
Net cash increase in cash and cash equivalents	**8,260**	**3,143**
Cash and cash equivalents at beginning of year	9,709	6,566
Cash and cash equivalents at end of year	**17,969**	**9,709**

Cash flow stronger than profits = positive working capital

Capital expenditure not excessive

Lots of cash

Keep it simple

Hopefully the preceding analysis and commentary shows the financial component of the sharemarket is not overly complex. If after several attempts you cannot understand or reconcile the numbers printed by a company, just walk away. If there are too many red flags then look for another story that reads as simply as a children's book.

Chapter 9

Margins, ratios and all that jazz

As a stock picker I feel compelled to discuss the fundamental analysis that we used at Wilson Asset Management in a bid to outpace the overall sharemarket for more than a decade. The aim of this part of the book is to convey the message that studying company numbers is not rocket science: it is within the grasp of the average investor. The discussion will not be comprehensive, but hopefully it will point you in the right direction and kick start an intrigue with companies and the results they produce.

> Studying company numbers is not rocket science: it is within the grasp of the average investor.

Every sharemarket expert has a favourite ratio they claim unlocks the secrets of outstanding stock picking. It seems that if you haven't got a trademark method you can get lost as just another face in the swelling crowd of promoters, and your brand starts to fade.

The reality is that no one ratio or one set of figures is pivotal to getting a decent return from the sharemarket. If a single ratio solved the mystery of why stocks go up and why stocks go down, then everyone would have clambered on board the train many years ago. We know this is not the case. Active share investors, though, should be acutely aware of the various financial ratios that market participants pore over every day because most of them are essential for analysing a stock. Ignoring or dismissing them will be harmful to your performance. Remember that these ratios are not high-level mathematics, but simple additions, divisions and percentages.

PEs—the bee's knees

Wherever you look, people talk about PEs. In newspapers, on television, in stockbroker research and in company commentary everyone is happy to wax lyrical about valuations based on the PE. It is the gold standard of ratios. PE actually stands for price to earnings ratio or multiple. In simple terms, this is the amount you pay for a company (price) in relation to the net profit (earnings) it produces in a given year. If a company earns a net profit of $10 million this year and the market capitalisation is $100 million, then the PE ratio is 10. If the market capitalisation is $200 million, then the ratio is 20, and so on. The market capitalisation is simply calculated by multiplying the number of shares on issue by the current share price. Increasingly, the PE ratio is being expressed in Australia, as it always has been in the United States, on an earnings per share (EPS) basis. Using our example, a company that earns $100 million and has 100 million shares on issue, generates an EPS of $1 a share. So at a PE of 10, the share price would be $10, and at a PE of 20, the shares would trade at $20.

A PE ratio can be a farce if the earnings published by the company are accounting trickery and not real cash (see chapter 8). So before you fall in love with the PE ratio, make sure that it is the appropriate measure to use by first examining the company's statement of cash flows and balance sheet. As you saw in chapter 8, the PE ratios attributed to ABC Learning Centres and ION Limited were mythical and about as helpful as using a toothpick to eat a rump steak.

Once you have established that the earnings are real and supported by cash, then the PE can be a useful way of measuring how keenly priced a stock is. The overall market will allocate different PE levels to different companies based on a variety of matters, including certainty of earnings, calibre of company management, future growth and industry dynamics at that time. So a company that has high earnings growth, sound management, a large customer base, a bulletproof balance sheet and superior industry structure, should be allocated a higher PE than other stocks. Conversely, a company that possesses only some or none of these features will be dogged by a low PE ratio.

The overall market in Australia has a long-term average prospective PE ratio of between 14 and 15, with a range from about 8 after a crash to just under 20 at the peak of a boom. Resource stocks, which have vastly more cyclical earnings, experience a greater range of PE ratios. For most resource stocks, investors have abandoned the PE measurement, opting instead to value these companies with a discounted cash flow measurement. A discounted cash flow is all the estimated future cash flows of a business discounted back to today's value. It tends to work best for mining companies because the assets have defined lives, while industrial and finance companies can operate forever.

It is important to understand a company's long-term PE ratio and every investor should pester their broker to run a chart displaying this. If a company that has traded for many years in a PE range of 8 to 12 suddenly trades at 15, serious questions should be asked. This does not necessarily mean you hit the sell button, but you do need to find a convincing argument to hold the stock. A company's PE ratio expands at the crest of a boom or industry purple patch, when earnings are at a cyclical peak. Investors are regularly lulled into a belief that these abnormal, strong periods of growth are sustainable. Invariably they are not and investors suffer when the share price starts to head south. When the purple patch ends, you get the double whammy of declining earnings and a contracting PE. For example, consider a company with a PE ratio of 20, that is earning $10 million a year and has a market capitalisation of $200 million. Suddenly the earnings decline to $8 million and the

PE ratio contracts to the long-term average of 10, and the share price fall is an overwhelming 60 per cent. That will rock your confidence as an investor for some time to come. In figure 9.1 you can see the dramatic spike in the PE multiple of Australia's largest engineering contractor, Leighton Holdings, from the beginning of 2005 until early 2008. The long-term average PE was in the range of 10 to 20, but quite suddenly Leightons was trading at a PE of 28 as the mining and infrastructure boom took hold. Then in 2008 the PE collapsed to less than 10 before recovering to 15—the middle of its long-term range. During this period the company experienced several earnings downgrades and the share price fell from a high of $61 a share to just $21 a share. So the PE has declined by 46 per cent, while the share price has suffered a larger 65 per cent decline. This is a seminal lesson in checking historical PEs (see figure 9.1).

At the other end of the spectrum a stock may be trading outside its long-term PE range at 6. Suddenly it experiences a jump in earnings of 20 per cent because of improving economic conditions and the market rushes to buy the shares, expanding the PE ratio to 10. The end-result is a 20 per cent upgrade, which can lead to a 50 per cent kick in the share price. Happy times!

Figure 9.1: long-term average PE ratios for Leighton Holdings from January 1990 to January 2011

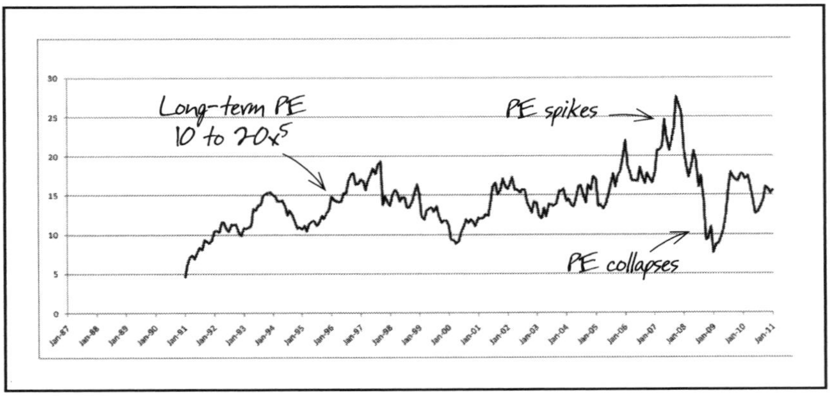

Source: Macquarie Research

EBIT, EBITDA, yah, yah, yah

To outsiders, sharemarket terms EBIT and EBITDA are part of a language akin to baby talk. Despite their oddness, these two measures of company profitability are ignored at your peril.

EBITs, EBIT multiples and EBIT margins

EBIT stands for earnings before subtracting interest and tax. This is my preferred profitability measurement, because it eliminates the possibility of variable tax rates, which can bolster a company's net profit number. Now that we have the EBIT definition, we can use it to calculate the EBIT multiple, which is a critical measure of a company's valuation. In calculating an EBIT multiple, you must take into account not only the market capitalisation (calculated by multiplying the number of shares by the price of the shares) but also the net debt of the company. This is commonly referred to as the enterprise value of the company, for reasons that are well beyond me. So if the EBIT is $20 million and the enterprise value is $160 million then the EBIT multiple is 8 times.

Here is the way each of these measures is calculated:

EBIT = net profit + interest + tax

Enterprise value = market capitalisation + net debt

EBIT multiple = enterprise value ÷ by EBIT

Once again it is worthwhile working out the long-term average EBIT multiple that a company has traded at and then comparing it with where the figure is today.

Another fertile use of the EBIT number is working out what profit margins the company is posting. To calculate the EBIT margin you simply divide the EBIT number by the revenue number. The revenue can be found in the profit and loss statement the company reports twice a year in its earnings results. This gives you a clear indication of whether a company is keeping its costs under control while increasing its revenue. In addition, today's EBIT margin should be compared with the long-term average to work out whether you are in a normal period or an abnormal period. It is the abnormal periods that usually trigger you to sell the stock or possibly buy it. I will never forget talking to former fund manager Alan Crozier who said he had no inclination to invest in GUD Holdings, maker of Sunbeam appliances, because its EBIT margin was sitting at around 16 per cent, when its long-term average was closer to 11 or 12 per cent. The stock was on a tear and the earnings outlook seemed incredibly rosy, so I could not understand his dogmatic approach. Sure enough GUD's margins trended back down to below its long-term average and the stock price halved. There are virtually always forces at work, whether it be rising costs, competition or customer revolt, that will ensure that margins start to track towards their long-term average.

EBITDA

A company's EBITDA is an extension of its net profit and EBIT measures. It stands for the earnings generated before interest, tax and the non-cash items of depreciation and amortisation are deducted.

Depreciation is an accounting measurement that a company uses to spread the cost of a capital asset over its useful life. For example, if you buy a truck for $30 000 and it has a useful life of five years, you will pay for it upfront, but depreciate it at $6000 a year.

Amortisation is the way a company spreads the cost of the goodwill it paid for when it acquired an asset or business. If a company buys an asset for $20 million and amortises it over 20 years, then it will have an annual amortisation charge of $1 million.

Both depreciation and amortisation are effectively annual non-cash items. Although they are described as non-cash items, they are actually expensed in the company accounts but they do not require the company to pay cash for them in any given year. For some reason, some professional investors like to use EBITDA as a proxy for the cash generated by a company. Find me a company that generates genuine free cash flows equal to its EBITDA and I will show you a pig that doesn't like getting dirty.

Many investors also like to value companies by their EBITDA multiple. This is calculated by dividing the enterprise value (market capitalisation plus debt) of the company by the EBITDA in a given year. I think this method is flawed because it can be deceptive at several levels. If you disagree with this view and want to use the EBITDA multiple as your key valuation method, then I would urge you to add the company's capital expenditure to the enterprise value (market capitalisation plus net debt). In a normal situation the depreciation and amortisation charges will be offset by the cash item of capital expenditure (capex). While this may sound slightly confusing we did see how critical capex is to working out the true value of a company when we examined ION Limited and ABC Learning Centres in chapter 8. The message is clear — if you omit capex from your calculations, you risk the administrators being called in to have a look at what is going on.

Cash into the future

Professional analysts focus on the valuations discussed above, but for the most part they prefer to use a measure called the discounted cash flow. In its simplest form this approach involves calculating the cash flow the company produces that will be available to the shareholders into the future. The future usually means 10 years, but for a limited number of sectors, such as mining companies and toll road operators, the future is the useful life of an asset. The analyst will calculate a terminal value for the company, which is effectively guess work for the long-term future (after 10 years).

Each year's cash flow is discounted back to today's value. How the discount rate is calculated will vary from company to company, depending on a range of factors, including the risk to future cash flows and the cost of capital. A large income-producing asset, such as a power utility, will have a lower discount rate than a smaller company, such as a retailer or building materials group, that experiences cycles in its cash flows. Once each year's cash flows are calculated, they are added up to record a valuation for the company. It is critical to understand that cash flow in the future is worth less than cash flow today, because time erodes the value of money. Therefore, each year's cash flow must be discounted back to today's value.

While analysts love this valuation technique, mainly because it is taught extensively in financial courses, it has some major shortcomings. First, history tells us that trying to accurately calculate a company's cash flows beyond two to three years is imprudent. At Wilson Asset Management our valuation methods concentrated on a rolling two-year forecast of cash flows and profits. We found any predictions beyond this point usually undershot or overshot the mark by up to 50 per cent. Second, a slight variation in the discount rate can radically alter the valuation of the company. If an analyst wants to crank up a valuation because the prevailing share price of the company is higher than his own valuation, he can simply tweak the discount rate down and, bingo, you get your number. I would rather deal in the reality of today than in the possibilities of the future.

If you are presented with a discounted cash flow valuation of a company, listen but be highly sceptical of its accuracy for most cases. If this valuation technique is restricted to companies that own assets with defined lives and regulated returns (such as gas companies, toll roads or single mine resource stocks) then it does have merit.

Don't take my word for it, though: you should do your own examination and reading to see if you believe discounted cash flow is superior to the other valuation measures mentioned above.

Returns that matter

If you start your own business you are acutely aware of the returns being generated. For example, if you buy a business for $1 000 000 with a combination of debt and equity and the business manages to earn you just $50 000 for the year before you even pay the tax and interest on the loan, you can quickly work out that the business is giving you a 5 per cent return on your capital invested.

Take this one step further and assume you have financed the $1 000 000 purchase with $500 000 of debt at an interest rate of 7 per cent, and the remaining $500 000 with your own cash. That means your interest bill for the year would be $35 000 (let's not worry about paying off the principal at this stage), leaving just $15 000 profit. That is a woeful return on your capital. It would have been much better not to exert the effort and put your money at risk. Instead you should have put that $500 000 in the bank at a 6 per cent interest rate. This would generate a pre-tax return of $30 000, double what the business has generated for you. Our example shows the business you have purchased is so poor that it hasn't even covered your cost of capital.

All of this seems simple, but surely it cannot apply to big businesses run by professional managers who know all about cost of capital? Well, it does. All businesses (big, small, listed and unlisted) should check if the return they are getting outstrips their cost of capital. Many industries, especially the mining services, need boom conditions to cover their cost of capital. For the remainder of their lives, they stumble around attempting to raise sufficient capital just to survive until the next boom appears. When a company listed on the sharemarket fails to cover its cost of capital, you can safely assume that it is going backwards, so try to make sure you don't invest in these companies. On the flip side, a company that produces a return in excess of its capital cost is always worth a look, especially if the PE ratio is not too high.

While the example of a private business discussed above is all pretty straightforward, it is slightly more difficult to work out the ratios of return on capital and return on equity for a listed company. Don't be scared, though; it's not difficult and anyone can do it.

See what your equity is earning you

Two measures, return on equity and return on capital, will give you an idea of what your equity is earning for you.

The company's return on equity in its simplest form is the profit before that tax a company makes divided by the total equity shown at the bottom of the company balance sheet. McMillan Shakespeare (see figure 9.2) is an exciting example of a company generating excess returns. In the year to 30 June 2008 McMillan Shakespeare posted a pre-tax profit of $24.9 million. If we look at the bottom of its balance sheet for that year, total equity amounted to $48.2 million, and so the return on equity was an extremely healthy 51.6 per cent. No matter where you get your capital from, it won't cost you that much. This number looks even better if you take out the net cash on the balance sheet of about $17 million, but we won't concern ourselves with that now. Just as importantly, the return on equity has been improved from the previous year's impressive 47.3 per cent.

The company's return on capital was also stunning. To calculate the company's return on capital, divide the EBIT number by the total assets recorded in the balance sheet. In 2008 McMillan Shakespeare delivered a return on capital of 40.3 per cent, while in 2007 the number was slightly less at 35.6 per cent. In other words for every extra dollar management put into the business, whether equity or debt, an extra 40.3 cents of EBIT pops out — a payback of around 2.5 years. If you could spend $1 and it earned you 40.3 cents a year for the rest of its life, you would do that every day of the week.

Figure 9.2: McMillan Shakespeare (MMS) share price, March 2004 to June 2011

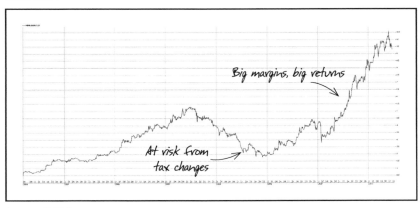

Source: IRESS

Nothing is a certainty, though

Both the return on equity and return on capital are vital ratios that must be calculated by any sharemarket investor wanting to pick stocks successfully. Before anyone gets too excited, though, there are major pitfalls to these ratios, which can be best explained by the old saying, 'Rubbish in, rubbish out'!

The first trap that you need to be aware of is how high levels of debt can boost the return on equity. A company that has no debt will have a relatively high total equity, compared with total assets on the balance sheet. Add debt to the liabilities (the amounts the company owes to other individuals or companies) and suddenly total assets start to streak away from total equity. That basically means a highly geared company should be able to create a higher return on equity than an ungeared company. So, when it comes to a highly geared company, I would suggest that you ignore the return on equity measure and concentrate solely on a return on assets.

The second trap is that return on equity and return on capital is based on the earnings of the company. As we saw in chapter 8, sometimes earnings are a ruse.

If we look at ION Limited's accounts for the year to June 2003, you can see what I mean. The company announced an EBIT of $81.3 million on total assets of $620.36 million. This equates to a return on capital of 13.1 per cent. Not brilliant, but acceptable for an industrial company whose cost of capital probably sits a percentage point below that. Because the company had high levels of debt, the return on equity sat at 31.7 per cent. This suggests the debt levels are far too high. Moreover, after looking at the cash flow statement, we know the profit and loss statement was virtually useless because of the company's enormous cash outflow. The fact is the company was leaking cash and its returns were plummeting as earnings went backwards. So before you dive into your ratios, make sure you check the discussion of the three key pages outlined in chapter 8.

If you want to find more ratios for analysing a company, you will have no problems. You can cut the numbers forever and any way you want, and many people do. But at the end of the day it is better to keep most aspects of life as simple as possible, so you don't get confused. If you stick to the approach I have outlined it is difficult to go wrong.

This leaves us with one crucial aspect to cover.

Profit forecasts — it's like forecasting the weather

Professional investors are obsessed with profit forecasts. Beat the forecast profit and be lauded by all and sundry; miss the forecast and be prepared to cop the wrath. To make matters more complex, a company that beats its profit forecast, but announces that analysts are too optimistic for the year ahead, will suffer a fresh wave of negative sentiment that will undoubtedly result in the shares being sold off.

While professional investors will always try to convince their clients they are long-term investors who are not rattled by short-term events, the reality is somewhat different. Consistently, a disappointing earnings result or a downgraded forecast will create an instant negative reaction. If I was to select a single financial indicator that professional sharemarket investors examine most closely, it would be the earnings forecast that the company itself or stockmarket analysts are predicting. The immediacy of this has escalated in recent years, with companies being forced by the regulators to provide updated earnings forecasts under their continuous disclosure rules.

I will state it now: whatever research you do into a company, the most vital piece of information you need to gather, regardless of the situation, is the earnings forecast for the year ahead, simply because the rest of the market is so sensitive to it. Professional investors are a reflection of general society and when great expectations are not met, severe disappointment sets in. Charles Dickens thought this was a subject relevant enough to dedicate a whole novel to.

Putting it into action

Once you have worked out all the key ratios and think you know how to value a company, you need to do two things. First, you need to work out the long-term average PE ratios and EBIT multiples for a company. At the same time, you need to work out what the market is forecasting the company can earn during the next two years. There is no benefit in attempting to calculate beyond this time frame because it becomes too much like trying to read the long-term weather forecast. You may be right, but it will be more about luck than good management. Numerous studies over the years have shown that market analysts can regularly be 50 per cent out on company profit forecasts when they try to estimate two years out. Not a great track record. There would hardly be an analyst on Earth who could precisely forecast a company's earnings five or ten years into the future.

Another imperative is to take the time to study and understand the industry a company operates in. There is no point allocating massive PE and EBIT multiples to a company that is experiencing strong industry tail winds. It never fails to amaze me that boom times last long enough for investors to be convinced the boom is the new normal. They merrily buy the shares of these companies only to find out the new normal is actually just a peak period in the same old, same old.

Once you have the forecasts in hand you can make an assessment of whether the market is too optimistic or too pessimistic about the future. Then, when the actual results are announced, you can determine if the market is going to be excited by the event or in deep depression. This requires constant vigilance, so don't fall asleep when companies announce their profit forecasts. Occasionally a company will pre-announce a result, some weeks before the end of the financial period, which can be a celebratory upgrade or a mournful downgrade. An upgrade can also lead to stock price re-rating, and a downgrade can work in the opposite direction. It is a dynamic game and there is never a dull moment.

None of these ratios require high-level maths. If you still feel uncomfortable about them, the only way to overcome this is to pull out your calculator and attempt to work out some real-life examples. Like most aspects of life the first few times you attempt a new activity it turns out badly, but eventually, with persistence, things start to click, so just keep on reading those numbers. As famous

South African golfer Gary Player liked to say, 'The more I practice, the luckier I get'.

Our approach

At Wilson Asset Management we had a simple but effective way of picking stocks. Our valuation template concentrated on forecasting the next two years earnings, working hard to get a firm grip on the rate at which earnings per share (EPS) could grow. We would then divide this EPS growth by the PE in the relevant years to get a valuation filter, ensuring that we were not paying too much for the growth. Finally, we would, after several meetings with company management, rate both the management and the industry the company operated in. This template would spit out a score. Ideally we were looking for a company that could grow its EPS at twice the rate of its prevailing PE ratio.

If a company produced a high enough score we would then take a further three steps. First, we calculated the return on equity to ensure the company was growing profitably and not in need of major capital injections. This was followed by a cash flow calculation to ensure the company could grow without having to raise future equity that would dilute existing share holdings. Finally, we looked for a catalyst that would change the value of the company in the market's eyes. If the company ticked all these boxes we would start to buy.

Two-minute free cash flow

We have already discussed how to calculate the return on equity, but we haven't really covered how to derive a free cash flow number. Investors and analysts all have their own method of calculating cash flow, but we preferred to use a very conservative and simple method.

First, we added the net profit to the non-cash items of depreciation and amortisation. We would then deduct the capital expenditure (capex), working capital increase and dividends.

This effectively gave the free cash flow before any acquisitions or asset sales.

Let's have a look at a working example.

A company earns $10 million in after-tax profit and has a total depreciation and amortisation charge of $1 million; then $11 million is deposited into its bank account. From this, they have $5 million outgoings in capex, an increase in working capital of $2 million and a dividend of $5 million. This amounts to $12 million going out the door. At the end of the year the company has recorded a negative $1 million cash flow. It has to pay for this by taking on more debt or by using any surplus cash it has. Ideally the company should have paid a dividend of $4 million or less to ensure it could pay for the dividend from operational earnings rather than borrowing from the bank. To check if your calculations on cash flow are correct you can check the movements in debt and cash on the balance sheet. This was discussed at length in chapter 8.

To summarise:

Free cash flow = (net profit + depreciation + amortisation)
           − (capital expenditure + change in working
           capital + dividends)

Working out working capital

To round out our two-minute free cash flow method we need to discuss working capital. In various industries companies will have enormous investment in working capital and management needs to keep a meticulous eye on this to ensure it does not blow out. Other industries are lucky enough not to need a big working capital component.

The critical components of working capital are inventories, receivables and payables. These items will all appear on the balance sheet. On the asset side sits the inventory and receivables, and on the liabilities side sits the payables. A quick working capital calculation is to add the inventory and receivables together and then deduct the payables. To gauge the change in working capital, we simply do the same for the previous year and deduct the number from this year.

Let's look at an example.

In 2010 a company had $10 million in inventory, $10 million in receivables and $10 million in payables. This would mean the company has a total of $10 million tied up in working capital. If we move forward to 2011, the company has $12 million in inventory, $12 million in receivables and $12 million in payables. Working capital now sits at $12 million, up 20 per cent from 2010. The company has to fund this increase by taking on more debt or by using existing cash.

To summarise:

Working capital = inventories + receivables − payables.

For our working example in 2010, our company working capital would be $10 million + $10 million − $10 million = $10 million. In 2011 the company working capital would be $12 million + $12 million − $12 million = $12 million.

If you calculate the 2011 free cash flow, the change in working capital would be $2 million from 2010 to 2011.

In our example, the expansion of working capital should be met by an increase in sales of about 20 per cent. If sales are flat then the company is experiencing a leakage of money and questions should be asked. If the company can grow its sales by 40 per cent and only expand working capital by 20 per cent that is a great improvement.

Over the years I have come across some companies that have got into financial difficulty because of a blow out in working capital. It is critical in your analysis to keep a close eye on this. Invariably in a major company turnaround the first move a new management team undertakes is repair of the balance sheet by reducing working capital.

You may be different

That was how we did it. This fairly simple method may suit your investment style or it may not. That said, I would urge every sharemarket investor to spend a lot of time working out the cash flow and the return on equity for companies they are interested in to understand the company's true health. It is imperative, as we are about to find out.

Chapter 10

All companies are different

Like human beings, all companies are different. They operate in a variety of industries, have individual management teams, have unique balance sheets and respond differently to changing economic conditions. In a bid to corral this vast diversity, sharemarket investors sort companies into specific categories. This is a natural coping mechanism and it is terrifically helpful for investors to more fully understand what they are investing in. Ideally, an investor would be able to borrow the sorting hat from the JK Rowling's *Harry Potter* books so they didn't have to guess which part of the world each company belongs to. Alas we don't have an official sorting hat, but we can apply our own methods to achieve a similar outcome.

Once you have worked out which investment category a company belongs to—growth, turnarounds, asset plays, cyclicals or PE plays—you can adjust your expectations about how a stock should perform through an economic cycle. A growth story should be viewed differently from a turnaround, and a turnaround should be viewed differently from an asset play. Understanding the various categories will also give you some genuine parameters to refer to when determining when to sell a company's shares—a key part of the investment process that too many investors ignore when they charge off to buy what seems like a stunning idea.

It is important to understand that these categories have nothing to do with the real world of business: they are the invention of professional investors over the years, to help their own investment process—in particular, to determine how to value a stock. By categorising each company, an investor can start to come to grips with its expectations. For example, a growth stock with a high rate of earnings growth should trade on a higher PE multiple than an asset play, simply because investors factor in profits from future years. If a company that has the ability to deliver 20 per cent profit growth for many years to come is trading on a relatively low PE, of say 8, it might be worth closer inspection. Inevitably the market will get excited about the story and the PE multiple will start to increase.

Growth is the drug

It is virtually impossible for any company to attract new investors if it offers absolutely no earnings growth. Growth is the drug of the market and once a company loses its earnings growth, it has effectively lost its appeal. Investors will dramatically de-rate the company, selling its shares and heading to the exit door en masse. For a company to be recognised as a growth stock, the market must feel comfortable that, over the long term, the company can grow its revenues and profits at a much higher rate than the prevailing general economy and the overall market. Commonly, growth stocks post revenue and profit growth of around 20 per cent, or possibly higher, each year. Most investors who buy these stocks have great expectations that this level of expansion will continue into the foreseeable future, and so they are willing to pay for this by placing a steep PE multiple on the stock.

A growth stock can come from anywhere in the market, but it tends to emerge from industries that have low barriers to entry (such as retail, or industries where a company has a niche, such as in medical devices or technology). They rarely come from mature industries, such as building materials, beverages, manufacturing or banking.

The best time to get into a growth stock is before the rest of the market has had time to discover it. That sounds great in theory but it is harder to achieve in reality. To achieve this goal you must be prepared to get down and dirty, and look at stocks that are much smaller than many of the blue chip names that your financial adviser is willing to recommend. In addition you must have a sense of vision, because you are banking on growth down the road, which most of us find difficult to see. This kind of investment also has a large degree of risk attached.

Over the years, most growth stocks I have discovered in Australia have been nestled in the retail or technology markets. In the retail game the headline acts in recent years have been electronics group JB Hi-Fi, car parts outfit Super Retail, and discount company The Reject Shop. Investors love these stories because you can accurately extrapolate earnings into the future. Once a retail chain has a footprint of stores and the concept is proven, investors can then work out how many shop fronts the company can roll out across Australia and possibly New Zealand. For example, a company may have 50 stores operating when it lists on the sharemarket. The management tells everyone that it can deliver 300 stores over the course of the next seven or eight years without having to raise any fresh capital from the market. Investors listening to the story will try to work out whether the concept is sustainable, and then wait for some financial results for confirmation of the story. If the company's earnings meet, or even beat, prospectus forecasts, investors will start to get on board. They begin to believe in the concept and figure that if the company can earn $10 million from 50 stores they should be able to earn six times that with 300 stores. Investors also start to build into their financial modelling store revenue growth of 4 per cent per year, which gives earnings a nice little kicker. That all adds up to a major re-rating of the stock.

As the company rolls out its stores and shows profit growth of 25 per cent a year, the PE can go from it starting position of 8 to 12 and eventually 20, by the time the whole market has woken up to the fact that a party is going on. For an investor, this is the sweet spot because you are getting the double whammy of earnings growth and PE expansion. Initially the company earned $10 million and traded on a PE of 8, meaning it had a market capitalisation of $80 million. Five years on, the company prints a profit of $60 million and its PE has ballooned to 20, and the market capitalisation will inflate to $1.2 billion—a gain of 1500 per cent for those who were set in the stock at the beginning.

Once the PE ratio ratchets up to nose-bleed territory, investors should be aware that further multiple expansion will be tremendously difficult to achieve. In addition, once the company approaches its complete 300 store roll out, future growth will ease and the multiple is likely to contract, unless a new retail concept can be discovered. That is a much higher risk play.

A fantastic roll out

This story has unfolded on numerous occasions in the Australian sharemarket. Despite knowing the life cycle drill I have managed to miss some eye-popping performers, such as JB Hi-Fi, Flight Centre and Super Retail. One stock that I do remember fondly, though, was furniture retailer Fantastic Furniture. Fantastic floated in 1999 after the company was bought out of administration by Julian Tertini and Peter Brennan, both experienced and sharp operators in the retail sector. The company's float was being underwritten by small Perth-based stockbroker Hartley Poynton at the top of the tech boom. The market was extraordinarily volatile at the time, and no-one was really interested in companies that didn't have a whiff of technology, media or telecommunications. Because Fantastic was a manufacturer and retailer of what was categorised as cheap and nasty furniture, it was forced to list on a PE ratio of just 8, compared with the overall market rating of around 15.

In a bid to muster institutional interest in the float, Hartley Poynton organised a site visit to Fantastic's manufacturing facility in the west of Sydney. My contact at Hartley Poynton told me that around 10 institutional investors from Sydney and Melbourne would be on the trip and insisted that I be on time, as the bus would be chock-a-block and it was a tight schedule. Taking his advice, I arrived 10 minutes before departure time, even before the bus had arrived. Eventually the bus turned up with two people on board.

Both were from the underwriting stockbroker firm. I clambered on board to get a prime seat up front so I could try to avoid my motion sickness affliction. I sat and waited and just as the departure time arrived, another fund manager—Graeme Burke from Colonial First State—arrived. We waited another 10 minutes to see who else was coming, with the broker claiming he had received several phone calls from other institutional fund managers who had to pull out at the last moment. After about 30 minutes we drove off with just the four of us on the bus—it had become obvious to me the stockbroker had no institutional interest in the float, and I had been the victim of a good piece of selling and was being taken for a ride—literally. This was going to be a long day.

An hour later we arrived at the site. We met the managing director, Julian Tertini, and his offsider, Peter Brennan, who were both pleasant and seemed to have detailed knowledge of the discount furniture market. We then went down to the factory and watched the company workers assemble lounges that were being made to be trucked off to one of 20 or so retail stores across New South Wales. While it seemed like a somewhat backward, manual process, we were stunned to learn that a lounge could be built from start to finish in just seven minutes. Graeme Burke and I looked at each other without saying a word, but nodding as if acknowledging how impressive the whole process was. During the walk around the factory, Julian made it clear that they would have to consider putting on a second production shift because demand for Fantastic's products was firming.

On the way back to the city I scanned the numbers in the prospectus and saw the following. The company had net cash on the balance sheet; a return on equity well above 20 per cent; and an ability to roll out four times the number of stores over the next five to ten years. This inviting combination was being floated on a PE of just 8 times prospective earnings. I was slightly befuddled and wondered why no-one in the market was really interested.

If memory serves me correctly, only two Australian institutional investors, including us, were on the register when the company announced its top 20 shareholding to the market. The rest was made up of management, staff and retail investors. As a novice analyst I had spent a lot time convincing my boss Geoff Wilson that it was worth taking a slice of a company that made cheap furniture and had recently been in administration. The company went to market with an issue price of 50 cents a share, only to slump in the first two weeks of trading to 42 cents a share. Market sentiment had turned sour and new floats in that arena usually were being spurned by investors, who thought the furniture was ghastly, unable to comprehend who would buy it. In addition there was no corporate history to rely on. I have found over the years that professional fund managers are poor judges of what sells to the general public, mainly because they spend their money on products generally out of reach of the average family.

Fantastic's PE ratio fell below 7 and we decided to buy more on the proviso that Geoff could meet up with management, which I organised with alacrity. I would come into work each morning, call my broker at Hartley Poynton and abruptly ask if he had discovered any interest in the stock. As usual there was a lot of positive commentary but no evidence of a buyer in sight.

Soon afterwards, market sentiment improved and the stock managed to climb back up to its issue price as sellers took time out. The love affair with technology was souring and investors were seeking out value in the industrial market for the first time in several years. In the coming days we met the management team and Geoff agreed with me that they seemed like good operators and the stock was cheap. He shocked me by deciding to buy more shares. Eventually the company released its first set of results and, while they didn't shoot out the lights, they were slightly ahead of the prospectus numbers. That is all it took. With the tech wreck in full swing, investors had turned 180 degrees and were desperate to discover cheap industrial stocks that actually earned a decent return on capital. Suddenly Fantastic was on the radar. In the end we were able to sell most of our stock at around $1.40 a share, happy with the result and in deep gratitude to the management team that did a fabulous job. The share price kept motoring along to hit $2.80 as the market became enamoured with the store roll out and the returns being generated (see figure 10.1). The company was trading on a PE of close to 20 within a couple of years, and I still regret that we sold so early.

Figure 10.1: fantastic result—share price for Fantastic Furniture from September 1999 to December 2003

Source: IRESS

Technical growth

Technology stocks or niche operators who manage to take their business into offshore markets also tend to get re-rated upwards by the local sharemarket, as they display an ability to notch up high growth rates and tremendous margins. This allows them to grow without having to go back to the market for fresh capital. Some examples of this in Australia have been ear implant group Cochlear, share registry operator Computershare and sleep mask manufacturer ResMed.

In recent years the players that emerged from the internet tech boom of the late 1990s have become the new growth stocks. Companies such as accommodation booking group Wotif.com, real estate advertising site REA Group and automobile auction group carsales.com.au have, from a standing start, become top 200 companies.

> In recent years the players that emerged from the internet tech boom of the late 1990s have become the new growth stocks.

If you fail to discover these growth stocks early, you have some major decisions to make. Once the company shows the market that it can deliver above-average profit growth over several years, the valuation of the stock will start to expand as investors start buying.

The investors in the company believe the earnings will eventually grow into the large PE. In other words, you have to pay up big time and be a major believer in the story. This is a dangerous game to play for the following reasons: the most obvious is that if something goes wrong and earnings stall, then the stock will suffer a larger share price decline than a cheaper stock. A stock trading on a PE of say 22, compared with the market average of just 14, has no room to slip up. In 2007 Credit Corp, trading on a PE of 22, announced that it would miss its 2008 earnings forecast by 25 per cent: it watched its share price drop immediately by 40 per cent, and then another 20 per cent before a future downgrade.

Another problem with growth stocks is that one day the growth will begin to fade. This has happened to many companies, including Billabong, Lend Lease, Brambles and Harvey Norman. Even if the company continues to grow its earnings at a decent rate, but less than previously, it will not prevent the stock's decline. The PE contraction, from say 25 to 12, ensures the share price is a long-term underperformer.

Growth investors have some fabulous years, but studies show they tend to underperform their arch rival—the value investor. The value investor tends to ignore highly priced growth companies preferring to concentrate on companies that are relatively cheap compared with the rest of the market. That should not deter those who have a great vision for the future and the ability to be ahead of the market and pick long-term growth stocks.

Turnarounds

The market loves failure. Professional investors stalk the market trying to find companies that have tripped at some stage, causing everyone to eventually give up. This drives the share price down to lows that did not seem possible at any stage while the group's earnings were chugging along okay. To find a turnaround play, you need to constantly read the 12-month lows and pick over the names, wondering whether there are better times ahead for particular companies.

A turnaround is a risky play. You have to decide whether a company's fall from grace is permanent or a fixable situation. I must admit that I have found this play can go either way and have been fooled by what looked like a prime turnaround, only to sit on a huge loss. If you do get it right though, the turnaround play can be an incredibly profitable trade. That is why they are so hard to ignore. Just to taste how bountiful a turnaround play can be we should remember that Peter Proksa bet his last remaining capital on biotech company Prima Biomed being able to turn its circumstances around. He went from the outhouse to the penthouse in the twinkling of an eye.

A company can only qualify for a turnaround play if at some previous stage it had performed at a certain level, and poor decision making or unforeseen circumstances then undermined that performance. As a consequence, a new company cannot be categorised as a turnaround. Investors should clearly understand that if a turnaround does take place, there is no further upside to the share price. Don't be fooled into thinking the new era will result in better earnings, higher margins and a higher rating from the market than the last era.

In the aftermath of the GFC, we picked our way through the market each day looking at stocks that had fallen on hard times because the market had thrown them on the scrap heap. We found some superb opportunities that proved to be major contributors to our performance. One that Geoff Wilson identified in early 2009 was the debt-laden McPherson's Limited, which had sunk to a PE multiple of just over 1. That is not a misprint. The market had written off the homewares wholesaler because of a currency hedging shambles and a sizeable level of debt. After a cursory look at the accounts, we thought it worthwhile meeting with management in a bid to get some comfort that the company was not going to be the latest outfit to enter administration as banks became increasingly skittish. We walked away confident the company could keep its lenders at bay. Once the debt problem was put to bed and the currency started to improve, we reconciled that historically McPherson's traded at about 8 times earnings. This meant the stock could go from around 30 cents a share right through to $3.00. We would have been happy to see the stock rise 50 per cent, but the stock did indeed climb all the way to $3.00 in about an 18-month period.

Second time unlucky

So much for the good turnaround story! At about the same time as the McPherson's story was unfolding, we took a position in white goods retailer Clive Peeters. The company had started to fail well before the GFC took hold, on the back of a disastrous expansion away from Victoria and Queensland and into the large Sydney market. To top off all the bad news, an employee decided to use her bookkeeping skills to steal $18 million from the company by funnelling the money into her own electronic banking account. Eventually, the share price fell to the point where investors were only willing to attribute value to the company's inventory level. We started buying shares in the belief that we could only lose if the group went broke. The initial investment was boosted by the news that the woman who had stolen the $18 million had a fetish for Melbourne residential real estate, which could be sold by the company to recoup most of the money.

Pleased with our ability to discover the downtrodden and forgotten, Chris Stott and I went to visit the company in Melbourne to get an update. Catching a taxi from the city, the driver went the wrong way and the meter caught my attention. As the fare went through $90, I turned to Chris in the back seat and said, 'This better be a bloody good investment to make up for this bloody cab ride.' By the time we pulled up at the Clive Peeters car park, the meter read $104—the largest I can ever remember paying. I should have known then and there that things were destined for failure. The management team were living in hope that things would turn around in the months leading up to Christmas, but it was obvious this was just a hope and not a reality, because it didn't have the funds to invest in desperately needed inventory. A retailer without sufficient stock is like a one-legged Olympic sprinter. The share price started to decline at a swift pace and we took a major haircut on our investment. It wasn't long before the administrators were called in (see figure 10.2).

Figure 10.2: not so easy. Share price for Clive Peeters from September 2005 to June 2010

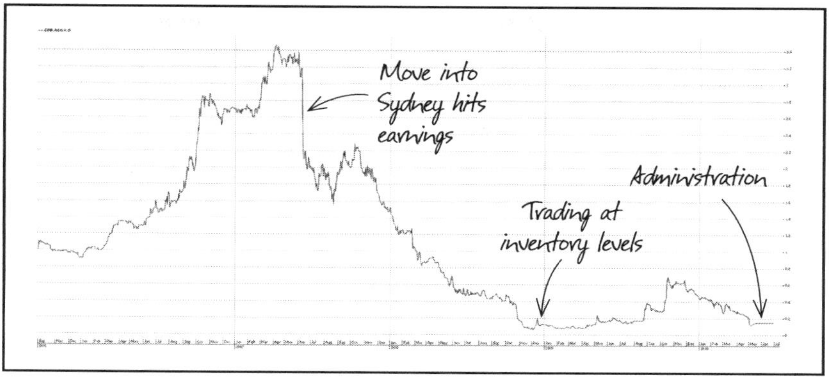

Source: IRESS

Turning the wrong way

The third type of turnaround story is the one you miss altogether. In 2001, I went with David Smith from Paradice Investment Management to visit equipment hire group Coates Hire at its modest headquarters at Miranda, a suburb in Sydney's south. The stock had been a much-loved story in the market during the 1990s, but after the Sydney Olympics, things had turned ugly as demand for hire equipment slumped. The company suffered from being overstocked and labouring under a hefty debt burden. The share price had declined about 60 per cent, which sparked our interest. Our conversation with the chief financial officer revealed that the company's bankers were very interested in proceedings and were in daily contact with the company. His parting comment was, 'The only way we can fix our utilisation problem is if they dig a bloody big whole and push half of Sydney's equipment into it and then cover the bloody thing up'. As we sat in the cab on the way back to the city I said to David, 'There is no way I can invest in that; they are likely to call in the receivers any day'.

The stock price bottomed at about 62 cents on the day of our company visit. Soon after, Coates announced a merger with arch rival Wreckair, a subsidiary of the much larger company Brambles. This was the catalyst to get the market excited and the stock never looked back again. In the private equity boom of 2007 Coates was taken over for $6.70 a share. If we had bought stock on the day of our visit, we could have nailed a gain of more than 1000 per cent.

With that I would leave you with these thoughts. A turnaround is a risky proposition and investing in them could easily be described as playing Russian roulette. For the most part I would not even contemplate buying into a turnaround unless a management change was undertaken to orchestrate the improvements. The people who presided over the decline are unlikely to be capable of making the improvement necessary. On top of this, you must be comfortable that the company's bankers will support a turnaround and, finally, you do not want to buy a turnaround in an industry that has a history of companies going broke—the mine drilling industry is a standout example.

Rich in assets

For true value investors only one thing exceeds the ecstasy of finding a company that is trading at below its hard asset value—finding a company that trades below the net value of cash on its balance sheet. It was these companies that the father of value investing, Benjamin Graham, wrote about so fondly in his seminal book, *Security Analysis*.

It is not uncommon to find companies listed on the market that trade below net asset value as stated on the balance sheet. It is important, before you put a company into this category, to calculate the intangible assets on the balance sheet. Sometimes an intangible asset is a genuine asset, such as a television licence, but mostly intangibles are goodwill that can disappear overnight if operations turn sour. Once you have deducted the intangibles from the balance sheet and discover that the company's share price is still trading at a level below its hard asset backing, you should feel compelled to investigate. After the GFC a large batch of companies, especially in the wounded listed property trust sector, traded between 10 and 40 per cent below their hard asset values. At Wilson Asset Management we tried to make money out of many of these companies, only to find the discount persisting with investors, who show little interest in taking advantage of an undervalued share.

A classic example of this was AV Jennings, which was trading at a 50 per cent discount to its stated asset backing, but no-one in the world was interested. It would seem the market is going to ignore these asset plays for some time unless the board of the company decides to sell assets at their book value to crystallise the value. The other alternative for investors is to stay incredibly patient, and hope the value will eventually be reflected in the share price. Investors who enjoy this end of the market are usually referred to as deep value players.

One asset play that did work after the GFC was an investment in Perth-based property group Cedar Woods. We had followed the company for about 10 years and concluded it had an outstanding management team and a collection of quality assets in Melbourne and Perth. All along, the management team had indicated the property assets on its balance sheet were conservatively priced. The problem for us was that it was impossible to tell by how much. At the depths of the market decline in 2009, Cedar Woods share price fell to below $2.00. In 2011 the company received an informal bid of $5.50 a share, but knocked it back, publicly declaring to the market for the first time that its assets were worth north of $6.00, some 50 per cent more than the balance sheet showed. This may still provide an opportunity for investors, with the share price in July 2011 hovering around the $4.00 mark following a rebuff of the takeover offer.

Sticking with Western Australian stocks, Wilson Asset Management analyst Chris Stott did a great job in identifying car parts distributor Coventry Group as an asset play that we could pluck. A perennial underperformer, Coventry's share price fell so far during the GFC that it was trading below its inventory levels. Effectively, you got the other assets on the balance sheet, including several parcels of land and an operating business, for free. The overall net asset value was above $2.00 a share, while the actual share price was languishing way down at 70 cents. No matter how badly the management performed, there was enough margin of safety in the share price, to borrow Benjamin Graham's terminology, that you could not lose. The management team did prove slightly disappointing, but the share price forged higher as investors searched out the value. By mid 2011

Coventry's share price was trading at about $2.30, which was a gain of 400 per cent from the dark days of 2009.

Money for nothing and your cash for free

The most alluring asset trade occurs when you discover a company that trades below the value of the net cash on its balance sheet. The only real piece of research required here is to establish whether the cash will be preserved or burnt by the company and its management team. The best way to determine this is to look closely at the last cash flow statement released by the company and see if it recorded a loss. It would also be useful to try to contact the company and ask what its plans are for the cash. If you derive a level of comfort that the cash will be retained, you have found the lowest risk play in the sharemarket that any asset class can deliver. Many professional investors ignore these opportunities because they like to buy operating companies that grow their earnings and have good prospects. That means fewer people are trying to buy cash at a discount, leaving it for people like you and me. Effectively, these opportunities allow the sharemarket investor to buy $1.00 of cash for 90 cents, 80 cents, or possibly even less. Where else does this happen? I can't think of one place on the globe.

In 2001, when we were surveying the debris from the tech wreck, Geoff Wilson made the comment that we wanted to unearth companies that would become so unloved that they would trade below their net cash backing. I dismissed him by saying that won't possibly happen! He said, 'It will. You just have to be patient'. He was right and I learned a great lesson. Unfortunately this situation is uncommon, but it does happen and when it does, you should get on board.

The one example of this that delivered us the best return following the GFC was in a stock called RHG. RHG had floated on the sharemarket near the peak in 2007, as the owner of mortgage provider RAMS Home Loans. The company relied heavily on wholesale funding and when the GFC hit and wholesale funding dried up completely the stock price fell like a stone. From its issue price of $2.50 a share, the stock bottomed on 30 June 2008 at just

4.6 cents, a decline of just over 98 per cent. The RHG management team reacted quickly, deciding to rid the company of its debt by selling its branch network to Westpac, leaving the mortgages already written in the listed entity. RHG struck arrangements with its financiers, and the business was put into run-off. In other words no new mortgages were written; operating costs were cut to the bone; and the remaining management team simply collected the money coming in to pay off the mortgages already in circulation. As the loan book started to run off with the customers paying back their mortgages, the cash started to flood in. Enormous value was being created. The stock started to rise gently, but was trading at only a quarter of the net cash on the balance sheet, with no value attached to the future cash flows that would be accumulated from the remaining mortgages still being paid down. In total, we thought the company was worth about $1.40 a share, while the stock was way back at 30 cents. The bulk of the run-off would be complete within about four years and the cash would be just sitting there. In addition, a pile of franking credits was being generated every time the company posted a profit. It was a gold mine. Luckily for us, independent analyst Mark Hancock had kept an eye on the company from the time of the float and brought it to our attention when the run-off started to get traction. If you can find an analyst like Mark then don't let them get too far away.

Cyclicals

Cyclical is a word that people in the sharemarket, such as economists, use liberally. Where are we in the economic cycle? Has the economic cycle peaked and when is the cycle going to turn? How long will this economic cycle last?

When it comes to the sharemarket, investors have deemed it appropriate to label a whole group of companies as cyclical. What does this exactly mean? Effectively, a cyclical stock is a company that will produce enormous profits when the industry it operates in is enjoying strong demand for its products. This normally runs in tandem with robust economic growth. Classic examples of cyclical stocks are building material, mining and retailing outfits. All of these companies enjoy tremendously strong periods of earnings, followed by frightening periods, as demand turns down abruptly.

When dealing with cyclical stocks there are some crucial factors to be aware of. The first of these is the stunning swings between peak and trough profits. A relatively small change in revenue can lead to an enormous variation in profit, due mainly to the high fixed cost base and intense asset nature of these businesses. Let's take the building materials sector and the recent decline in the US housing market. Australian-based building group Boral spread its operation to the US in the 2000s to diversify its geographical base and in search of growth. When the US economy was humming along in 2006 and houses were being built in record numbers, Boral printed earnings before tax of $185 million. When the housing downturn arrived in 2007, the company's pre-tax earnings in the United States disappeared and a $65 million loss was printed only two years later: a mind-blowing difference of $250 million in just 24 months.

In these tough times the cyclical company will reduce costs by laying off people, closing plants and squeezing suppliers. Importantly, when housing demand eventually returns, a company like Boral should see profits rocket as costs lag renewed demand. This sweet spot can last for up to two years, providing a marvellous opportunity for investors to get on board. In these circumstances a 10 per cent increase in revenue can lead to a 50 or 60 per cent increase in profits.

A second point you must remember about cyclicals is the way the market will price them. When a cyclical is on its knees, such as Boral during the US downturn, the sharemarket will, more often than not, place a high PE ratio on the stock. When the tide turns and demand starts to pick up and earnings surprisingly jump, beating all expectations, this PE will stay fairly constant. However, when the cyclical upturn becomes more mature, possibly after two years, and the company is printing record-breaking profits, investors will start to sell the stock in anticipation of a future downturn in the cycle, pushing the PE lower despite stellar profits being recorded. Effectively, that creates a high PE in bad times and a small PE in good times! In other words you have to be quick and constantly on the ball to get the full benefit of the share price upswing when it comes along.

While not a foolproof approach, a good way to play cyclical investment is to watch which way official interest rates are moving. A cyclical's share price will start to move higher when official interest rates are cut, as investors forecast better economic conditions down the track. Alternatively, when the central bank decides to lift rates, investors will start to move out of cyclical stocks in preparation for a future downturn, even though the company may be recording record profits. Whatever you do, don't be hoodwinked into believing a cyclical company can avoid the cycles, as many people believe in good times.

The PE game

Most professional investors tend to play the game of PE multiples and dividend yields. They will narrow down their universe of stocks and then work out which companies represent the best value, based on their forecast earnings growth. While some investors will startle you with their elaborate investment process, the mainstream professional fundamentally looks at the same group of stocks and spends most of their time working out what PE and what yield each company should trade at. This is a very rewarding approach if done properly and, if the market moves higher, it is possibly the best way to invest a larger pool of money.

To do this it is worthwhile getting your broker to run some long-term historical PE or yield charts of the stocks you are interested in. For example, you may be looking at investing in the banking sector and you notice Westpac is trading at a 12-month low and the share price has fallen away quite dramatically. You call your broker and ask what PE and yield Westpac is trading on and how these compare with the long-term average. Your broker says the company is trading at the bottom of its PE range and at the highest yield in many years. This may be enough to trigger a purchase on its own. On other occasions the investor will do more research to ensure there is no reason for the collapse in the share price, and then wait for a catalyst to buy into the stock. A catalyst is a trigger that causes a stock to re-rate. The most common of these triggers is an earnings upgrade or even confirmation of earnings forecast if a stock has fallen far enough. Alternatively, it could be a purchase of a new business or a sale of an underperforming asset. In the case of the banks, the catalyst could have been the government's decision in 2008 to support the banks with its AAA sovereign credit rating and the insurance of customer deposits. There are always catalysts, and the truly great investors over the years have been able to identify them and move quickly to maximise their profits. Vitally, an investor should not get carried away with claiming the catalyst, believing it will drive the company's PE ratio to new historical highs. Always be very cautious if a company that has traded in a PE range of 12 to 15, suddenly sticks its head above this range.

It is incredibly valuable to ask your broker at all times to check the long-term PEs and dividend yields of the stocks you are sniffing around. It is one of the best screens for analysing stocks that I have come across, and it is one we use to great effect in all kinds of market environments.

Conclusion

As you can appreciate, investors like to categorise companies into various groups. Importantly, this is not about the sectors the company operates in, but the individual characteristics the outfit is exhibiting. If you are able to get a firm grip on categorising companies as described in this chapter, you will reap great rewards.

Chapter 11

The perfect company

Striving for perfection is a dangerous game. If you are an idealist and believe that perfection can exist in any aspect of human endeavour, then you will be overwhelmed with disappointment at some stage. This phenomenon was on full display in the golfing community in 2010. An army of fans around the globe had followed Tiger Woods religiously for more than a decade, believing he was superhuman, winning major golf title after major golf title. Not only did they admire his stunning golfing ability, they heaped praise on his sportsmanship, his off-course demeanour and his ability to succeed as a person from a mixed-race background in a sport traditionally dominated by Anglo-Saxons. Then, in 2010, it was revealed that Woods had cheated on his wife. None of Woods's behaviour was illegal, and for any normal human being his activities should have been his own business. However, the golfing community and many among the general public were shocked. They had put a golfer up on a pedestal only to find out that he was human, just like the rest of us.

When it comes to the stockmarket, the problem with believing you have discovered perfection is that you will inevitably lose money. If this adulation is obsessive, the amount of the loss could be devastating, because you will never see the imperfection on the horizon.

In 1998 we thought we had discovered the perfect stock and to make the situation even more tantalising, the rest of the market seemed oblivious to the chance of a lifetime. The ASX was listing on itself. The ASX had all the key elements of perfection—a monopoly with pricing power, positive working capital, stunning margins, a bulging cash balance, no debt, double-digit revenue growth, no need for extra capital and infinite returns on equity, simply because it didn't require any. The only weak link we could find was a pedestrian management team that had operated under the protection of an unlisted monopoly. The stockbrokers who had forked out $25 000 to become members of the ASX years earlier were going to become marvellously rich by receiving shares for their membership. We did our own straw poll before the ASX listed and most analysts told us the company should trade on a PE of around 12 because of the cyclical nature of the equity market. We were stunned, given that was a discount to the average industrial PE across the market.

When the company listed at around $4 a share, the members all became instant millionaires. Our pre-listing poll of brokers proved conservative, with the stock's first trades valuing the company at just five times earnings. As some of the members cashed in their windfall, a small bunch of fund managers swooped, driving the stock up to $15 a share in five months. The PE was now a hefty 20 times earnings. A great trade if you were quick enough to snap up the shares the moment the ASX listed.

A few years later the ASX merged its business with the unlisted Sydney Futures Exchange, possibly the only other monopoly business in the country with the same perfect qualities. It was renamed the Australian Securities Exchange and suddenly, you had a top 50 company consisting of two monopoly exchanges. This proved to be the awakening for many investors, as they sat up and took notice of the business, drooling over its bulletproof balance sheet and high level of growth. Nine years after listing, the company's share price had climbed to $61 a share, with a market capitalisation in excess of $10 billion and a PE hovering around 25.

Corporate perfection, though, is only ever fleeting. As we now know, the sharemarket topped in Australia on 1 November 2007. It then proceeded to fall 54 per cent over the next 16 months as the GFC punctured the confidence of every investor. The share prices of companies with high levels of debt were slaughtered to levels that no-one could have possibly imagined only a year earlier. A monopoly company like the ASX, with mountainous cash levels, should have fared relatively well in such an environment, but it moved down in lock-step with the market. It eventually bottomed at the same time as the overall market, hitting a low of $27 a share, equating to a PE of just over 12. For a short time the members of our poll some 10 years earlier were spot on with their forecasts.

> Corporate perfection ... is only ever fleeting.

This brutal sell off by investors is a sharp reminder that regardless of the qualities of a business, the market will eventually decide to focus on valuation. The key message in this story is that you must never, ever, take your eye off the price of a company. As I mentioned earlier, investors don't really understand what makes a business tick and deliver exceptional performance. However, they do understand what valuation is, and is what is acceptable. In good times, much higher PEs are the norm, but when pessimism turns into the black dog of depression, only low PEs will do.

In recent times, the ASX's perfection has been damaged. The federal government through its regulatory body, the Australian Securities and Investments Commission (ASIC), have decided to issue licences to newcomers who want to establish rival exchanges. This decision followed similar moves in other countries, such as Canada, which has seen the trading market shares of the original monopoly fall away quite dramatically when several new players have entered. Australian investors have viewed these changes with a high degree of caution and the ASX's share price has floundered, despite a takeover bid from the Singapore Stock Exchange in 2010. It just goes to show that perfection can only last for so long before a catalyst ushers in a new era of imperfection. All those people who were happy to buy the perfect company in 2006 and 2007 are, five years later, nursing a painful loss. So much for perfection!

10 points of perfection

So let's dream a little and imagine that the perfect company does exist. What would it look like and what would be its key characteristics? They can be summed up as follows.

1 The company's balance sheet has net cash rather than net debt.
2 The company shows profit growth in all economic conditions.
3 The business is experiencing fast growth.
4 The business is unique and cannot easily be copied.
5 The company can grow without buying other businesses.
6 The company does not exist because of government regulation.
7 Poor management will not be terminal.
8 The business has many customers.
9 The share register will be free of institutional shareholders.
10 The financials will be as easy to read as a children's book.

The company's balance sheet has net cash rather than net debt

The best performing companies have net cash on their balance sheets. This attribute is commonly criticised by company analysts who are quick to label the company as having a lazy balance sheet. Instead, they would generally prefer to see a degree of gearing on the balance sheet to enhance the company's return on equity. This approach is straight out of the textbook and is technically correct. However, a cash–laden balance sheet tells me several things. First, it virtually rules out the chances of a company going broke, which, as we learned in 2008 and 2009, is a distinct possibility for a raft of companies. Second, if, in addition to having net cash, the company has positive net assets, then it's a sign the company is healthy because it can meet its financial obligations in the coming 12 months, effectively ruling out the administrators being called in.

Net cash on the balance sheet also tells me the business is self-funding. Self-funding is a crucial concept, because it means the business is of sufficient quality to not only finance its own growth, but also to produce excess cash to pay dividends for the shareholders to enjoy. This cash can be deployed over time as special dividends or to make strategically important acquisitions without having to take on debt or raise extra capital from its shareholders. This comment is made on the proviso the company has not raised fresh equity to achieve the net cash position.

To be in the position of having a healthy net cash position, a company must not have the heavy burden of regular capital expenditure, negative working capital or skinny profit margins. In other words, cash on the balance sheet is usually code for a company having high returns of 20 per cent or more on capital and equity—a vital measurement of quality. Over the years, businesses that have been able to grow their revenue at levels above general economic growth and still generate surplus cash are financial software group IRESS Market Technologies, education giant Navitas, stock exchange ASX, accounting software outfit Reckon, automobile auction site carsales. com.au, real estate listing company REA Group and salary packaging leader McMillan Shakespeare, to name just a few. You only have to look at the charts on the ASX website and see how well these companies have performed over the years to know what I am talking about.

I will never forget when educational company Navitas floated with net cash of $20 million on its balance sheet. At the time I asked Rod Jones, its energetic managing director and major shareholder, how much the company had paid in dividends to its shareholders over the years when it was an unlisted public company. His response was an astounding $200 million. All that money had been stuffed into shareholders' pockets and somehow there was still $20 million left for the new shareholders. Since listing on the sharemarket in late 2004, Navitas has managed to grow its earnings before interest and tax (EBIT) from $42.9 million to a hefty $90.5 million in 2010. In the same period the company's share price has appreciated 300 per cent compared with a meek 20 per cent gain by the sharemarket overall. Importantly, the company's net cash balance has grown from the initial $20 million, to $60 million, even though a steady stream of dividends has been paid to shareholders.

The company shows profit growth in all economic conditions

Outstanding companies are able to grow earnings in all economic conditions. The vast majority of companies require tail winds in some form to produce decent earnings growth. For example, retailers need consumers to be spending; builders need construction levels to be high; miners thrive on high metal prices; and exporters need a low Australian dollar. The search for those rare companies with the ability to clock up decent earnings growth in all conditions is endless — and commonly fruitless.

During the GFC many growth companies were exposed as good-time Charlies. And some companies that survived the horrors of 2008 and 2009 suckered many investors by performing terribly in 2010 as the government spending stimulus faded and interest rates rose. The Reject Shop was one example of a company that performed outstandingly when the supposed crisis was raging, only to fall flat on its face a year or so later.

Realistically, only a handful of companies fit into this category at any one time. Typically they emerge in a niche industry and are in the process of becoming the dominant player in their space, which gives them the ability to lift prices regularly. Examples of this dynamic over the years have been share registry operator Computershare, medical centre manager Primary Health Care, share trading system IRESS Market Technologies, taxi payment group Cabcharge Australia, accounting software provider MYOB, online vehicle trader carsales.com.au and bionic ear implant manufacturer Cochlear. All of these companies managed to either create their own niche industry or revolutionise an industry through the implementation of new technology. They have enjoyed stunning growth in all conditions as their products and services have been rolled out across their various industries.

These competitive advantages will eventually disappear and the premium rating attached to the company will dissolve before your eyes. At some stage, one of three things is almost certain to occur. First, as in the case of Computershare, there is a limit to how far the niche can extend globally. Second, a regulatory change is introduced that breaks down the barriers to entry that previously existed. These companies have luxuriated in fat margins for many years. The most obvious example is the ASX, which is under threat from new exchange licences being issued in Australia. Third, and most commonly, a management decision takes the company in a new direction that undermines what has been a fabulous business. Primary Health Care going from a pure medical centre operator to a large player in pathology and radiology in 2008 is one such example.

The business is experiencing fast growth

For a company's share price to appreciate over time it needs above-average earnings growth. In chapter 10 we rummaged through the various types of possible investments, such as turnarounds, asset plays and growth stories, and what you should expect out of them. All of these have their moment in the sun, but eventually their shelf life expires and investors demand the company produce healthy earnings growth. At Wilson Asset Management we had a very simple ratings sheet for each company that concentrated heavily on trying to predict earnings growth in the next two years. We thought it was too difficult to predict the performance of most companies beyond this time horizon, and each year we would roll out the forecast another two years.

It is common for professional investors to talk about market darlings having their share price de-rated because they have gone ex-growth. In other words, the earnings growth has slowed to levels that do not deserve the same PE multiple. So a company that has pumped out 20 per cent plus earnings growth for several years but suddenly experiences a growth rate of 8 to 10 per cent will see its share price decline. The most common example of this is in the retail sector. Most specialist retailers prove their model with a handful of shops; they then list on the sharemarket and proceed to roll out the concept around the country. The roll out means they can avoid the negative impact of an economic slow down by simply adding new stores that generate fresh sales and earnings. Investors froth at the mouth at the earnings growth being clocked up and push the PE ratio up to a hefty number. Inexorably, the roll out comes to a close and the PE deflates. Prime examples of this in recent times have been Harvey Norman and Fantastic Furniture.

The business is unique and cannot easily be copied

For a company to be seen as offering perfection, it must have a business that is virtually impossible to replicate. One of the most fruitful investments we were lucky enough to make at Wilson Asset Management was in stevedoring group Lang Corp. At a company conference held by a stockbroking firm in 2001, Lang Corp managing director Chris Corrigan was asked from the floor why the company was coy about charging higher prices for its services. At the time Lang Corp was thriving in a benign duopoly, so aggressive pricing was possible and seen as the best course of action on behalf of shareholders. Corrigan made the salient point that if they were to increase prices this would have flowed through into higher returns on capital, which already stood at around 25 per cent. Corrigan said if we ramped up the returns any further, the result would flush out a third market participant, even though they would have to invest hundreds of millions of dollars to get a foothold in the Australian market. I considered his answer and concluded that I was happy to take a business that achieved returns of 25 per cent, was growing its revenue at 10 per cent each year and was in a cosy industry structure.

The Lang Corp example goes to show that practically every business can be replicated, but there are many (such as the ASX, IRESS Market Technologies and Cochlear) who have tremendous market shares and insurmountable leads. If they are managed fittingly, they can keep the party rolling for many years to come.

In contrast, many businesses are constantly under pressure from rising competition. Industries such as transport, recruitment, equipment hire, stockbroking, retail, construction, travel, property and financial services are under relentless pressure from fresh competition. These industries and the companies operating within them are far from perfect, and over the long term they will, by and large, suffer from declining returns. It is not unusual for a throng of companies in these industries to post such poor returns that their cost of capital is not even covered. If you can't generate your cost of capital then you might as well stop operating.

The company can grow without buying other businesses

The perfect company rarely requires the burden of making acquisitions to bolster its earnings momentum. Ideally, the longer a business can generate double-digit revenue and earnings growth for extended periods without having to venture outside its core competency the better off the shareholders will be. This does not mean a company should not undertake the occasional strategic acquisition, but a string of mergers is not ideal. Strangely, investors get tremendously excited about a company making an acquisition — especially if the acquisition is earnings per share positive and requires a capital raising. To me, the purchase of another company carries enormous risk, both financially and culturally, and should be avoided in most circumstances. In contrast, if a company has growth as far as the eye can see without needing to spend copious amounts of money on capital or goodwill, then start counting the money.

The company does not exist because of government regulation

Companies that have a right of way because of government regulation or legislation should be viewed with great suspicion by investors. A perfect company must stand on its own merit and not be artificially supported by a third party that can remove that assistance at any stage. Examples of this over the years have been the duopoly operators of the Victorian poker machine market Tabcorp Holdings and Tatts Group, which both suffered enormously from a decision by the state government to remove their right to be the only two operators of the lucrative poker machines in the state. The federal government's decision to no longer provide tax breaks for collective agricultural schemes was the death of companies such as Timbercorp and Great Southern Plantations. The recent decline in Telstra's share price can be attributed largely to the government's move to roll out the national broadband fibre network as a replacement for Telstra's copper wire network.

Poor management will not be terminal

A good company can generally survive and move forward without great management but a perfect company cannot. We have seen this in recent years with mining giant Rio Tinto. Australia's second biggest mining company delivered shareholders fabulous returns during a resources boom that kicked off in 2003, despite the best efforts of management to bring the behemoth to its knees. For instance, at the peak of the 2007 resources boom, Rio Tinto went out on a limb and purchased Alcan for a boom-time price of $39 billion. No-one will ever work out why Rio Tinto made the purchase, but maybe fending off its own takeover offer from BHP was a key factor. The Alcan purchase meant Rio Tinto had to leverage its balance sheet to dangerous levels and, when the music stopped in 2008, the company was almost forced to relinquish control of its business to Chinalco, one of its Chinese customers. Eventually the Australian sharemarket bailed out managing director Tom Albanese and his board from this embarrassing situation by putting up a chunky $15 billion in new capital through a share issue to pay off debt.

Over the years many of Australia's largest and best known companies have been able to keep shareholders relatively happy in spite of management. A decision by NAB, first to enter the highly competitive US market and then initiate a foray into the UK banking sector, destroyed enormous amounts of value. BHP, under current CEO Marius Kloppers, has squandered hundreds of millions of dollars simply trying to make an acquisition in the current resources boom. Fortunately, he has not succeeded in his attempts, given some of the historically high prices he and his team have been willing to pay for local mining rival Rio Tinto and a potash company in Canada. Corporate advisors, lawyers and accountants hope that he keeps up his obsession with acquisitions so that money can be transferred to them away from shareholders. I get the feeling the shareholders will eventually lose this battle.

Imagine if these companies had been run by astute managers who understood what delivering shareholder value was really about. Imagine if a manager like John Rubino, of mining services and engineering group Monadelphous Group, had been at the helm of a company like Rio Tinto in the current boom. Since the boom started in 2003 Rubino has presided over a capital gain of approximately 5700 per cent, compared with a 260 per cent gain by Rio Tinto. A stark difference, particularly when both companies operate in fundamentally the same industries.

While a great company might not need great management, a perfect company unquestionably does. I will discuss the qualities of top notch managers in chapter 15.

The business has many customers

I have learned firsthand that a company with a high concentration of customers is a grenade that can go off in your hands at any time. An agricultural management company we held an investment in for many years, Select Harvest, relied heavily on managed investment scheme (MIS) operator Timbercorp. Select received fees for planting, managing, harvesting and marketing Timbercorp's high-yielding almond crops. It was a prosperous relationship that heavily favoured Select and, as a shareholder of the company, Wilson Asset Management was thrilled. Select was generating returns on equity in excess of 25 per cent, while also accumulating a mountain of cash on its balance sheet. I thought I had found another bulletproof stock, as our investment doubled, tripled and quadrupled in price in four years from late 2001. As tends to happen, the market proved I was living in a fool's paradise. Without warning the federal government decided that it would legislate to remove all horticultural MIS schemes. Investors could no longer claim an upfront tax deduction for the cost of the scheme, dramatically watering down the attractiveness of the investment proposal. That was the beginning of the end for Select's ascending share price. Timbercorp's share price started a spiral that eventually led to administration in 2009. Select was spared this devastation, but its bull run was over and its share price lost 85 per cent over five years—the result of having one customer.

The perfect company has many customers and, if possible, thousands. If one, two or even three customers disappear, because it prefers a competitor's product or because of its own difficult financial situation, then the change will hardly cause a blip on earnings. The upshot is that a company with a heavy concentration of customers or one major customer will trade on a low PE ratio compared with the rest of the market. A company with a spread of customers will be viewed more kindly by investors. It has amazed me that investors have been willing to place Australian mining companies on historically high earnings multiples, when one country—China—has created all the incremental demand for their products in recent years. To compound the problem, it is possible that China as a country is one single customer because it has a centralised government that controls the decisions of many of the country's companies.

The share register will be free of institutional shareholders

An aspect of the perfect company that rarely gets air-time is the share registry. At Wilson Asset Management we loved to stumble across companies that had no or very few institutional investors on its share register. This absence of professional investors could mean several things, including a lack of size or genuine lack of interest in the company's story. However, when it comes to small companies that have not been actively explored by the investors, it is usually a sign of the company being undiscovered. This might sound like a stock-picking cliché, but it can happen and it can reap enormous rewards. Some of our best investments were initiated when we discovered there were next to no other professional investors on the company's share register. If a company looked like it had several perfect qualities and we could identify a catalyst to re-rate the stock, then we would buy a small stake. We would place this in what we called our incubator category. We would buy a small stake in the company and carefully follow its progress. If events turned out favourably, with the earnings growing strongly, we would buy more shares and take it out of the incubator section of the portfolio. Over time we would hope to see a re-rating of the stock as larger institutions turned their attention to the stock and started to buy it.

This has proven to be a highly profitable method of stock picking. Some of our best performing stocks over the years, including accounting software group Reckon, wine producer McGuigan Wines, grocery wholesaler Metcash, Wide Bay Building Society, agricultural merchants Roberts, salary packaging group McMillan Shakespeare and branded herbs and spices company Burns Philp, were beneficiaries of this system. Sure, this approach requires courage, but if you trust your judgement and keep on top of the story, then the downside to an under-owned stock can be only minor.

The financials will be as easy to read as a children's book

The accounts of a perfect company are always easy to digest. What has simplicity got to do with perfection? When you look at our three important pages — profit and loss, balance sheet and cash flow — they should be undemanding on their reader and effortlessly connected to each other (see chapter 8). I say this because businesses, in their most pure form, are not complex and their accounts should be straightforward. There are revenues and there are costs. You subtract the costs from the revenue and you have the profit. This profit should be close to the cash generated by the business before any dividends are paid out to the shareholders.

When I have looked at the accounts of companies that are going through perfect patches, I can read their accounts like a children's book. It is difficult to hunt down these companies but at various times I would put the stock exchange ASX, travel retailer Flight Centre, entertainment retailer JB Hi-Fi, online real estate site REA Group and four-wheel drive accessory group ARB Corporation in this category.

When events start to turn sour for a company, the financials become increasingly difficult to read and comprehend. Towards the end of its life as a listed company, the accounts of Babcock and Brown became so complex that I spent close to a full day trying to find the cash flow statement let alone attempting to understand it. There were so many tables of numbers cut and diced in various ways that trying to find the real statement of cash flow was harder than solving the Da Vinci code. Once I recognised which table of numbers was the actual statement of cash flow, it took several more hours to work out whether or not the company had made any cash for the period. From my best guess, and that is all I could call it, the company had lost close to $700 million in cash for the period compared to a reported net profit of $500 million. That seems far from perfect.

If you invest long enough some companies become lucky charms—they make you money regardless of underlying fundamentals. For Wilson Asset Management, private hospital owner and operator Healthscope was one of these companies. We discovered the stock in 2000 as it was just kicking off a major operational turnaround implemented by a new managing director, Bruce Dixon, and we enjoyed a fabulous run. We made money years later when the company had expanded rapidly and, finally, we were able to play a profitable takeover arbitrage as private equity swooped in 2010. Fortunately, we missed a sizeable earnings downgrade that sent the stock plummeting in 2005. Given the fairytale ride we enjoyed, I should not be critical of the company. However, it was hard not to notice how the simple accounts of the early years turned into a long list of numbers. In a bid to keep profits ticking and cash flow obscure, the company started to add extra lines to its investing cash flow section. The standard property, plant and equipment (capital expenditure) was itemised to include money allocated for greenfield projects (start-up hospitals), brownfield projects (development of existing hospitals) and finance leases. If this clumsy structure had been a one-off then it could have been ignored, but when it reappeared over the following years, questions had to be asked. I concluded that the company was aiming to boost the profit number by capitalising costs rather than expensing them. The company trumpeted strong profit growth and expanding margins, but when all the numbers were added up there was no cash, and the return on capital was below the cost of capital.

If the accounts throw up more questions than answers then it is probably a safe bet to leave the company alone.

Never forget the price

If you are lucky and discover a company with the 10 perfect qualities, it is still essential to consider the price. No matter how investors try to avoid bringing valuation into a stock selection it can never be ignored. Most of the thousands of companies that filed through our offices at Wilson Asset Management over the years delivered their spiel with their capital structures stuck at the back of the presentation. Geoff Wilson would always force the company management team to run through its capital structure first before hearing the pitch. His reasoning was, 'What is the use of having a look at a magnificent house and falling in love with it, only to find out it costs twice as much as I can afford?' That made a great deal of sense to me and I have adopted the same rule over the years.

If you somehow stumbled across the perfect company, which is the equivalent to discovering the secret to eternal life, it would still be highly risky to simply avoid considering what price the company was traded at. At the peak of the tech boom in the United States, bellwether equipment supplies group Cisco Systems was trading at a price close to 80 times earnings. This meant investors buying the stock would have to wait 80 years to see a return on their outlay. Assuming most investors don't buy shares until they are adults, they would probably die before seeing a return on their Cisco investment. That doesn't seem to make a lot of sense. If Cisco did manage to continue to grow its earnings at the startling rate that was being achieved in the run up to the fear-driven Y2K problem predicted for the year 2000, then it would represent half the US economy within a decade. That is quite some investment. Of course, the tech bubble burst and Cisco's flame started to fade, resulting in its share price falling from $US77 to its current level of just $US15, just 11 years on.

The message here is that perfection, even when only in the eye of the beholder, is only transitory. Investors should never forget this and when they are done drooling over a stock, take care to check out the price.

Chapter 12

Trophy cabinet to rubbish bin

I have come to the conclusion that most companies listed on the sharemarket are rubbish—they just have good periods. If you trawl through the sharemarket tables in any of the metropolitan daily newspapers it will feel like you are walking through a graveyard of dead bodies. Most of the companies listed promised the world at some stage or another. They sprang to life with great expectations, only to collapse as disappointment set in. They sit on the tables wallowing at a disturbingly low share price without anyone taking any real interest in them. Even the big companies that investors like to call blue chips have some fabulous periods, followed by long and unexplained lean periods. If you have been playing the market virtually every day for 13 years, it makes you feel queasy just looking at the names of some of the stocks that you invested in at some earlier stage. Today, they are penny dreadfuls with an uncertain future.

If you think most of the companies you investigate and research are rubbish, how can you possibly make a good living from picking stocks on the sharemarket? The key is to view the market as a game of snakes and ladders. Like the board game, the ladders go up and the snakes go down, and your job is to jump from ladder to ladder and avoid the snakes where possible. Nirvana is when you land on a ladder that rises and rises for years—unfortunately this is the exception rather than the rule. If you do happen to find yourself standing on a snake you must try to make sure it is a short ride down by getting off as soon as you can see that you are heading lower. This sounds difficult but you have a better than even chance of still making money because the overall sharemarket powers higher by about 7.5 per cent each year. Your return grosses up to around 10.5 per cent once you add in dividends.

Despite being rubbish, most companies do have fabulous periods of share price appreciation at some stage in their evolution, and that is when you should be aiming to jump on board and go for the ride. Some fabulous periods can be brief or for others it can go on for years but eventually they end, or at least experience an extended pause.

Darwin alive and well

If there is one part of society that is living proof of Charles Darwin's theory of evolution, it is the sharemarket. The process of natural selection is always evident as investors roam the market looking for the best story of the day, rushing to throw capital at it. This results in various stocks and sectors having their day in the sun, only to be replaced by a different stock or sector the next day, year or decade. To give you an idea of what I am talking about, only one company of the current crop of 30 was in the original Dow Jones index from the day the index was put together more than 100 years ago. That company is General Electric, which in that time has morphed from a single-purpose entity to one of the largest conglomerates in the world. The other members of the Dow Jones have disappeared because of new technologies, shrunk in size or been taken over by a rival. It is a process of natural selection that will go on for many decades to come.

Endless inefficiency

Ironically, the social justification for the existence of professional investors is the argument that they play a crucial role in the efficient allocation of capital. Supposedly capital finds its way into the companies that deliver the best returns, and over the long term this is indubitably the case, but in the short term it is hogwash. If the sharemarket was a highly efficient mechanism to allocate capital on all time frames then you wouldn't get so many meteoric rises in individual stocks followed by monumental collapses soon afterwards. The examples of this are endless but let's explore a few.

Aristocrat Leisure

Aristocrat Leisure (see figure 12.1, overleaf) is a poker machine manufacturer that listed on the Australian sharemarket in the mid 1990s. The company had been founded by Len Ainsworth back in the 1950s and was a clear leader to the domestic poker machine industry. When the stock listed on the sharemarket in 1996 investors had never seen a poker machine manufacturer before, but within the space of a few years most people had become experts. The company's story started to resonate with institutional investors as it surpassed profit estimates and grew market share. The introduction of poker machines to states outside New South Wales meant the company expanded rapidly. Its pride and joy was the poker machine game Queen of the Nile.

From humble beginnings the stock started to rise, and before long it was a market darling, climbing past $10 a share with buy ratings from all the stockbroking analysts in the market. Such was the company's success that it began to make its highly successful machines for the offshore market, a concept that Australian investors latched onto quickly and another reason for the stock to trade at a higher share price with a much higher PE.

Out of nowhere the company announced that it had shipped a batch of machines to South America, but had not received payment for them, and there were no expectations of payment. Management had not done its homework on its new offshore customers. The result was a downgrade in earnings and soon afterwards the departure of the chief executive officer, Des Randall. The stock headed south at a rapid rate and, before anyone could catch their breath, it was back at 90 cents a share, a fall of more than 80 per cent from the top.

A change in managing director and a focus on offshore markets restored investor confidence at a surprisingly brisk pace. The potential growth in the US market hypnotised investors who jumped on board for a second spin of the wheel. The US market dwarfed the Australian market and as the US economy boomed through the first decade of the new millennium the share price powered past its previous peak, eventually hitting $19 a share—a 2000 per cent gain from the bottom. The Aristocrat PE also expanded as investors grew more and more confident about earnings growth prospects from the company.

Figure 12.1: the ups and downs of Aristocrat—share price from July 1996 to June 2011

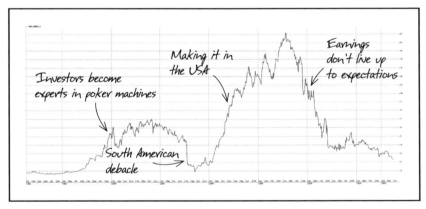

Source: IRESS

Then the rot started to set in for the second time. Due to the highly competitive nature of the US industry, the projected earnings failed to materialise and analysts begrudgingly cut their ratings on the stock. The share price drifted lower when the GFC hit like a hurricane flattening towns like Las Vegas, and for the second time in less than a decade the company's share price was in free fall, eventually sinking below $3 a share.

To date there is no sign of a recovery in the share price. The glory days of when the Queen of the Nile dominated the local scene are long gone and the hard slog of competing against the dominant American manufacturers is constantly with the company. The PE has shrunk back towards the market average and the great expectations have vanished for now.

So with Aristocrat you had two opportunities to make some stunning gains and two opportunities to almost lose the lot, all in the space of around 15 years.

ABC Learning Centres

I first met Eddy Groves in 2001. I was sitting at an outdoor cafe with Geoff Wilson when he came strolling down Macquarie Street with a stockbroker, planning to pitch the float of his childcare company, ABC Learning Centres. If memory serves me correctly, he was wearing a light grey suit with an open neck shirt. He didn't quite fit the textbook profile of a CEO, with his shoulder-length blond hair and Cuban-heeled boots. When I said to Geoff, 'Here they come', he leaned over and said, 'How are we going to invest with this guy? He looks like Johnny Farnham'.

Over the next hour Eddy, still only in his thirties, was subjected to a range of tough questions, but to his credit, he wowed us with his knowledge of the childcare business. At that stage the company only had 31 centres in its portfolio but Eddy knew every employee in every centre, every rental charge per square metre, the occupancy level of each centre, the waiting lists and so on. He was also disarmingly honest, telling Geoff and me straight up, 'The key to our business for the shareholders is the occupancy levels at our centres. If occupancy is above 90 per cent then we start to make a lot of money.' He repeated that comment several times during that session and in many subsequent meetings. I have not met a CEO before or since that day who demystified a business so rapidly for incoming investors.

At first we weren't convinced. Still sceptical of this young Queenslander, and never having come across a childcare operator that relied heavily on government spending, we decided to give the float a miss. Before the company listed on the sharemarket a couple of months later, I met Eddy at least twice more and said to Geoff that we needed to look at this company more carefully, because this guy really knew his stuff. Not many people were prepared to look at the company because it was so small, but I thought it fitted into our sweet spot—undiscovered and fast growing.

The stock listed and Eddy got busy buying more centres and spreading the gospel of his company to investors. He had enough energy to run a power station. It wasn't long before the broader market discovered the company and its colourful chief executive. In those early days he worked exceedingly hard with only a handful of stockbrokers hovering around sniffing for fees as the company needed to raise capital to fund its endless list of childcare centre acquisitions. Whatever Eddy Groves was doing, it was working, and the share price increased threefold in a short space of time. It was only then that we wilted and decided to help buy a parcel of shares in ABC held by Hunter Hall, who had profited nicely. Luckily for us, though, Eddy was only just getting started. His empire around Australia was expanding exponentially and over the course of the next year or so we watched our investment triple before our eyes. Things got so hot and steamy the company thought it necessary to split its stock to create more liquidity and give the impression it was not so expensive. The pièce de résistance was the merger with Australia's other largest childcare centre manager—Peppercorn. The brokers were now lining up to support the company, which was like a fee-generating machine on the back of so many capital raisings and mergers. ABC now stood at the top of the mountain.

Then the 20 per cent plus growth that investors had become accustomed to started to become harder to achieve. Eddy turned his attention offshore and before you knew it he had bought businesses in the United States, followed by operations in the United Kingdom. Following a series of capital raisings, the market capitalisation of the company had soared into the billions, while the PE kept travelling north to well above 20 times forecast earnings as investor interest started to emerge from all over the globe.

There had been some public detractors of the stock, including well-known analyst, market commentator and fund manager Roger Montgomery, who made the prescient observation that returns in the business had gradually declined over time as more and more acquisitions were made. He was, like Winston Churchill, a voice in the wilderness, with the share price rising each day as investors, including me, ignoring the financial fundamentals.

In 2006 I went to a presentation by ABC at a big brokerage firm where there was standing room only. I was lucky to grab a seat near the door but due to the size of the crowd I couldn't see Eddy — but I could hear him. I had decided to come along just to get an update on the latest acquisition and find out how the business was travelling. There were a lot of new investors in the room asking questions that long-term investors had asked many times before, so I was guilty of not concentrating and reading something else. And then one person piped up and asked the question: 'What are the occupancy levels of the centres in the US?' Eddy replied that it wasn't important to concentrate on occupancy levels. I nearly fell off my chair. Another person asked why that was the case and Eddie launched into a long-winded answer that didn't really make much sense.

I didn't stick around to hear the rest of the presentation, sneaking out the door that I was sitting near. I raced back to the office and as I walked in I said to Geoff, 'We need to seriously think about selling our ABC Learning shares'. He said, 'It's fine with me'. We spent the next few days re-examining the accounts and we had a lot of questions, including what had happened to $400 million of cash that had seemingly disappeared. Fortunately for us the stock was still trading in tremendous volumes and we were able to sell our shareholding at slightly more than $7 a share.

As is well documented, ABC Learning hit the wall in 2008 when the GFC hit. The company, which had enjoyed investor support to the tune of more than $1 billion through a series of equity raisings, had somehow found a way to fall prey to a multi-billion dollar debt burden.

There were many lessons to learn from the ABC Learning experience, but the point here is that stocks can be in the limelight for days, months or even years, only to become a disastrous investment down the track. Invariably as a story spreads across the market and more and more people get interested, more exotic reasons are created to buy the stock. Stockbrokers will place price targets for the stock near the current share price level, and when the PE ratio goes from say 10 to a head spinning 20, the analysts will generally follow with their valuations of the business. Things like sagging returns and higher debt levels are conveniently pushed to the side by investors and brokers as they all get sucked into the vortex of a rising stock price. At some unknown time in the future the share price will reflect the financial fundamentals and start to fall. For the investor the hardest aspect is timing when this will happen rather than if it will happen.

Our croupier Peter Proksa learned this the hard way. In his bid to avoid paying too much for a stock he has limited his investments to shares or options that trade at 1 cent of less. This method also removes the possibility of his becoming enchanted by the story rather than concentrating on the facts presented in the accounts.

The reality was, however, that if you were onto the ABC Learning story early, like the Hunter Hall investment team, then you could have made many times your money. The key was seeing that things were changing and working out when to sell. Roger Montgomery picked it and was happy to tell the rest of the market, which should have listened more carefully. Things had changed at ABC Learning over the years and Eddy admitted it in that meeting, but most people holding the stock just weren't listening to the message he gave everyone.

> The key was seeing that things were changing and working out when to sell.

There are snakes and ladders everywhere

Many people will argue these two examples do not apply to the big end of town, where a special breed of stocks called blue chip resides. And there is a grain of truth in this. There is very little chance of a big company going broke in Australia due to an unwritten contract between investors and company management who know they are too big to fail. That does not make them immune from being shocking investments.

The classic example is Australia's largest manager of super-annuation and life insurance products, AMP. Its demutualisation into a company during the late 1990s and subsequent listing on the Australian sharemarket came with much fanfare and could be viewed as one of the biggest events in the nation's business history. Such was the rush to buy stock on day one of trading that an investigation by the regulators was launched in a bid to determine how the shares had spiked to briefly trade at more than $40 a share before settling to close on day one at around $20 a share, closer to most analyst valuations. Since that day back in 1998 the stock has consistency fallen and today it sits at just under $5 a share. Investors who bought the shares 13 years ago with the intention of holding onto a profitable blue chip have watched their money fade to grey.

Even the biggest can do nothing

Stockbrokers often talk about how investors should take a bar bell approach to the Australian market. On one side of the bar bell sits the significant banking sector and on the other are mining and energy giants BHP, Rio Tinto and Woodside Petroleum. About 50 per cent of the Australian market capitalisation is represented by this handful of companies. The stockbroker is basically saying that investors should simply own both sides of the bar bell and they will benefit over the long term.

Research by market historian and observer Ashley Own that was published as 'Buy and hold or buy and hope', carefully tracks the performance of some of these stocks over the long term. His findings show that investors in Australia's largest company, BHP, have struggled through extended periods where they have not made money. Investors who took the plunge into the Big Australian at the back end of the 1960s resources boom had to wait until the 1990s before they generated a real return from the stock. Even worse, investors who dived into the stock at the top of the 1880s boom had to wait 75 years for a real return. It just goes to show how cyclical mining stocks are and investors should tread carefully at the current (mid 2011) point in the cycle, with China's industrialisation driving commodity prices higher.

Owen has also studied Australia's oldest bank, Westpac. He found that investors who took the plunge in the buoyant time of late 1972 would have made a real return on the shares only once over the 39 years since then, and that was at the market peak in late 2007. Once dividends are taken into account Westpac has delivered a total return of just 1.6 per cent better than inflation over the last 50 years.

The premise of Owen's article is to show how crucial it is to get your timing right when buying stocks and markets. For me, it also shows that all stocks have their grand periods, when earnings race and the underlying operating environment is supportive, while other periods with be plagued by underperformance. This can happen from the smallest to the largest companies.

The list of big companies that have had tremendous share price appreciation followed by a protracted decline is as long as the River Nile. Among them are financial services group Macquarie Bank, property company Lend Lease, Chep pallet operator Brambles, general insurance outfit QBE, major bank NAB, media conglomerate News Corp, grocery chain Woolworths, shopping centre owner and manager Westfield, newspaper publisher Fairfax, paper group Amcor, beer giant Fosters and engineering construction company Leighton Holdings. All of these companies at some stage had a golden period on the sharemarket where earnings rose strongly and PEs expanded as investors built into their minds an expectation of above-average earnings growth forever. The fact is that the world is dynamic and things change every day. Rest assured that the market darlings of today will underperform the overall market at some stage, with the much loved mining sector most susceptible to a hiccup in the phenomenal Chinese growth story.

It may be difficult to believe just now, but global superstars like Google and Apple will join the long list of companies that will become friendless, just like Microsoft and Cisco have in recent times. Cisco's share price almost hit $US80 a share in 2000 but today it sits at just $US15. Both Google and Apple, with a combined market capitalisation of $US500 billion, will no doubt make billions of dollars of profits, but the extreme growth they are currently experiencing will slow and investors will de-rate the stock. As sure as Collingwood winning another wooden spoon, investor enthusiasm for those stocks will change but you can't pick exactly when that will happen. So as an investor you must keep watching and reviewing. You can't just be happy with companies that have historical track records of strong profits and a growing stream of dividends. It is future earnings that matter.

Small diamonds can turn into big rocks

Down at the small end of the market, history shows us a pit full of broken ladders and snakes. Unlike the big end of town, a small company has a lot more risk attached to it and that means the gains can be colossal, but the losses can also be up to 100 per cent. In other words a small stock can go broke, something not even the worst management teams can achieve at the big end of the market, due to their unspoken contract with investors.

Stocks such as child care provider ABC Learning Centres, financial engineering outfit Allco & Co, tourist operator MFS, shopping centre owner Centro Properties and financier Babcock and Brown became the symbols of the sharemarket crash of 2008, falling like dominoes as credit dried up around the globe. All of these companies had the same problem—too much debt. What is quickly forgotten, though, is that each one had tremendous runs as it grew from an unknown company into a sharemarket sweetheart. Investors who owned these companies as the core of their portfolios became rich on paper and spellbound by the magic of a sharemarket. Unfortunately very few of these investors were nimble enough to recognise that in 2007 the tide was turning as the decade wore on. They did not jump off the ladder, opting instead to increase their bets by taking out margin loans and buying more shares. As a company grows, margin lenders come into play and are happy to enhance your returns by lending a higher proportion of your overall investment. At the same time most high-growth companies are piling on debt to expand their businesses. The end result is debt on debt at a time when the PE has expanded from an acceptable level to well over 20 times optimistic forecast earnings, which is not sustainable. Instead of copying those investors you should be looking to jump onto a new ladder that might take your wealth higher and not down a long snake. A stock that has risen exponentially in the past should always be thoroughly reviewed with a large degree of sobriety. A lesson that took Peter Proksa more than a decade to learn!

Fundamentals are everything

When it comes to stock picking, no matter how good the story is you constantly have to go back and check the financial fundamentals to make sure you are not carrying too much risk. Even the believers who pick a bunch of large blue chips with consistent earnings and dividends need to tweak their portfolio on a consistent basis. For those of you who prefer to take on more risk and ferret around in the market, you must review the fundamentals regularly. The key is to make sure you do not get caught up in the excitement as the market becomes aware of a star in the making.

In my experience the key is always to step back and look at the fundamentals to make sure that you are still on a winner and not a loser. You have to make sure the stock is not trading well above its long-term PE, a figure that your stockbroker should be able to provide for you. You should also ensure the company's debt levels are not too high—a situation that became painfully obvious for the stocks that collapsed in 2008. Finally, and harder to identify, you must be aware of the industry a company operates in. If the industry is enjoying an unusually high level of activity for some reason, make sure you don't get sucked in. Some classic examples of this were the technology services and software companies leading into the year 2000; oil companies leading into 2008, when the oil price tripled in a short space of time; building material companies when the housing cycle is towards its cyclical peaks; and money management companies when the market has been jumping 20 per cent a year for five years. In the future we might see mining companies decline suddenly as investors realise that the Chinese economic miracle will have many ups, but also some nasty downs.

All of this seems fairly rudimentary but, as many readers will know, as a stock price heads higher and higher it becomes mesmerising, and it is easy to forget the financials that will probably ruin a great feeling.

If you can always go back to the fundamentals, then the following important things will happen to your portfolio of stocks. First, you are almost guaranteed of missing the last leg of gains a stock delivers because share prices will shock you with their ability to move higher and faster than you could ever dream of. Second, you should be able to avoid sudden and emotionally charged share price falls that invariably happen following a steep gradient rise. Finally, keeping a close tab on financial fundamentals could keep you in a stock for many years as earnings growth persists and superior management keeps on delivering.

Some ladders seem to go into space

All of this suggests you should be jumping in and out of stocks every day. This is not true. While you should definitely check the fundamentals of a stock every day and make sure the rot doesn't set in, you will still hold onto stocks for years as the story unfolds and the fundamentals continue to add up. At Wilson Asset Management we were lucky enough to hold a handful of small stocks that just seemed to keep on delivering well beyond our expectations. Accounting software group Reckon was a core part of the company's portfolio for the best part of nine years, while salary packaging outfit McMillan Shakespeare was still there after five years. Another stock that we held for several years that we did not have great expectations for was Tasmania-based rural merchant Roberts, which was eventually taken over in a corporate play delivering us phenomenal returns. All of these companies started out at ridiculously cheap prices and the management kept delivering by adding shareholder value along the way without strapping on excessive risk; though this does not make them immune from poor performance into the future. The holders of winners like these should not grow complacent just because the stocks have performed so well for so long.

Chapter 13

Don't fight momentum

In the 1990s no-one was a tougher trader on the floor of the Sydney Futures Exchange than Brian Price. He drove to work in a large, petrol-guzzling car with massive shark teeth painted on the doors, turning heads when he sped past. Suited up in military fatigues, he would stride onto the floor, flanked by two trusted lieutenants also kitted for war. Trading on the futures floor was not a game for wimps and no-one messed with the Canadian-born Price. He had cut his teeth trading futures, leading up to and through the war zone that was the 1987 stockmarket crash. He then rose from the ashes to carve out a very profitable stint as a local on the floor (a local trades their own money and not an institution's). He had managed to make millions and lose millions over the years, but he was well ahead by any measure. Nothing spooked him and no trade was too big or too risky for him.

In the mid 1990s the US sharemarket was rampant, progressively hitting fresh highs as the latest recession faded to memory and investor infatuation with everything tech was starting to emerge. Price started to wonder why, with little inflation to speak of, equities could be rising in value so quickly. By 1996 US Federal Reserve chairman Alan Greenspan agreed, describing the unfolding bull market as 'irrational exuberance'. It was about this time that Price thought prices, especially in the tech-laden Nasdaq, were stretched and stocks overvalued. Like a natural trader, he saw an opportunity to make a kill and he started to short the Nasdaq—he was taking a large bet the Nasdaq would fall and he could profit from it. The market accelerated higher through 1997 and Price held firm. Like a man at war he kept his nerve under fire. In 1998 the Nasdaq rose a further 65 per cent and still Price, like Charles Atlas, stood as the strong man holding back his lenders who were now pounding at the door. Certain the collapse was near, Price kept adding to his short position. And then at last, more than three years after he had started shorting the US tech market, the Nasdaq cracked and the bull market was over. It would lose 70 per cent of its value over a period of two and half years. At last Price could relax: he was right and the market had at last caught onto the idea. But Price had been forced to close out his Nasdaq short in the last few months of 1999 because his lender would or could no longer bear to back the trade. He missed the eventual demise of the Nasdaq by a matter of months, tallying up losses thought to be between $20 and $30 million. He was ordered to close his short at exactly the time it was sitting at is largest paper loss. It was his biggest hit on an individual trade since he had started in the futures game and, if he hadn't managed to offset it with some highly profitable trades, it could have been the end of his trading. It doesn't always pay to be right.

There are several lessons to learn from the highly talented Price. The first is about taking risk. If you don't have a vast reservoir to absorb risk, you should not place all your bets on one trade, and when the bet starts to work against you, it does not pay to increase the bet. Our croupier Peter Proksa tasted this bitter lesson by attempting on more than one occasion to average down the cost of his investment by buying more stock as the price fell before he realised that there were easier ways to keep the spoils of victory. The second and more important lesson is that when a market has momentum, don't stand in its way. One of the most surprising aspects of

> If you don't have a vast reservoir to absorb risk, you should not place all your bets on one trade, and when the bet starts to work against you, it does not pay to increase the bet.

the sharemarket is how long and how far a trend will go. The tech boom of the 1990s continued and actually gathered pace for more than three years after the Federal Reserve chairman made his famous comments about irrational exuberance. Economist John Maynard Keynes best summarised the perils of momentum when he said, 'Markets can remain irrational longer than you can remain solvent'.

Golden opportunity

Momentum can also occur in individual asset classes represented on the sharemarket. For example, respected Australian fund manager John Hopkins went overweight in gold in the late 1990s. Hopkins thought that gold, hitting cyclical lows, was underpriced while equities were dramatically overpriced. With the goodness of time, Hopkins's crystal ball proved spookily correct, as sharemarkets hit significant turbulence in the first decade of the new century, while gold started to head north and has never really stopped. Unfortunately for Hopkins, his investors did not have the benefit of hindsight and could not wait for his vision to play out. His fund shut down. Once again it didn't pay to be right.

Stepping aside

We all get hammered by momentum at some time or another. As world equity markets crumbled in 2008 and 2009 to lows that a limbo champion could not wriggle under, at Wilson Asset Management we tried to go back into the market. We gritted our teeth on more than one occasion and jumped into the market, before being spat out with our tail between our legs. Eventually, after much pain, we got lucky in March 2009 and this time the market decided that going down was no longer that much fun.

Momentum is also a factor that must be considered when looking at an individual stock. The speed at which a stock rises can sometimes accelerate as time marches on. There have been plenty of examples of this in recent years with Zinifex Minerals, Fortescue Metals and rare earths miner Lynas Corporation (see figure 13.1, overleaf) to pick a few high-profile names. The best way to observe this phenomenon is to ask your stockbroker to send you the long-term charts of these stocks and see how they initially start rising gently, only to pick up pace. Towards the end of their bull run the chart looks like it is vertical. If you are an investor in these companies then you feel fantastic as you watch your investment initially going up 0.1 per cent a day and later 1 per cent a day and finally 2, 3 or even 4 per cent a day. The only problem is such enormous gains are not sustainable over the long term, and when the momentum stops the share price won't just go sideways, it will turn and head down at a rapid clip. I have never seen any stock rise sharply over an extended period only to flat line.

Figure 13.1: volatile Lynas Corporation — share price from January 2009 to July 2011

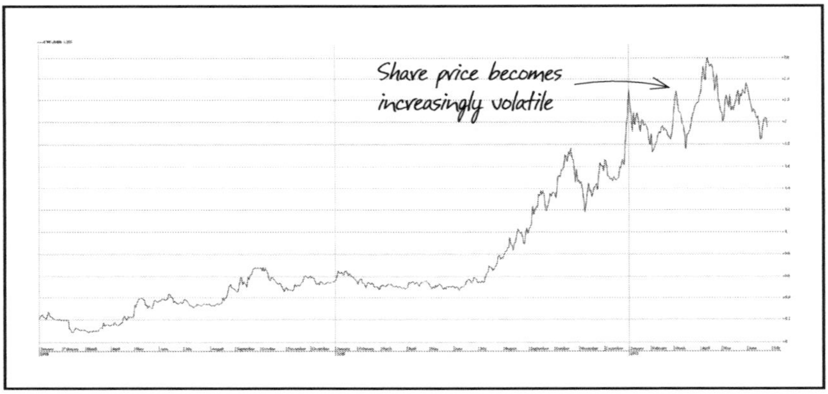

Source: IRESS

So how do we handle this scenario? Some investors will argue that you ride the raging bull until you are bucked off. For me, that always sounded an awfully painful way to make a living. My preferred approach is to sit still in the early stages of the rise and then gradually offload the investment over time. While you will never get your timing perfectly right, there is a reasonable chance that you will have sold a significant number of your shares by the time the momentum peters out and gravity starts to kick in.

Sometimes it is obvious that an asset or individual stock is entering bubble status, and sometimes it is not so obvious. In mid

2011 it is obvious to me that mining stocks, especially in the small end of the market, have entered a period that will be remembered as a bubble in years to come. Inspired by a genuine economic boom in Asia, propelled by industrialisation of China, commodity prices have gathered momentum as more money is pumped into the global economy by various central banks. On several occasions we have tried to pick the top for many of these stocks and bet they would start falling by short selling a select number of stocks. This has been the wrong bet each time, but eventually it will be right, so we should just wait until the market is ready to agree with our view.

It might also be obvious to some, but I believe the US economy will fall into recession for the third time in about a decade because the US government has to solve what seems to be its insurmountable debt problem. Taxes will have to rise rapidly and spending will have to be cut even more quickly. All this adds up to recession. So should we short the US sharemarket? Maybe — but as it currently stands the US market has added 100 per cent in just two years since hitting its decade low in March 2009.

The greatest attraction to trying to buck a market trend is getting it right and proving everyone else is wrong. Australian fund manager Bankers Trust (BT) successfully grew its business strongly for more than a decade by picking the October 1987 crash. The brains trust at BT became increasingly nervous about the rapid rise of the sharemarket in 1987 and decided to protect their funds against a collapse by taking a protective option position. This cemented its reputation as a premier institution in the country. In the lead up to the GFC, famous author Michael Lewis dedicated a whole book called *The Big Short* to the individuals who managed to identify the looming financial crash in the United States and profited from it.

That is all fine but, as Brian Price's example shows, going against momentum is a risky business. So do you stand in front of a truck hurtling down the highway or do you change lanes? If you are getting suspicious that a certain share is getting overheated or that a whole market is getting seriously expensive, then the best option in my mind is to de-risk the situation by selling out of shares and moving to the sidelines. Just remember that there is no stage when you have to have any money invested in the market. You might miss the big turning point, but what is wrong with waiting for a change in direction. Crucially, we should recall that when a market changes direction after a bull or bear market then that new trend could last not only for months but probably several years.

Chapter 14

Traps

The idea that the sharemarket is littered with landmines is greatly exaggerated, especially in protracted bear markets. The overall trend of the sharemarket is generally up, so if you embrace the key rules discussed in chapter 6 then you will see your portfolio swell in value over time. At the same time, it would be naive to believe that you can drive a car with a blindfold on. You must stay alert at all times, keep your nerve and exercise sound judgement. It does not mean you have to be the smartest guy in the room to navigate the sharemarket, but it does mean you have to exercise common sense.

With those overarching comments planted, let's explore a variety of situations that should be handled with caution.

Floats

Floats are not just a potential trap—they are a complete lottery. Many companies floated on the ASX in recent times have become tremendous performers over the following years, including share trading software group IRESS Market Technologies, online job board Seek, automobile auction site carsales.com.au, diversified retailer

Super Group, rental and leasing outfit Thorn Group, and oil and gas engineering company Worley Parsons. On the flip side, a multitude of companies have shot out of the blocks, been written up as stars and then, as time marches on, they have deflated without too much fanfare. In this category you can put companies like commercial air conditioning company Hastie Group, Babcock and Brown, advertising placement group Adcorp Australia, technology outfit Data Dot Technologies, material manufacturer Gale Pacific, mail order retailer Undercover Wear, education provider Kip McGrath, life insurance giant AMP, telecommunications group Telstra, wagering and gambling company Tabcorp Holdings, Ellex Medical Lasers and marketing conglomerate Photon Group. The list is almost endless.

Investors should be cautious about floats because they are brought to the market with heightened excitement and slick promotion, but very little track record. The positive commotion surrounding the company is predominantly created by the promoting stockbroker who stands to make a substantial fee in successfully listing the stock. It never fails to amaze me how investors, both professional and amateur, chase floats with such gusto, despite a dearth of knowledge about company management and the relevant industry cycles. To further complicate matters, most floats surface in bull markets when investors are hungry for new products to throw their plentiful money at. These conditions can hardly be described as ideal for astute buying.

A rookie's pain

The first float that I participated in was at the pointy end of the technology boom in 1999—my venture was akin to a baby trying to safely crawl across a six-lane highway. The volatility in the market, especially for technology stocks, was so extreme that a doctor would have diagnosed his patient as suffering from schizophrenia. Some weeks the market was totally convinced that any stock with the slightest aroma of technology was a world beater and the scramble for shares led to arguments with the underwriting stockbroker. The next week investors would toss the prospectus of a new float into the bin without reading a word. Investors who had committed to taking shares in a tech float would wait anxiously for the stock to actually list on the market. This wait, on average, would be six weeks, in which time the tech sector could be in and then out of vogue several times over. Making money out of these floats required a great deal more luck than any innate stock-picking talent.

Geoff Wilson was away on holidays in 1999 when I, after about a year in the job, agreed to help underwrite the float of a company called Isis Communications. Isis (see figure 14.1 on p. 193) had a combination of businesses, including some cutting edge internet plays in education and mapping. The company was run by a young gun called Adam Radley, who dressed in slick casuals and spoke with assuredness that convinced me this company was a winner. Radley had cobbled together a bunch of untested internet assets, together with an old world business in the form of an outdoor broadcasting unit. The company was floating on a valuation of $141 million, despite the fact that it was forecast to lose $10 million in 1999. Even with a hockey stick improvement in the year 2000, the company was being priced on a heavy weight multiple of 25 times forecast earnings. To make matters worse I had made the decision to sub-underwrite the float (committed us to taking stock) in the full knowledge that I had no idea what the company actually did, and how it was supposed to make money in the future. In my haste to prove I could play the tech boom as well as anyone, I agreed to sub-underwrite $2 million worth of stock, a hefty 15 per cent of our total funds under management at the time. The standard approach during the tech boom was to bid the house down for new floats in the comfort that you would be dramatically scaled back. On this occasion the promoting broker called and with a jolly voice announced we had got 100 per cent of the stock we had bid for. I instantly felt sick. There can be no surer sign that a float is on the verge of failure than when you get slotted with the total amount of stock you applied for.

Before the company listed on the market, the view on tech stocks had turned sour again. This flip-flop attitude of the market meant a company could start trading at 40 per cent below its issue price if it happened to list on the wrong day. If a tech company bombed on listing, there was very little hope it could recoup the loss, if liquidity was poor and it had a flimsy business model. If the market did not improve quickly, we were looking at a 40 per cent down trade, stripping 6 per cent of our fund's value in blindingly quick time. This would have wiped out our fund performance figures for the month and possibly for the best part of the year. Geoff was calling in from his holidays increasingly nervous and I was losing sleep over the whole incident. I was looking at the Nasdaq each night hoping it would rally 2, 3 or even 4 per cent. Any rally, though, rapidly failed. I had given up hope and wondered whether this would cost me my job.

Then Isis decided to temporarily halt the float process as it agreed to acquire a new asset that required additional information for investors. I was hoping this was a game changer for sentiment. To my disappointment it did little to make the world more optimistic. I must have read the underwriting agreement 20 times, and with that my luck turned on a dime. The decision to acquire a new business during the float process triggered an out clause that I had to take advantage of. The phone call to the company telling them we were not proceeding with our underwriting made me bilious, but it could have saved us a lot of money.

Isis did eventually list, initially falling 20 per cent, holding up quite well in the circumstances. About three months later, the tech market swung back into favour and the Isis share price took off, spiking an amazing 200 per cent in the space of just half a year. If we had taken our $2 million worth of stock and sold at the top, we could have made close to a 40 per cent gain for our fund. My concerns, like most things in life, were overplayed. If, however, we did not sell at the top we would have lost everything as Isis crashed with the rest of the tech sector, before eventually failing completely and being used as a corporate shell for a new company called Staging Connections, which specialised in managing conference centres.

I learned several lessons from this experience, including that floats might sound great, but many companies that come to market

> Floats might sound great, but many companies that come to market are untested

are untested and do not have a robust business model that can sustain the company through various business cycles.

Figure 14.1: the float trap—the Isis Communications share price from September 1999 to June 2001

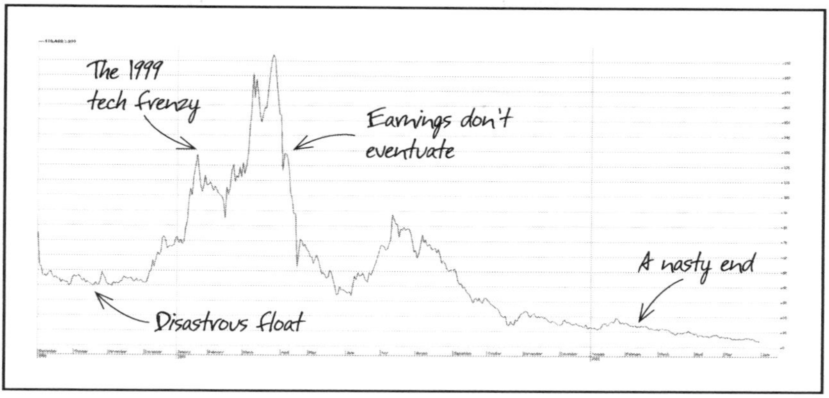

Source: IRESS

Benjamin Graham's book *The Intelligent Investor* quotes a study by professors Jay Ritter and William Schwert. It revealed that investors who spent a total of $US1000 at the issue price in every initial public offer (IPO) from January 1960 and sold out at the end of that month, then invested anew in each successive month's new crop of IPOs, would have built a portfolio worth more than $533 decillion by the end of 2001—to make that clear, a decillion has 33 zeros. This fact strongly suggests you should try to take as many floats as possible, but move them on hastily. I believe a more prudent approach would be to take any floats that appear interesting and presume that you are going to sell them in the first week, unless you are absolutely convinced the company is cheap and has a bright outlook. That way you might limit your downside and still not miss some great opportunities that have delivered 400 or 500 per cent returns in less than a decade, such as IRESS Market Technologies and blood products behemoth CSL.

Why are floats risky?

So why be so careful about floats? Most companies that float are relatively small, have only a short track record and have no listed peers. All this equates to high risk. Investors have no idea of how these companies will perform in varying economic cycles and their management has no track record the public can scrutinise. Investors have to rely on a prospectus document, which is sanitised by the regulators. Presentations are generally restricted to professional investors who are the guests of a stockbroking firm that is receiving fees to underwrite or, at the very least, promote the company.

It is also crucial that investors look carefully at why a company is floating. Is it simply a way for the major shareholder to cash in his chips or capitalise the value of its holding? Ironically, it is those companies that don't need to float, those that generate fabulous returns and spew out cash, that you really want to get aboard. Finally, the number of floats tends to boom when the overall market is rocking and rolling, and one can only conclude the sale to the public is opportunistic. There have been many examples of this, but in bull markets investors still line up with their cheque books and pens poised. In recent times mining and mining service companies have rushed to the market in a bid to capitalise on the boom in commodity prices. Another prime example was the mortgage broker RHG Group, which listed at $2.50 a share in July 2007, only to succumb to the GFC, when the share price was savaged and fell to just 4.6 cents in just 11 months. There is no guarantee that the elevated industry conditions of mid 2011 will continue into the future, and investors should be aware.

Companies that float and do have a listed peer in their industry are automatically priced off that peer. This is a considerable leap of faith from the investment community given the existing listed company has usually spent many years proving itself to the market.

All these warnings should not scare you off looking at floats. Larger, established companies, such as rail operator QR National and insurance group Promina, have delivered outstanding results to their shareholders. Both of these examples floated into an environment of scepticism, with the seller under financial pressure to offload the asset. However, the assets had relatively long histories of delivering acceptable returns and the sales were pitched at a reasonable price.

The value trap

Everyone wants to find value. Professional and retail investors scour the market every day in the hope of finding a quality business that is trading on a low earnings multiple and a high yield. For most sharemarket buffs this is better than finding God and is simply too good to walk away from. And for the most part these types of companies should not be ignored, but investors need to concentrate on the word 'quality', not the seductive numbers.

Quality is fleeting when it comes to the corporate world. There have been many companies that for a specific period looked like industry leaders with good management and deserved to be labelled as quality outfits. Within the space of a few short years, a regulatory change, a management move or increased competition can see the quality tag vanish. The result will be a share price decline, despite earnings initially holding up and dividend yields surging higher. Effectively the market is reacting ahead of time and predicting that today's strong earnings will either decline or stall in the future.

The Telstra trap

The greatest value trap in Australia in recent years has been telecommunications carrier Telstra (see figure 14.2, overleaf). Privatised in 1997 by the federal government through the sale of three separate tranches of shares to the general public, Telstra became the most widely owned stock in the nation's history. Everyone cheered the shares higher as it motored from the $3.30 issue price to a high of $9.00 a few years later. For many investors this was their first taste of the sharemarket and they must have felt like they had discovered a money printing press. The drivers for the share price rise were the enormous costs that could be taken out of the business and a buzz around the globe regarding mobile phones and the internet. In the early days the managing director, US import Frank Blount, played the game beautifully, ripping out the excessive costs that had ballooned from years of government ownership. This was all happening as Telstra used its financial clout to grab the lion's share of the mushrooming mobile phone market, leaving its two competitors in its wake. All this was tremendously exciting to the market, which was inebriated from the tech boom. Telstra's PE ratio climbed from around 11 at the time of the float to 17 by early 1999.

Figure 14.2: the Telstra trap — company share price from November 1997 to July 2011

Source: IRESS

Then things started to change. The global tech and telco markets crashed around the world, forcing investors to reassess the true value of companies in this space. In Telstra's case, investors also noticed that the bottom line growth was stalling with the cost-cutting story coming to a conclusion. Soon afterwards, mobile phone growth started to mature as almost everyone in the country had at least one handset. Without much hype, Telstra's share price had begun its long journey south, with the PE contracting and the yield pushing up. This is when the value trap first started to raise its head. The dividend yield climbed from just 3 per cent to 4, then 5 and eventually 6 per cent. For the army of people who owned the stock in their superannuation funds, these dividends looked like gold, because they came with an imputation credit, meaning a tax refund. People who fell into the value trap failed to appreciate that for every juicy dividend they received, they were losing that, plus more, on the capital depreciation of the stock. The stock's multi-year decline was punctuated by some major rallies that sucked in investors like a black hole sucks in stars. It wasn't long before these investors watched in amazement as Telstra's shares tumbled to new, unexciting lows.

As the first decade of the new millennium wore on and Telstra lured more and more people into its carefully laid value trap, the smart phone appeared on the horizon. Led by the Blackberry and rapidly followed by Apple's iPhone, the buzz came back to the mobile phone market as consumers scrambled to be attached to the internet as they strolled through the streets. Consumers were no longer interested in their carrier—they only cared about which brand of handset they could parade. This technology switch came at a time when Telstra's board decided to import American executive Sol Trujillo to run the company in 2005, a lamentable tenure that was characterised by disappointing profit results and constant sparring with the company's largest shareholder—the federal government.

Finally the government, having at last exited its entire shareholding, announced it was going head to head with Telstra by building its own fibre network (the national broadband network), which would replace Telstra's copper network that led into every Australian home. The last vestiges of Telstra's monopoly were being dismantled. Investors bailed out of the stock and by late 2010 the share price had sunk to around $2.60, a 65 per cent topple from the peak. The dividend yield climbed all the way to 11 per cent fully franked, an amazing 5 per cent more than the cash rate.

Investors who bought the stock on a yield of 6 per cent fully franked were stung by a 40 per cent decline in capital value, and a few years on many would have departed the share register. They had been sucked into a value trap. Instead of blindly looking at the numbers and convincing themselves that the share price could go no lower, they should have taken a holistic view of the industry and the environment and realised the market wasn't done with its selling. It is again a matter of using your judgement and trying to determine what is important for the stock's outlook.

Will the stock reach a yield of 11 or possibly 12 per cent? I have no idea. The key is trying to determine whether the market believes a lot of the imponderables are now baked into the share price and investors are more comfortable with the outcome. A possible way of making this decision is to look overseas and see what other telcos are trading at, and whether there has been any improvement, especially in countries that are technologically ahead of Australian in telecommunications and broadband. At Wilson Asset Management, we started buying Telstra stock in early 2011 at around $2.70 a share in the belief that a resolution to the national broadband network battle would lay to rest many of the market concerns. The stock has traded up to $3.00 a share, but if this is just another rally in a decade-long bear market—only time will tell.

Not worth the paper it is written on

Another more obvious value trap in recent years has been newspaper publisher Fairfax Media, which owns Melbourne's *The Age* and *The Sydney Morning Herald*. Its stock has gradually got cheaper and cheaper, after reaching a share price peak of more than $6.00 in around the year 2000. Today, 11 years later, the stock is trading just above $1.00 a share—a fall of about 80 per cent. During this decline the stock has looked incredibly cheap compared with historical averages, but the numbers have been deceptive.

The real story has been the stunning decline in the newspaper revenue streams in the form of classified advertising, which have been transferred to online specialists at a speed that not even the most pessimistic investors could have predicted. All attempts by management to arrest this slide have failed and investors have given up. A look offshore, particularly in the United States, shows investors had fled newspaper companies some years earlier, leaving their stock prices to fall rapidly.

Investors should have been looking offshore for their lead, and not at the façade of attractive company financials. Keep reading everything you can, even if that means leaving the reading of your local newspaper to others.

A similar value trap could well be emerging as you read, with the internet rapidly changing the face of shopping in Australia and indeed globally. Investors should be careful of shopping centres and department stores as they get cheaper while all the time business is slipping away to the electronic world. A similar fate could be dealt to free to air television with the onset of online television.

Buying the world

Everyone likes an acquisition. Managers like them because they get a bigger car to drive; the company chairperson and his or her board glow in the limelight of the announcement; and investors get to use their analytical skills to work out if the whole shebang will improve their earnings per share. If the acquisition is struck at the right price, stockbroking analysts can put through earnings upgrades and the share price will invariably motor higher, to the delight of shareholders. Nothing could make more sense.

Acquisitions, though, should be viewed with a healthy dose of cynicism. For a start, buying another company comes with risks that most stakeholders won't or simply can't acknowledge at the time of the purchase. From a financial point of view, an acquisition is struck at a price based on future earnings. I have never encountered an acquirer telling the investment community that the earnings of the business they have bought will decline in the years to come. Even if there is no organic earnings growth, management will preach that they can get earnings growth through cost and revenue synergies from putting the companies together. Earnings only go in one direction—up.

So what, most of you say. After all, virtually every investor buys a company on what it is going to earn in the future and not what it earned in previous years. The difference is that when a company takes over another business it is entirely different from an investor like you or me buying a small stake. The most obvious of these being that a company buys 100 per cent of the other company and, if the financials don't unfold as forecast, then they can't just dump the stock. It is like a parent having a child: you are stuck together for life. Just ask building materials group CSR: it bought Pilkington Glass for near on $1 billion, only to face a write down in value to a quarter of that in a few short years. Other, much larger, companies (such as News Corp, NAB, BHP and Rio Tinto) have all suffered the same fate. Not so obvious is the fact the vendor is usually selling out its complete holding—it can just take the money and run. Occasionally some vendors stick around to drive the business further and stronger, but on most occasions it takes off for the new owners to blithely wander into the future. When we buy a company's shares, we are backing the installed management team to generate increasing wealth for us.

If you are lucky enough to get over the possible financial hurdles that an acquisition brings, then you have to deal with the less transparent cultural issues. When I have asked a company why an acquisition hasn't worked, more often than not they say it just wasn't a cultural fit. Despite culture being blamed for most failed corporate marriages, it is one of the most elusive pieces of the jigsaw to fit into place. Realistically, no company is able to fully appreciate its own culture, let alone the one that walks through the door on the back of an acquisition.

The problem of a successful marriage

Acquisitions are an interesting trap for most companies. On many occasions a company will initially pull off a terrific purchase that is well priced and strategically clever, displaying to shareholders an ability to deliver. As investors show their appreciation of the management's capital allocation process, they pump up the share price. Simultaneously they can pump up the ego of the management team, who start to view takeovers as the easiest route to long-term success. One has only to look at blue chip company QBE Insurance, which for many years was seen as the stand out stock in the industry, cementing its position as number one in the local market before carving out a global presence through a string of acquisitions. The spree of purchases, kicked off by the gentlemanly John Cloney and sharply accelerated by his successor Frank O'Halloran, was roundly applauded by the sharemarket, which pushed the share price higher and higher, making it a top 10 listed company by market capitalisation in Australia by 2007. The share price peaked at over $30 a share.

QBE has not abated its acquisitions of businesses around the globe, but shareholder enthusiasm has waned as returns have declined. It is a painful example of a company feeling enormous pressure to keep growing its earnings to appease investors, rather than making sensible investment and capital management issues that would have, in the long run, created more value for shareholders. The capital allocation is now under question from many followers of the stock.

The QBE story has been mirrored in many other companies, including marketing specialist Photon Group, engineering construction company Leighton Holdings, integrated transport provider Toll Holdings and dominant share registry operator Computershare. While none of these companies has come completely unstuck the theme is the same—in the long run, serial acquirers rarely create a lot of value.

For investors attempting to analyse the performance of a company that has made a rash of acquisitions, the task becomes increasingly difficult and, on occasions, near impossible. Each purchase adds more revenue and more profits, but the numbers generated by the original business slowly get lost in a sea of financial data. In fact, some investors are suspicious enough to claim that some managers deliberately make a bunch of purchases to cover up a crumbling core. This may not always be the case, but the message is loud and clear—be extremely careful of a company that is addicted to buying other businesses.

Don't chase downgrades

When a company downgrades its forecast earnings, there are three immediate reactions—one group of investors bails out; another group goes into denial and hangs on; and the active buyers cancel their buy orders. The net result is for the stock to fall by an amount equivalent to the downgrade: if a company downgrades its forecast earnings by 20 per cent, then the stock also falls 20 per cent. In times of heady bull markets, like in 2007, the fall of the stock price can easily outstrip the size of the earnings downgrade. When debt ledger purchaser Credit Corp downgraded its 2008 earnings by 25 per cent in November 2007, the stock price slumped 40 per cent as investor optimism was pulverised.

Once the dust has settled and the company has explained why the earnings trajectory has been altered, investors begin to wonder whether to start buying into the stock. After all the stock is now

20, 30 or even 40 per cent cheaper than it was only a few days before. Those investors should save their energy. An investor should never buy shares if a company has recently downgraded its earnings forecasts by more than 10 per cent. Occasionally, a company's shares will bounce back quite quickly, but this is the exception. Most of the time the stock will not rebound, and it will actually continue to fall, resulting in a loss for its investors.

In 2007 Macquarie Equities undertook a study of companies that posted earnings downgrades, finding that about one-third of companies that downgraded earnings once will suffer from a subsequent downgrade. The study also found that the larger the share price tumble on day one of the downgrade, the more those shares would underperform on the overall sharemarket in the following six months. Finally, the study uncovered that if a stock is a market darling, with every analyst branding it a buy, then it will be severely punished by investors if a downgrade is announced.

Overwhelmingly, the message from this is keep away from companies that experience a downgrade in earnings, no matter how attractive the share price decline may seem. In fact the more attractive the stock may look, the further you should run.

Chapter 15

The mystery of management

The greatest stock pickers on the globe have one skill that separates them from the pack—they can identify which companies have superior managers before anyone else can. In my 17 years of participation in the Australian sharemarket I have not met a professional investor who has a firm grip on scoring management. Not a single one, and I include myself in this category. I will never forget asking one of Australia's greatest stock pickers how he measured the quality of a company manager and his team, and he responded: 'I don't really know, so I just rely on the numbers they produce.' This is such a disappointing aspect of the professional investor because most companies perform appreciably better when they have a management team that understands the needs of their stakeholders and in particular their shareholders. Just imagine the performance you would have enjoyed over the last decade if you had had the ability to select managers such as Brian McNamee at blood products group CSL, Graham Turner at retail travel company Flight Centre, John Rubino at mining services outfit Monadelphous, Allan Moss at Macquarie Bank, Pat Grier at private hospital operator Ramsay Health Care, Ron Hancock at building society Wide Bay Australia, Tony Robinson at insurance broker OAMPS and Clive

Rabie at accounting software provider Reckon, to name just a few. This portfolio would have outstripped just about any other, especially one littered with companies that had incompetent managers.

In 2002 I was lucky enough to interview a highly successful managing director who was leaving his job on his own terms. He commented at the time that he was so confident of the situation that he said, 'Bozo the Clown could run the company over the next two years'. Unfortunately the incoming managing director wasn't quite as talented as Bozo the Clown. Earnings stalled and the share price drifted downwards. Sometimes you cannot truly comprehend how good a manager is until he or she leaves and new blood takes over.

When it comes to investment books I would recommend you read Jim Collins's *Good to Great* before you even contemplate any other tome. Surprisingly, Collins lays no claim to being an investment expert; he is an academic from Boulder, Colorado who has spent the best part of his working life trying to work out why some companies perform better than others, and what role management has played in delivering this performance. Collins, in typical American style, coined the term 'Level 5 Leadership', and argues that a company can only achieve sustained excellence if the management team possesses a fierce resolve with a large dose of humility. Maybe Collins has solved the mystery, but my guess is he is only part way there.

My desire to demystify management led me to write a book on the subject. I interviewed 13 of Australia's best performing CEOs in a bid to unearth the key ingredients to their success. It was a fruitful exercise and changed the way I approached investing from that time onwards. Instead of simply looking at the numbers and deciding what represented value, I slanted my examinations towards assessing the various individual qualities of senior managers of companies. This required a different line of questioning and crosschecks with employees, customers, service providers and competitors. I have no doubt this has improved my stock picking, even though I am still a lifetime away from nailing the subject.

Most professional investors simply avoid trying to accurately assess management. The preferred approach is to analyse all the tangible aspects of a company, including the industry it operates in and the financials it produces. The extreme version of this was Benjamin

Graham's value style of investing. Graham tried to minimise all forms of risk, including the quality of management, by inventing and applying what we termed the 'margin of safety.' Effectively, Graham wanted to buy shares in companies that were trading at or below their net current asset valuations. In other words he would only pay for the cash, inventory and receivables of the company minus any outgoings over the next 12 months to creditors. This totally discounted any future earnings and the value of any hard or intangible assets on the balance sheet, and eradicated the need to investigate the ability of the management. Confirming the benefit of Graham's non-humanistic approach is the fact that, over time, value investors have performed significantly better than their growth-based investor peers.

Graham's most famous student, Warren Buffett, took on board the Graham philosophy, but was clever enough to try to combine price safety with picking stocks that had top-notch managers. In fact, Buffett is the only money manager I can think of who has consistently put the ability of management at the forefront of his investment process, allocating enormous amounts of time to discovering exceptional people to lead the companies in which he has large shareholdings. Buffett's unique judgement and instinctive ability to pick human beings is a skill that has taken him to the top of the investment mountain.

> Buffett is the only money manager I can think of who has consistently put the ability of management at the forefront of his investment process.

Our own Peter Proksa has also discovered that management has an influential role in delivering value to shareholders. His decision to buy into Prima Biomed shares was solidified by his conversation with executive director Martin Rogers, who gave him confidence the company would not only survive but also prosper. These days Proksa makes a priority of contacting the management teams of the companies that he decides to invest in.

How do you crack the nut?

If professional investors who constantly interview management teams can't identify who is first rate, how can an individual investor at home do so? There is no easy answer to this riddle and it is an aspect of investing that I will find tremendously difficult to overcome when I am picking stocks at home instead of as part of a professional organisation. Given the importance of management, this difficulty doesn't mean we should ignore the issue. There are a number of prudent steps you should take as a minimum to help you avoid awful management and possibly lead you to some gems. These are:

- Read what the company is saying.
- Keep the story straight.
- Make sure there is no revolving door.
- Watch out for firms that put you at risk.
- Watch out for promises, promises, promises.
- Decide if you have a friend in bad times.
- Beware of hubris.

Read what the company is saying

If retail investors can't put themselves in front of management, then it is imperative to read the announcements a company releases through the stock exchange to the market. In recent years there has been an increase in the number of announcements because of the ASX's requirements of continuous disclosure. Put simply, if the management and board view a company event as price sensitive, they have to tell the general market about it.

The place to start your reading is the annual report. For the most part professional investors skip the front part of an annual report and delve into the back sections, where the much more instructive numbers sit. The front of the report usually carries a string of glossy pictures and some sterile commentary from the managing director and chairman—the front of an annual report is a marketing document. Many managing directors and chairs of larger companies don't even write the text themselves, preferring the investor relations officer to produce the report in a bid to avoid saying something stupid before signing off. Typically, the message is buried in corporate speak that skirts any real substance. This is incredibly disappointing and shows that senior management is totally out of touch with telling the company's story to its owners—the shareholders. It goes to show that many heads of companies do not value their shareholder base, especially retail shareholders who get little or no chance to talk to the management team during the year.

An exception to this is West Australian engineering group Lycopodium. The company's chairman, Mick Caratti, takes great time and care to pen his own chairman's letter to shareholders, writing in an easy-to-read-style. He is trying to tell his story in the best possible way and bring his shareholders along for the ride. Unfortunately, Caratti is the exception, but if you find a well-written personal letter from the CEO then sit up and take note, because it probably means that you have a management team that has its stakeholders, including its shareholders, at the forefront of their thoughts.

But it's in the numbers that you will find out, for instance, what the board and management are being paid. It is my experience that it is harmful to company performance if the people within the company are paid excessive amounts of money to do their job. Hopefully the remuneration structure will allow fair compensation with a portion attached to performance hurdles based on earnings and not share price movements.

Usually the remuneration packages for board members are more straightforward than those for management. To interpret these numbers, call your stockbroker and ask what the usual pay is for board members for a company of similar size.

When it comes to management, it can be immensely difficult to work out how much they are putting into their own pockets at the end of the year, with bonuses, performance hurdles, share issues and a range of other compensation tools. The best method I have used over the years is to take the total package of the CEO and the CFO and calculate their pay as a percentage of the company's profits. Over the years some managers have taken a massive chunk out of profits that should have been flowing back to shareholders.

A stark example in recent years of an overpaid executive delivering underwhelming share price performance was at plumbing and pipelines outfit Crane Group. Managing director

Greg Sedgwick — through a combination of salary, bonuses and share allocations — managed to get paid $30 million over his seven years with the company, from 2004 to 2010. At the same time the share price went backwards, falling 12.5 per cent from $8.82 in before Fletcher Building put shareholders out of their misery by making a takeover bid for Crane. During Sedgwick's tenure, the benchmark All Ordinaries index climbed 46 per cent higher. To make matters worse, the profit posted by Crane in Sedgwick's first year was higher than the one posted in his last year. In 2010 the Crane board attempted to pay him a total of $4.5 million for his services, but was foiled by shareholders who voted his remuneration package down. If it had gone through, Sedgwick's pay packet would have represented an eye popping 13.6 per cent of that year's profits. If Marius Kloppers, current CEO of BHP, was paid a similar percentage of company profits he would have collected a handy $1.7 billion. Kloppers's package normally comes in at around $10 million, or less in tougher years. Obviously he has the wrong board.

Investors should also be wary when the board and management of a company are able to accrue enormous extra benefits for simply performing their roles. A prime example of this was at engineering and drilling group AJ Lucas. Executive chairman Allan Campbell was paid a handsome $6.5 million fee in 2009 after the company sold a coal seam gas asset for a large price. This money should have stayed with the shareholders rather than the insiders, who still received hefty remuneration packages. AJ Lucas's share price has fallen from more than $5 a share in 2009 to less than $1 and has been suspended from trading since May 2011.

Another company that has underdelivered for shareholders over the years, though management has been paid a king's ransom, is entertainment group Village Roadshow. Here three executives received multi-million dollar pay packets that amounted to about 20 per cent of the company's net profit. A decision in 2010 to reduce executive remuneration has worked wonders for a rebound in the share price.

A final recent example of this was industrial contracting group Downer EDI. CEO Geoff Knox was given substantial incentives, in the form of share options, to boost the profits of the company. In his desire to hit the profit targets, drive the share price up and get his company shares, his decision making was impaired and he entered into a rail construction deal with the New South Wales state government in 2006 that has led to significant losses, which could haunt the company for years to come.

Keep the story straight

A lesson that I learned from researching the book *Master CEOs* was that the best managers had decided on a relatively simple business plan. Andrew Reitzer, CEO at grocery wholesaler Metcash, narrowed down his company's mission to its being the champion of independent retailers. He has stuck by this slogan and over the years his shareholders, employees, customers and suppliers have all come to know that is what the company stands for. The moment Metcash starts to diverge from this central theme is the day a shareholder would seriously consider looking elsewhere to put their money. This statement can be made about most companies. Individuals and organisations find it difficult enough to handle the business they are currently operating let alone diversifying into a completely new arena. There is the odd exception, such as mining and retail conglomerate Wesfarmers, but I would argue Wesfarmers is a holding company for a range of businesses that are deliberately kept separate and independent.

Make sure there is no revolving door

A sure sign that a company might be struggling or is about to enter a difficult period is when key staff, and in particular the chief financial officer (CFO), suddenly departs. The CFO has a crucial role to play in any organisation. Not only does he or she have to prepare the accounts for public consumption, but set targets for margins, negotiate bank loans and, on many occasions, act as a back-up operating officer. The CFO has an intimate knowledge of all the numbers a company is producing and is one of the first to identify if a company is on top of its game or floundering. The departure of a CFO is not announced with the same fanfare as a CEO's departure, but on many occasions it is a more significant warning sign of pending trouble. I can recall the sudden departure of many CFOs over the years, at such places as software group Solution 6, domain registration company Melbourne IT and debt collector Credit Corp that has been the forerunner to a major business downturn. The abrupt departure of the CFO is not necessarily the death knell of a company, but the investor should be on alert and closely review any announcements and financials released by the company.

A company that has amazed me in more recent times has been the highly successful industrial and mining services business UGL, previously called United Group. In the space of just four years, from 2007 to 2011, the company has employed three separate CFOs while there has only been one managing director — Richard Leupen. Either the board or the CEO has flawed recruitment skills when it comes to their CFO, or UGL is not a great place to work. To date, UGL has continued to perform admirably, delivering fantastic returns to shareholders over the last decade on the back of strong resources and infrastructure markets. A closer check will also reveal that many other senior managers have left UGL over the years and ended up in other companies. It will be interesting to see if the company can keep performing for its shareholders.

Watch out for firms that put you at risk

A good management team will never put the shareholders of a company under undue pressure. This does not mean a management team, regardless of the quality, can avoid the shares of their company falling, especially in times of a bear market like the one we experienced in 2008. The short-term ups and downs of a company share price have to be accepted by shareholders as the norm. What should not be considered normal is when a management team makes the decision to dramatically alter the risk profile of the company. For example, a company may gear up its balance sheet by paying too much for a major acquisition. Alternatively, a management team that gets a taste for making corporate plays can easily put shareholders' money at risk by undertaking a spate of hasty acquisitions. There have been many examples of this over the years: marketing outfit Photon Group is one that sticks in my craw, simply because we saw all the signs of heightened risk, only to hang on and ride the shares to unfathomable lows.

A prime example of a company putting its shareholders' money at risk was the decision by mining giant Rio Tinto to pay a whopping $39 billion plus $5 billion in debt to buy aluminium group Alcan in 2007. The next highest bid for the company was almost $10 billion less. The purchase was financed almost exclusively with debt, and the decision was made after a stunning increase in commodity prices over a three-year period, combined with the spectre of a takeover bid for Rio by its long-time rival BHP. Driven by supply and demand, commodities are cyclical and so when the GFC paralysed global growth in 2008 and 2009, Rio was under enormous financial pressure after forking out far too much money to buy Alcan. Matters deteriorated when BHP decided to shelve its takeover plans. In a desperate move, Rio searched the globe for an equity injection, eventually finding the Chinese company Chinalco. Chinalco would have become Rio's largest shareholder and would have exerted enormous influence over the operations and strategic direction of the company. In a further turn of fortune, the Australian equity markets, recovering from the demise of 2008, was bouncing and open to capital injections for companies under pressure. Rio eventually spurned the Chinalco proposal, happy to heavily dilute existing shareholdings by launching a massively discounted rights issue to raise $15 billion. During the course of 2008, Rio's share price fell more than 75 per cent (see figure 15.1, overleaf), compared with a 45 per cent fall by BHP, all due to management putting the shareholders at risk with a diabolical acquisition and gearing up the balance sheet. Luckily, for Rio CEO Tom Albanese his board forgave him and saw him as the best person to manage the company into the future.

Figure 15.1: drowning in Rio—share price for Rio Tinto from December 2004 to December 2009

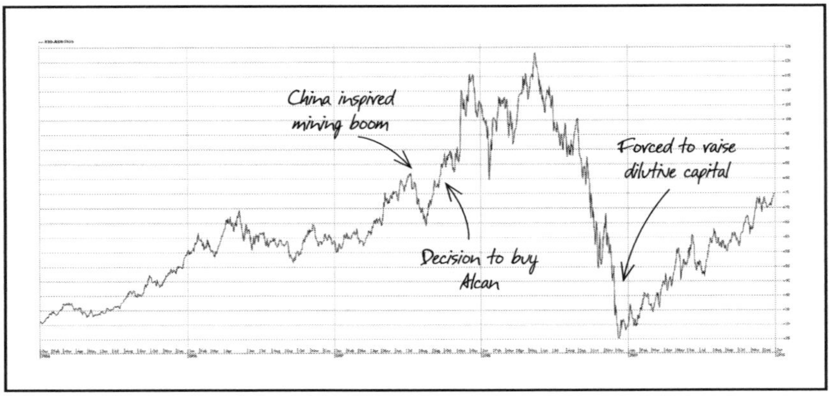

Source: IRESS

Watch out for promises, promises, promises

Underpromising and overdelivering is a common phrase used by managing directors to describe their approach. From my experience, this is easy to say and mightily difficult to do. However, a sure sign that your investment is in good hands is when earnings forecasts are set, and then achieved or even bettered. There is no real excuse for missing a forecast. If external events, such as a sharp rise in the currency or interest rates, work to undermine earnings then the management team should have been sufficiently aware of these variables and never made a forecast in the first place. Companies make regular profit forecasts and they are announced on the ASX under the continuous disclosure rules. The chairman of mining services group Monadelphous, John Rubino, takes this one step further by saying, 'You must always aim to deliver a positive surprise not a negative surprise. If you think you are going to be able to produce 100 and you know you can achieve it, you say you can do 99, and then deliver 100. It is always important to deliver that positive surprise to your client'. Rubino hits the earnings forecast nail on the head.

Decide if you have a friend in bad times

A theme that keeps popping up is the critical need to exercise sound judgement. For example, if you have a friend who only calls you when they need help, then you will eventually close the door on the relationship. This simple line of logic can also be applied to investment in companies. The board and management team of a listed company should regularly communicate with their shareholders, given they are the owners of the business. In addition to the compulsory annual report and half-yearly results, a company's managing director or chairman should take the time to write a quarterly report to explain what the company is trying to achieve and updating how it is progressing. When I worked at Wilson Asset Management we were responsible for managing three listed investment companies. We not only had to comply with the usual company disclosures, we also had to write a monthly net tangible asset report. We saw this as an ideal way to talk to our shareholders and reveal what we had invested in.

If a company does not attempt to communicate with shareholders, but comes knocking when it needs help—usually to raise money to repair a damaged balance sheet—then you should seriously consider looking at investing in a different company with a different attitude.

Beware of hubris

A sure sign that a management team is of the lowest quality is extreme arrogance or hubris. Once again this is much easier to spot when you have the opportunity to meet face to face with a management team and conduct a conversation. However, there are always signs that you can pick up on if you stay alert and read all the communication the company publishes. The surest sign that a management team has grown too admiring of its own ability is the constant reference to the achievements they have made in the past, and the increasingly audacious activities they undertake. You might pick up on this if you are in a position to attend the annual general meeting or a company presentation, but you must be alert and observe the body language of the management and movements of the company.

One company that suffered from the disease of hubris in the lead up to its eventual demise in 2008 was Allco Finance. Originally brought to market as Record Investments with a core business of aircraft leasing, the company's belief in its own ability got out of control as the bull market ran into 2006 and 2007. In 2006 the group, led a consortium of investors, including the equally self-confident Macquarie Group, to launch an $11 billion takeover offer for airline Qantas, a valuation the airline had been unable to reach at any time before. This was a quantum leap in Allco's activities and totally unrealistic, given the heated nature of the market. The bid failed and Qantas's share price has never looked like hitting the $5.60 a share bid price.

Soon after the Qantas bid failed, the company decided to launch a bid in 2007 for the property management company Rubicon, which included among its major shareholders two Allco directors. This was not an arm's length transaction and was undertaken at a time when credit markets were starting to freeze. Rubicon's core business was to manage a batch of highly geared property funds that were coming under pressure from their creditors in the lead up to the GFC. The fact there was a deteriorating funding environment and that this was a related-party transaction didn't seem to faze the company chair, David Coe, and his management team, who were happy to put the matter to shareholders. Allco shareholders eventually paid an inflated price for the Rubicon management company, which was in the process of watching its main assets disappearing like the rest of the property market. The deal smacked of arrogance at Allco, and its team showed little regard for unsuspecting shareholders who had placed their misguided trust in the company.

Allco collapsed under a debt burden in 2008, not long after the Rubicon deal. David Coe said the company had been hit by a perfect storm of negative external events. He should have claimed that management had found the perfect way to dismantle a company.

Conclusion

The job of determining the quality of the management is not easy, especially when you cannot meet people face to face: you will have to rely largely on the material publicly produced and the public actions of the company. But given the poor record of professional investors in recognising sub-standard management, I would not lose heart but instead work hard at keeping a close eye on management teams. Hopefully with the roll out of the broadband network across Australia in the near future, companies will undertake more video sessions with investors over the internet. This should give you a better fix on the people who are the stewards of your company and your investment.

Part IV
Exploding the myths

According to the *Oxford Dictionary* a myth is 'a widely held but false belief or idea'. Unfortunately, over hundreds of years the sharemarket has become polluted with investment myths, which have caused many investors significant pain. In this section we try to attack some of these myths in a bid to ensure that you are not sidetracked by issues that detract from rather than add to your ability to make money.

Chapter 16

Skin in the game

Investors are always looking for some comfort. Whether it is a strong earnings result, a higher dividend, superior management or talk of a takeover, every investor longs for a modicum of extra comfort in the decision they have made to invest in a company. Investors are particularly vulnerable because, more often than not, they are passive. They are not invited to drive the bus and are forced to sit in the passenger's seat hoping the driver can steer the vehicle in the right direction.

Without doubt, many professional and private investors feel the most comfort in their decision making, when the company management and board have skin in the game—they own shares in the company they help run. To the investor skin in the game or blood money is akin to walking arm in arm into enemy lines—it is a jungle out there and it is simply too dangerous to go it alone.

A decision by key insiders of a company to buy shares or have their pay packets linked to a rising share price, does seem attractive. In reality, it is cold comfort. The old saying 'pay peanuts and get monkeys' may be right, but there is no truth in believing that management having skin in the game will deliver superior returns to shareholders. The facts are that some managers who own shares perform well;

some who have shares perform poorly; and some who have never considered buying large chunks of stock in the company they run can deliver exceptional returns. Many managers are driven to succeed simply because they are competitive and want to do an outstanding job. Increasing their own wealth is a consideration, but it is far from front of mind when they are trying to run the company to perform at its best. Money will also fail to buy good judgement. Never underestimate the innate skill of judgement in any vocation, especially the management of a publicly listed company.

> Never underestimate the innate skill of judgement.

An even more disturbing investor belief is that a founding major shareholder or principal has his or her interests aligned with those of minority shareholders. A major shareholder who has strong influence over the company's strategic future should be viewed not as a positive by shareholders, but as an accident waiting to happen. There are exceptions, but big, influential shareholders regularly have their own agendas, which can prove to be a weapon of mass destruction for the minorities. This list includes News Corp, Seven Network, Westfield, Austar United and Primary Health Care. There are some successes, such as plumbing outfit Reece Australia, but these are rare. It would seem that large, prominent individual shareholders who stand back and let a professional manager run the company seem to achieve better outcomes. Ramsay Health Care is a clear example. We will return to this later in the chapter.

The message is that there are no ironclad guarantees that a sharemarket investment will work just because management has major financial incentives to make it work. Many market participants will disagree with this assertion, and the weekly newspaper list of the company insiders who have bought or sold shares is heavily scrutinised. I tend to concentrate on who has sold rather than focus on who has bought.

We like managers who buy shares

Justin Ryan took over as managing director of building materials and medical supplies conglomerate Alesco Corp in 2006. Ryan had been poached from a large private equity firm and groomed to run the company by its outgoing managing director, Kevin Clarke, in the five years leading up to Ryan's employ. On a visit to the company's headquarters in Chatswood on Sydney's North Shore, I asked Clarke why he was retiring from the job when he was so young. He looked left and then right, before pulling me into a spare room just near the reception. In a whispering voice he explained to me it was time for him to go. He then explained, with a heavy dose of conviction, that the company had hired a gun in Ryan. He went on to tell me how smart Ryan was, especially in terms of his grip on the financial standing of the company. From our one meeting with Ryan, we could do nothing but agree — he was sharp, articulate and affable. From what we could gather Ryan had been introduced to Clarke when Alesco had bought the B&D Door business from the private equity firm Ryan had previously worked for.

Ryan was originally hired by Alesco to be Clarke's assistant, but once groomed he would take over the top job. Even before graduating to the CEO role, Ryan made the decision to spend just under $600 000 of his own hard-earned cash on buying 75 000 Alesco shares. While this move was not entirely unusual, it was rare for a new, relatively young executive to buy shares with his own money. The more conventional method was to strike a remuneration package that included performance shares or options, keeping the blood money to a minimum. When asked about why he had purchased the shares directly, Ryan said he felt it was a sound investment and it demonstrated he was aligned with all other shareholders. This was skin in the game and shareholders felt some comfort.

Ryan got off to a stellar start after finally taking the top job at the end of 2006. He stamped his name on the position by deciding to spend $250 million of the company's cash, together with a large dollop of debt, on buying into the high-growth water industry. Alesco's share price rose and rose, as the market surged higher, with Ryan spending another $1.3 million on stock at an average price of $11.28. By the time Alesco's share price had peaked at $15 Ryan owned a total of 500 000 shares through a combination of his own purchases and performance rights worth $7.5 million. Now he had several layers of skin in the game.

As economic conditions began to tighten in late 2007 and early 2008, the Alesco share price started to fall. Then in January 2008 the early phase of the GFC started to buffet the market. Alesco, carrying large debt levels following the water business acquisition, was dumped by nervous investors.

As 2008 unfolded, the banks became nervous about the company's debt levels. To compound the problem, the initial results from the new water supplies and services business were poor. Investor comfort levels were declining. By early 2009 the share price had tumbled to below $1 a share and one of Alesco's major lenders, a French bank, was considering pulling all of its funding from Australia. In an unusual time of panic this raised the spectre that Alesco might not make it through the crisis. When it looked like the end might well be looming, Ryan and his team pulled a rabbit out of the hat by selling the group's highly reliable medical supplies business, for a thumping $175 million. This staved off the banks and the share price started to head north again. Within a matter of months the stock had risen to a remarkable $5, and the worst of the GFC was behind the market. Investors, inspired by the possibility of a major business turnaround got very excited by the Alesco story.

The turnaround, however, failed to materialise. The core building materials business was failing to gain any traction in a dead housing market, and the much touted water business proved to be a white elephant, as rain started to pour around the nation. The share price headed south again and the patience of the Alesco board and its investors grew thin. The facts were that under Ryan's watch the company had geared up to buy a business that had very little track record and then been forced to sell the business that had delivered the most reliable earnings for the company in previous years. It was an invidious situation. Ryan left the company in May 2010, with the share price sitting at around $3 a share. The incoming managing director eventually sold the water business for just $20 million, less than 10 per cent of the purchase price, and then set about restoring the profit margins of the group's various businesses. In the end Ryan was left with 950 000 shares at around $3 each, worth about 20 per cent of what they were at the peak, and well below the prices he had paid for on market purchases. Today, Alesco is trading at $2.60 a share.

Of the thousands of managing directors I've been lucky enough to meet, Ryan is one of the most honest and enjoyable to talk to. He possesses a sharp mind and shows genuine interest in a range of subjects. I'm not sure where he has gone since departing Alesco, but I do think he will succeed in whatever he chooses to do. However, when it came to running a listed industrial company, he seemed to lack the necessary judgement and attention to operational detail to deliver the best outcome for shareholders. In the end, the skin in the game delivered very little comfort and left Ryan financially poorer.

Ryan's situation is obviously a negative example of skin in the game. A poor acquisition, the GFC and a soft housing market all conspired to undo Ryan. It goes to show skin in the game is not the panacea that investors so desperately look for when they jump on board the bus. There are, however, also many examples of when an executive has skin in the game and everyone wins. Michael Kay at salary packaging group McMillan Shakespeare was given substantial incentives to increase the company's share price. It has more than doubled since he entered the top job in May 2008 and shareholders have been shouting his praises from the rooftops. However, there are no guarantees about any company and each situation should be judged on its merits.

Primary concern

Management having skin in the game is one thing, but the founder of a business holding a large shareholding is another version of skin in the game altogether. At Wilson Asset Management we have vigorously debated whether it is preferable for the person making the decisions at the company to have his or her own money on the line. The natural conclusion from a conservative fund manager is to say yes. But I would argue that fund managers can quite easily make the mistake of believing that principals have the same money-making objectives as themselves.

You only have to look at the performance of Rupert Murdoch's News Corporation over the years to understand this is not always the case. The fact that Murdoch organised for News Corp to have two varieties of shares—voting and non-voting—is a dead giveaway that his intentions were no longer about making money for shareholders. He became sidetracked by the aim of keeping control of the group and buying assets around the globe. News Corp's shareholder returns over the years have been negligible. Murdoch's more recent decision to buy Shine, a production company associated with his daughter, for about $700 million, despite negligible earnings, was another example of why investors should be careful of being part of this company.

Another example of the principal and founding shareholder making life hard for investors is medical centre developer and operator Primary Health Care. Founded by Dr Edmund Bateman, the group came to the market as a highly profitable business. Operating medical centres had proven near impossible for corporate Australia, but Dr Bateman had cracked the nut. A larger-than-life character, Bateman loved the sharemarket and firmly understood what investors wanted. If he could deliver a great return on assets, increasing profits and providing the genuine prospect of long-term revenue growth through the roll out of his medical centres across the country, the value of Primary Health Care's shares would rise dramatically. And that is exactly what happened. Not only did he have a roll out of medical centres for investors, but as Primary reported its earnings to the market every six months, it showed the established medical centres were growing earnings at a faster clip than investors initially envisaged. Investors fell in love with the stock and with Bateman. His personal fortune, on the back of his 40 per cent stake in the company, climbed above $300 million and Primary's PE ratio went from around 14 to more than 20. As one fund manager commented, 'I think that you just have to back the guy, he is a winner'. Being an investor in Primary I nodded my head with a grin on my face.

A factor the market underestimated, though, was Bateman's penchant for gambling. When rival medical group Healthscope bid for the much larger Symbion Group in 2007 the market was aghast, and Bateman was seething. He had always harboured an ambition to snare Symbion for himself, and now the moment was slipping by. Symbion offered Primary the chance to diversify away from a medical centre play and become a major operator in the highly profitable pathology and radiology markets. The only problem was that Symbion, with a market cap of more than $2 billion, was twice the size of Primary. Bateman, showing the skill of a seasoned merchant banker, outflanked Healthscope and won the battle for Symbion, paying $2.8 billion in 2008. Suddenly, Primary was no longer a fabulous small growth story, but a large healthcare stock, hobbled with a mountain of debt used to make the acquisition.

The timing of the Symbion purchase proved to be unfortunate. The more than $2 billion of debt used to buy the healthcare giant became an albatross for Primary, as the world lurched towards the GFC in 2008. Primary had always intended to offload Symbion's wholesale pharmaceutical distribution business, along with its natural healthcare operation, and when it received surprisingly robust prices for these two operations market concerns eased. But the calm was only short lived. Primary was still heavily indebted and investors were concerned, despite Bateman's feared reputation for being frugal. Declining returns on equity and capital were fanning the anxiety, and Primary's share price started to suffer. When the company announced to the market that major cost savings were in the offing from the merger with Symbion, the positive response from the investment community was only temporary (see figure 16.1, overleaf). As time went on and debt concerns escalated rather than eased, investors lost confidence.

When the federal government decided to vary its regulation of the Australian pathology market in 2009, the game was all but up for Primary. A series of earnings downgrades and several capital raisings punctured the share price, which deflated all the way back to $3, down almost 80 per cent from the heights of $14 a share before Symbion was purchased. Bateman had lost the confidence of investors.

Primary's story is far from finished. It could well be that it decides to offload the majority of the old Symbion businesses and once again concentrate on the high-returning medical centres. It would be back to the good old days. The lesson for now, though, is that a major shareholder may possess totally different ambitions and outcomes than the passive shareholders on the registry. Instead of expanding with a whale of an acquisition, investors would have been comfortable for management to simply concentrate on the core business and roll out medical centres across the country, relishing a return on equity of more than 20 per cent. In the meantime the company could continue to grow earnings at double digits and consistently pay rising fully franked dividends.

Figure 16.1: Primary concern—share price for Primary Healthcare from January 2004 to June 2011

Source: IRESS

Macquarie money

Possibly Australia's greatest skin in the game sharemarket play has been Macquarie Group. The primary reason the millionaire factory exists has been to make its executives and management rich, or at least richer than they already were.

When the company listed on the market in 1996 for just $3 a share, the board deliberately structured staff remuneration so that everyone could be captivated by the magic of a rising share price. The formula changed over the years, but generally the profits generated by the company were split 50–50 between insiders and external shareholders. This alignment with external shareholders was strengthened by the fact that a high percentage of the employee remuneration was received in shares rather than cash. The enchanting aspect of having equity is its ability to make individuals seriously rich if the profits rise. Leverage into a rising equity price has far greater wealth creation ability than just receiving a bonus each year. It also worked to tie employees in for extended periods of employment, rather than skipping across to another ravenous merchant bank.

The fact that Macquarie had created this structure attracted people who had similar money-making ambitions. Talented people joined the group from around the globe, resulting in innovative ideas that took the former merchant bank into ludicrously profitable areas, such as infrastructure ownership and asset management. Macquarie became the financial symbol of the great bull run from the early 1990s until the GFC of 2008.

There were grumblings from various sections of the sharemarket that Macquarie was generating profits by taking on huge amounts of debt through its satellite companies and manufacturing profits from asset re-pricing. The most vocal of these critics was US-based hedge fund manager Jim Chanos, who became a rock star when he picked Enron as a house of cards. The key to the Macquarie model was to gain control of a key asset, such as Sydney Airport, gear it up, and attach a management contract that produced enormous fees for Macquarie before it sold the asset back to the public through the sharemarket. As the manager of the asset, Macquarie would attempt to have the asset re-valued up each year, producing bulging performance fees and allowing them to add more gearing into the vehicle. A fantastic model if asset prices continued to head north. Cash flow was not always strong, but growth and opportunities were boundless. Macquarie Bank's share price hit $98 in early 2007 and the number of people in the eastern suburbs of Sydney and Melbourne who grew wealthy from Macquarie was staggering. When bonuses were paid at the bank and the share-selling window was open, real estate prices in those areas tended to reach yearly highs.

Then the bull market came to an end. Macquarie's share price peaked around six months ahead of the market top in November 2007. The GFC accelerated the decline in the share price, as investors became fearful that Macquarie would be caught up in a banking style collapse that was engulfing the northern hemisphere. To the credit of Macquarie's management, they had secured a banking licence in the lead up to the GFC and used this to shore up its funding when the federal government allowed Australian banks to rent its AAA sovereign credit rating, which was a life saver for many institutions. Macquarie aggressively shored up its finances and survived, despite doubters in the market who watched the share price fall to just over $15. Like the market, Macquarie's share price bounced strongly in 2009, as investors looked to get back on the bull market track. But after the initial sharemarket recovery, Macquarie share price has floundered, currently sitting at around $30 a share or about one-third of its peak price. Big acquisitions are not being made, and earnings growth has stalled. Things are a lot tougher and the employees can see the share price is not moving. Is the model broken? Quite possibly, but only time will tell. It is amazing how exhilarating a rising share price can be for employees who have shares, and how deflating for morale when the price is falling. People get retrenched and enthusiasm for the leverage-equity play fades. The individuals who set up Macquarie were entrepreneurial and understood the ups and downs of business, but the second generation of employees enjoyed the upside of a rising share price, but had no stomach for a falling share price and declining bonuses. Leverage works both ways.

It is another example that shows having skin in the game doesn't deliver a guaranteed outcome for external shareholders (see figure 16.2).

Figure 16.2: better up than down—Macquarie Bank share price from January 2004 to June 2011

Source: IRESS

No hard and fast rules

I have deliberately taken the path of negative skin in the game examples to make a point and, it would be fair to say, on many occasions skin in the game can be a terrific positive for all shareholders. However, the message must be heard loud and clear that blood money is not a sign that automatically means you are on a winner from the outset. The fact that many professional investors promote skin in the game as essential to a successful company is negligent and shows a genuine lack of independent thinking.

The only explanation that I can give for perpetuating this myth is that most professional investors assume that senior management teams are all focused solely on making money and making money for the shareholders. This reveals poor judgement about human beings. If management is totally fixated on the share price of their company they should switch jobs and take up investing, which is a job that concentrates solely on the share price.

In the book *Master CEOs,* I found that, of the 13 people interviewed, only one person saw shareholders as their number one priority. In fact, the vast majority of them thought that if you got the most out of your employees, looked after your customers and promoted a strong culture and brand, then the share price would look after itself. Each of these 13 managers had been in charge of a single company for more than a decade, all of which comfortably outstripped overall sharemarket performance. Some were paid well; some owned a decent number of shares; and some delivered staggering returns to shareholders without holding more than a handful of shares themselves. A CEO with the ability to deliver outstanding results does not need to be aligned with shareholders. Try to find comfort elsewhere.

The sell smell

Of more concern to investors should be insider selling of shares. There is nothing more disconcerting to investors than a manager or board member — those who know how the company is performing at all times — deciding to sell. A director is required to declare on the ASX a sale of shares in the company within five days of the trade. There is always a good excuse for selling shares, the most quoted being a house renovation, diversification of assets or payment for a divorce. Sometimes these reasons are true; other times it is a convenient excuse. The size of the sell down should always be taken into account. If a major shareholder or a board member decides to sell down 10 per cent of their entire holding to help liquidity, then investigate but don't slit your wrists. If, however, they decide to sell 80 per cent of what they own, which was the case when John Kinghorn floated his mortgage group RHG, be worried about what is going on operationally. Be very worried!

There have been many examples of insider selling over the years that has led to shareholder tears, making it difficult for the company to recover for a protracted period. A permanent smell follows the insiders and the board. Streetwear and skateboard group Globe International floated on the ASX in 2001, on the back of the highly successful Billabong listing some months earlier. Globe's shares shot out of the gate, moving higher at a phenomenal pace. Towards the end of the next financial year, but before the announcement of its profit results, the company declared it was making a major acquisition to boost its skateboard business. To fund this acquisition the company would raise new equity, assuring shareholders the transaction would be earnings per share accretive. As part of the overall transaction, the founders and major shareholders of the business, the Hill brothers, said they would sell down a $40 million parcel of their own shares at a price of $1.70 a piece in a bid to help liquidity for the market. Within months, the company announced an earnings downgrade and the shares fell like a stone. By the beginning of 2003 the share price had sunk to just 11 cents. It was a new company that failed to hit an earnings target, and the insiders had stuffed overpriced shares into the market. The company survives to this day, but the shares have never recovered and investors have never forgiven the company. Today Globe's share price flounders at just under 50 cents a share, well below the price when it floated ten years ago (see figure 16.3).

Figure 16.3: global mistake — Globe International's share price May 2001 to June 2003

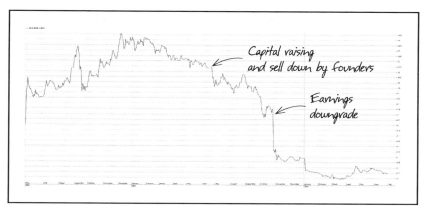

Source: IRESS

There are, of course, some notable exceptions. John Rubino, the chairman of mining services group Monadelphous, has sold down his shareholding over the years. He has sold at a fair price and, as a rule, the sale has been followed closely by extremely bullish earnings results. The same attitude has been adopted by the highly successful founders of travel retailer Flight Centre. This list is not long, and all investors should be on high alert if the insider pushes the sell button.

Chapter 17

Look for the catalyst not the company

Professional investors are often quoted as saying, 'I won't buy shares in a company unless I understand what it does'. The greatest living investor, Warren Buffet, preaches this view and it makes a great deal of sense. Why would you put your own money, and possibly other people's money, into something you don't fully understand?

In reality, though, it is highly unusual for any investor to fully comprehend what a business does and what drives its success. You might understand that a company sells shirts, develops real estate or manufactures ice cream, but that is a quantum leap from grasping the mechanics of the business, why it can be a success and what makes it tick. How else can you explain why some organisations outperform others in the same industry? The answer to this question must lie in the existence of a superior management team that has a better grasp of the business and an intimate knowledge of the fundamentals needed to produce healthier returns. Sure, investors study the historical financials, assess the industry and rate the management, but to suggest this is enough to claim complete knowledge is foolhardy. As one leading Australian fund manager said at a presentation

I attended, 'We allocate our funds to various company managers who look after it for us'. Experience tells me this is far closer to the truth.

You are in the market, not running a business

The job of an investor is not to acquire perfect knowledge of a business he or she is considering putting money into. You can think you know a company inside out and believe it is ridiculously cheap only to make the investment and fail to eke out a return. How can this possibly happen? Acquiring total understanding of a business is unlikely and can sidetrack you from the real job at hand—deciding whether a stock price is going to go up or down. Buffett has said that, for an investor, 'Investment philosophy is the clear understanding that by owning shares of stocks he owns a business, not pieces of paper'. That might be the case for him, but for the rest of us it is bunkum.

> The job of an investor is not to acquire perfect knowledge of a business he or she is considering putting money into.

At Wilson Asset Management we concentrated on what would make a share price go up or down. We labelled this a stock catalyst. This does not mean an investor simply ignores the operations of a business, but the old saying 'analysis, paralysis' is worthwhile considering. There are so many companies in so many industries that it would be arrogant to believe you could be an expert in every one of them—and a quick way to failing when it comes to making money on the sharemarket. This might sound like short-term trading but careful decisions on a stock purchase can result in holdings going up for many, many years. Contrastingly, a decision not to buy a stock may save you a lot of money and agony. We must remember that the sharemarket is not operating in the real world: it is only a derivative of the real world. The managers of a business are in the real world and it is their job to understand the business they are running, while investors sit in judgement, trying to work out whether a company's shares are going to go up or down.

If you can start figuring out what will make a stock re-rate in the eyes of the market you can achieve massive returns. For example, a business that earns $10 million profit and trades on a PE ratio of 10 has a market value of $100 million. If, over the course of the next five years the business doubles its profit and still trades on a PE of 10, its market value will increase to $200 million. That's a great 100 per cent return for its investors. If, however, over the same five-year period the earnings double and the PE also doubles to 20 times, the market value of the company increases to $400 million. That equates to making a 300 per cent return on your original investment. One or two investments like that each year can make all the difference to an investor.

Preoccupation with what a business does will not normally lead to these types of gains. and may even take your eyes off what is actually happening in the market place. Let's look at some examples.

Caught in a debt trap

Chris Stott joined Wilson Asset Management in November 2006. Chris distinguished himself in many ways as a fine analyst, and he had a unique ability to sum up a situation without uttering a word, opting instead to express his thoughts with a variety of sighs. A high pitched 'ahh' generally described a profitable announcement from one of the companies we owned. A flat 'ah ha' could be interpreted as an announcement that required more explanation. A stern 'mmmm' spelt bad news. On most occasions I didn't need to ask for an explanation, such was the clarity of his code.

On 6 November 2007, after the market had closed, Chris released one of the longest and sternest mmms I had heard in the year he had been with the company.

I looked up and said, 'It can't be that bad!'

His eyes on the screen, he said, 'I think it could be even worse'.

'Come on then, let me have it', I said.

Our largest individual holding, debt collection company Credit Corp, had posted a notice received (NR) with the ASX saying that its earnings forecasts would be revised down for the year to 30 June 2008 by 25 per cent. The size and suddenness of the downgrade was shocking. Only four weeks before we had visited the company and walked away feeling the business was powering ahead, justifying its lofty price of more than 20 times forecast earnings.

Both Chris and I felt sick that afternoon, left to ponder how far the stock price would tumble the next morning when the market opened for trade. Chris decided the stock would open between 25 and 30 per cent down, while I thought it could open closer to 40 per cent. Unfortunately, I was right. We decided to offload a portion of our shares but naively held on grimly to the rest. A few months later the stock downgraded its earnings for a second time. In the end Credit Corp's share price fell from a high of more than $12.99 in August 2007 to a low of just 39 cents a share in February 2009, a decline of more than 97 per cent. We had experienced companies going broke before but we had never clocked up a dollar loss of this magnitude in the nine years that we had been managing other people's money. The ghost of Credit Corp, four years on, still haunts the management team and our shareholders.

So how could we get it so wrong? The easy answer would be to say the management had not been straight with us in our meeting or with the general market. This would be misleading. The fact was that I had fooled myself into believing that I completely and utterly understood the business model. Credit Corp had grown at an astronomical rate in the years leading up to the fateful earnings downgrade, and we had racked our brains over what could possibly undermine the juggernaut that had seen the share price rocket and the company become a darling of the small cap market. Floating at 50 cents a share in 2000, on a modest PE of just 7, by 2007 Credit Corp, had delivered a magical 2500 per cent capital gain for all those who had picked the stock at the float and run with it all the way to the top. The company's business model was to buy 180-day-old debt ledgers from a variety of banks. They buy the book of debts for about 10 per cent of their face value and then attempt to collect the money. All going well, the money shelled out for the ledger can be recouped within 18 months and over about six years the company would hope to collect 2.5 times the ledger purchase. To buy the ledgers from the banks, Credit Corp used a mixture of shareholder equity and bank debt. Ironically, this creates a situation where the company borrows off a bank to collect the bank's own dated debts. The problem with growing fast and buying an increasing number of ledgers meant Credit Corp needed to borrow larger sums of money from the bank, increasing its own risk.

We always thought that as long as the management team did not pay too much for the ledgers and the banks kept selling the dated ledgers, then Credit Corp would grow its earnings for many years to come, with the return on equity strengthening. The industry was still relatively young and growth should not have been a problem in the foreseeable future. This was a naive view. Talented company analyst Andrew Hills had told us that we might also need to watch Credit Corp's collection rates closely, and that if the collection rate slowed the earnings would be under pressure and plummet. Sure enough he was right, and the company conceded that its collection rate had dropped away and was the prime cause for the downgrade, something that we never really acknowledged and never really understood, mainly because the company had not disclosed the information before. Hills, a former banking analyst, had learned over the years that collection rates were vital for any debt business. He knew what to look for and we didn't. And how would I know, given that I have never been part of a debt collection business and never worked at a bank.

And there lies the problem when you are an investor. The fact is that you can do as much analysis and work on a stock as you like, but unless you stumble across someone who has actually worked in an industry or has been unlucky enough to work out what can go wrong the hard way, then you will never know what the most sensitive aspects of a business model are. There are hundreds of different companies out there, some in retail, some in finance, some in wholesale, some in mining, some in mining services, others in agriculture, and the list goes on and on. No doubt when you are investing you do your best to understand what a business does, but knowledge is never complete. The idea that investors have perfect knowledge and the sharemarket is not a random walk is bordering on ridiculous. I have worked in three separate businesses besides professional investing and I know that investors have, at best, a vague idea of what makes those businesses perform.

What we should have been focused on with Credit Corp is not so much what could have gone wrong with the business, but the fact its price had rocketed to more than 20 times future earnings, which meant that if the slightest thing went wrong, our losses would be significant (see figure 17.1). In other words it was priced to perfection and the catalyst to sell the stock was the obvious one—the stock was too expensive. An earnings downgrade, coupled with a contraction of the PE would be tremendously painful.

Figure 17.1: no credit available—Credit Corp's share price from January 2002 to June 2011

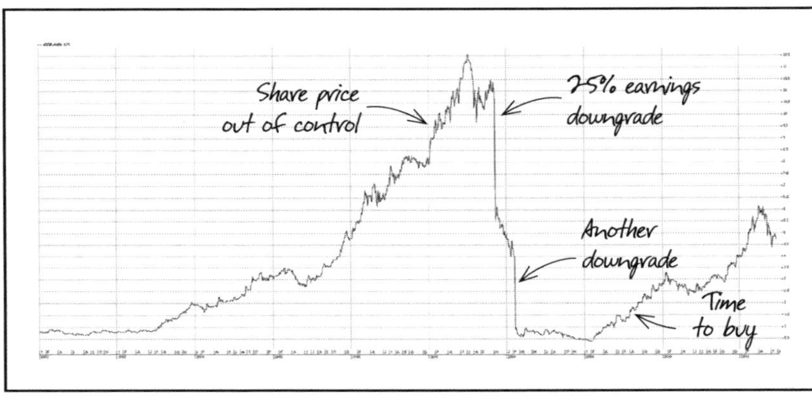

Source: IRESS

Feeling rejected

Sitting in a taxi in Melbourne in early December 2010, Chris Stott calmly said from the back seat that The Reject Shop had downgraded its earnings for the year to 30 June 2011. The discount retailer's bad news had come like death in the night—swift and without warning. The company had said, only five weeks before at its annual general meeting, that the first three months of the financial year had met budget and, as a result, the full-year earnings forecast was re-affirmed. In the space of just five weeks the company was forced to downgrade from those forecasts by 20 per cent. Ouch!

We extracted ourselves from the cab 15 minutes before our next company meeting. Of course, we attempted to work out what went wrong. The official reason given by the company was that, since the Reserve Bank of Australia had decided to lift official interest rates on Melbourne Cup day, 2 November, business had dropped suddenly and there was still no sign of recovery. This explanation had baffled us and most stockbroking analysts, because the company had won many fans in the market due to the resilient nature of its earnings. They sold low-priced goods that would benefit from a tough economic environment. Apparently not on this occasion!

Before that December announcement The Reject Shop had gradually, over the space of about five years, become a poster child of the retail sector. Initially met with scepticism by the market after being floated out of private equity, the stock gradually saw its PE ratio jump from about 8 to around 12 as earnings surpassed investor and analyst expectations.

Then the GFC hit the world. It was the making of The Reject Shop in the market's eyes. In early 2009 the consensus view was that all retail stocks would bleed on the back of the crisis as consumers tightened their belts. However, The Reject Shop powered ahead with earnings growth and store roll outs. The market increased the company's PE up to around 18 times, with many brokers claiming it was as defensive as food retailers, such as Woolworths and Wesfarmers. The central message espoused by the analytical community was that with the supply side running efficiently, not much could go wrong. And then, with the GFC fading into the distance, the company hit a road block—supposedly on the back of one interest rate increase.

While the interest rate hike may have knocked consumer confidence around it was hard to believe it could reverse company earnings. In our 15-minute discussion before our next meeting, Chris and I came to our own conclusions. The main source of problems for retail businesses is more often than not the quality of the inventory. I should have been more careful. I had remembered that when my wife had run her own discount variety store some years before, the key was having fresh stock appearing regularly to get people to come into the store each week. The single biggest mistake you could make was to have the same stock, or the wrong stock, sitting at the front of the shop each week and expect shoppers to be lured in. It was not like Woolworths or Coles where people virtually had to come into the shop to buy their bread, milk, nappies, and so on. In addition, the stock rotation had to be spot on, or you could have a build-up of old inventory very quickly that would take months to clear. Shoppers already expected a bargain, if you had stock they didn't want then you virtually had to give it away.

In The Reject Shop's case the stock problem was exacerbated by the time of year. The business had always made a significant amount of its profits in the two months leading up to Christmas and it would stock itself to the gunwales in preparation for the festive season. If the business had stock that was not moving at this time of year then it could be months, maybe years, before it was completely cleared.

In presentations to investors after the downgrade, management admitted they had made some poor inventory decisions. They had taken on some much larger, more expensive items, which their customers had shied away from. The result was tremendously painful.

The market's reaction was typical. Leading into the downgrade, there was not one sell recommendation in the market and so the stock fell in line with its earnings, the PE multiple did not shrink. The downgrade was generally viewed as a bump in the road, and investors believed that previous earnings growth rates would be quickly resumed. It wasn't until the Queensland floods a few months later severely damaged The Reject Shop's distribution centre that investors began to lower its PE rating as many offloaded their shares. It will be interesting to see where the market finally decides what earnings multiple to put the company on. The market, including Wilson Asset Management, was looking the wrong way when we crossed the road. It wasn't the macro-economic environment that was important to The Reject Shop, but the management of the business. We cut our holding in the belief the earnings downgrade would see the market slowly re-rate the stock lower, reflected in a lower PE ratio over time. We viewed it as a catalyst to the downside.

How do you make your money?

When meeting a company for the first time Geoff Wilson always asked the question, 'How do you make your money?' In 13 years of attending company presentations I didn't hear anyone else ask this simple question. Mainly because it is too embarrassing for a professional investor to admit they might not know how a company actually earns its profits. After all, any professional worth their salt can calculate the key financials of profit margins, cash flows, return on equity, stock turns or even the revenue growth rates into the future. To ask a straightforward question such as how a company makes its money was embarrassing. In fact, sometimes you could hear the fund managers and analysts around the presentation table chortle to themselves when Geoff asked his regular opening line. Geoff didn't care. He always viewed a group presentation as if he was the only one in the room with the company management team. However, each time a management team was kind enough to answer Geoff's question, most investors in the room started to write furiously in their notepads. Obviously many people still hadn't worked out how the company made its money. The question Geoff asked was so pure and so fundamental that it invariably revealed an answer that added a lot of value. It also led to a series of other questions that were also quite revealing. I'm not saying that it meant that by the end of the discussion we understood every possible outcome for the business, but it did move us a great deal further towards the Holy Grail.

Geoff's 'How do you make your money?' question also revealed many things about company management. Those management teams who could answer the question without hesitation and in a concise form gave you a lot of confidence they were on top of their game. Unfortunately, over the years many management teams simply repeated the question back to Geoff, before meandering through a clumsy explanation. Maybe the guys running the company didn't know how they made their money either. For those investors like Peter Proksa, who are able to wangle a one-on-one meeting with a company management team, I recommend you borrow Geoff's technique. Even if you meet a divisional head or a lower placed manager, it is always a good question to ask. The key is not to be embarrassed.

Even the big boys don't know what they are driving

The GFC of 2008–09 was a prime example of investors, both professionals and part timers, having only limited knowledge of a business model.

An example of this could be found with the Australian banks. To outsiders the local banking industry stood tall in the heady days of the financial crisis, but in reality many companies, including Suncorp, St George Bank and BankWest, were only a breath away from spectacularly failing like so many US and European institutions did.

Before 2008, investors generally assumed that funding would be available for banks to meet their obligations to their borrowers. In previous economic downturns investors had focused on the other side of the equation—the ability of the bank's customers to repay the bank. This time is was different and no-one was quite sure how to handle the situation. When world credit markets froze in August to November 2008, there was the very real possibility that a major Australian bank would not be able to access funds to lend out to its committed borrowers. Sure, it was an unusual situation, but Australian banks were big players in the international wholesale funding market, proudly roaming the globe with their rare AA debt rating pinned to their prospectuses. The reality though was that, for a four-month period in 2008, no wholesale funds were available to AA rated banks, meaning that when it came to refreshing short-term funding requirements there were simply no funds available. It raised the genuine prospect that one or more of our local banks could have been forced to call in loans from thousands of customers simply to repay their own lenders. It was only the alacrity of the federal government that prevented a financial crisis of our own. The government rented its own premium AAA debt rating to our banks, allowing them to secure wholesale funding that was simply not available to the standard rated bank. It effectively prevented a mass call on consumer and business loans. Investors ran for the hills, dumping bank stocks on the market at any price. No-one had predicted the avalanche of selling, because no-one knew the risks associated with wholesale funding. We live and learn—I hope.

Given the amount of equity subsequently raised by the banks and their scramble to build up alternative forms of funding, especially retail deposits, it also proved many bank management teams had been ignorant of the risks they had been taking in the years leading up to 2008.

A lack of resources

The ignorance displayed by investors towards bank funding in late 2008 was superseded by the clueless investing in our pride and joy — resource stocks. As the GFC took hold on equity markets in 2008, investors fled from the nasty banking stocks and into the safety of the mining companies. Financial and industrial stocks were viewed as victims of the crisis unfolding in the northern hemisphere, but mining stocks were still on a tear. After all, China, the single biggest buyer of Australian commodities was enjoying an economic miracle that could not be derailed by the calamity in the developed economies.

By July 2008 the All Resources index was hitting record highs, proving China could power forward without assistance from the rest of the globe, effectively decoupling from the world economy. Or so we thought. At about this time the Chinese, instructed by their central planning government, decided to run down their stockpile of all commodities because the nation's rampant export industry had grounded to a halt. It wasn't so much that decoupling was a myth, but that Australian investors and the management of our mining companies had no idea of how much the Chinese had been stockpiling commodities in the lead up to the crash. The consensus view was that China had about one month's supply of materials such as iron ore, coking coal and copper. The facts, calculated only later on, revealed China had much more than that — possibly six months supply of most commodities — and were no longer interested in buying materials from Australia. Investors panicked and dumped any mining share that sat in their portfolio, while companies across the industry raced to close mines and lay off workers just to stay in business.

The fact was that China had become the only incremental buyer of Australian resources. This was dangerous for two reasons — no business should rely on one customer and if you have only one customer, make sure you have a firm understanding of their motives. These risks had been totally ignored in the 2006–07 mining boom.

The Holy Grail

Understanding what makes a business successful and, more crucially, what factors have the ability to bring a business model undone, is the Holy Grail of investing. And for the most part totally unattainable. That sounds like a defeatist attitude but it is reality. The search for the Holy Grail should, through rigorous research, be pursued, but not obsessively. Investors should not delude themselves into believing they have complete knowledge of a company — this will only result in disappointment and ultimately result in a loss of confidence, which is a far more important factor in successful investing. The father of value investing, Benjamin Graham, tried to whip this problem by concentrating on companies whose share prices were trading below their cash plus inventory and receivables. After the Great Depression era of the 1930s in the United States, stocks regularly traded at these ridiculously low levels. Graham's margin of safety in the valuation meant that he didn't really need to worry about operational problems arising in the business — the value he was paying simply sat on the balance sheet.

Graham's approach is rarely achievable. There are only brief periods in history when you can buy a company below its cash backing. In 13 years at Wilson Asset Management we searched hard for these situations but only managed to find a handful. The tech wreck of 2000–02 threw up several gems, including a long-term holding in accounting software provider Reckon. The other major opportunity appeared in early 2009 after the GFC, when analyst Mark Hancock pointed us in the direction of financial outfit RHG. A third and final discovery was fund manager Everest Babcock and Brown, which was identified by Geoff. These were all highly profitable, low-risk trades, but you cannot make a living out of three trades in 13 years.

If no Holy Grail, then what? A story, of course

Australia's best ever small-company fund manager, David Paradice, believes that to be a successful investor your key objective is to identify the one or two factors that are going to make a stock rise or fall in the near future. At Wilson Asset Management we would describe this process as discovering a catalyst that will cause the share price to be re-rated. In other words the market would be happy to change a stock's price to earnings ratio from say eight to ten. For most investors, this has to be the right approach. The combination of rising profits and a rising price to earnings multiple is the sweet spot for investing in a company. The reverse can be a diabolical outcome, as shown by the Credit Corp and The Reject Shop examples. The fact is this: you are not running the company, instead you are buying a company's stock in the belief its share price will rise in the near to medium term so you can sell your shares for a profit.

A highly successful fund manager once told me that when he invests in a company he adapts the view that he owns 100 per cent of the company. That way you can fully appreciate the business more completely and understand what management is trying to achieve. I nearly choked when in the next breath he described a company he was looking at as a 'good story'. No-one who owns a business believes their company is a story that has a beginning, middle and end. Polly Mazaris, the founder and major shareholder in highly successful recycling company Baxter Group, would say when she visited us from Melbourne, 'My company is not a story, so stop calling it that'.

For the most part company share prices don't move dramatically, but endless searching will unveil great opportunities to get on board a stock that is going to rise. What will make a stock re-rate in the near to medium term can be one of many things. To help you identify a stock that might move, you need to acquire a vast amount of knowledge of the company, especially when it comes to financials and management. A re-rating of a stock can include an upgrade in earnings, a change in management, an acquisition of another business, a business sale, the disappearance of a competitor, or the discovery of a new resource. The list of catalysts can be endless. Sometimes, such as in the gloomy days of early 2009, a company's outrageously low share price can prove to be the only catalyst needed for a re-rating to occur. Wholesaling group McPherson's sunk to a PE of almost 1, compared with its historical average of about 8. That is a catalyst staring you in the face.

Looking for a catalyst

If there is one thing that took up most of our time at Wilson Asset Management it was the search for a catalyst. Every Friday morning we met for two hours to discuss our portfolio and we would shoot the breeze about all the stocks we already owned, constantly asking the question, 'What is going to make this stock re-rate?' There were obvious catalysts, such as the possibility of an earnings upgrade, or a downgrade. A change in a company's management can be a positive or negative catalyst. Other catalysts are there, but we just needed to search hard to find them. Let's have a look at some examples.

Day of reckoning

In 2003 we started buying stock in Reckon Ltd. Reckon was the listed company name of the group that owned the Quicken Accounting Software business in Australia. As far as we could ascertain at that time, Quicken and rival MYOB had a combined market share in excess of 80 per cent of the Australian accounting software market. The catalyst to buy the stock was the fact it was trading at below its cash backing in the carnage of the tech wreck.

The ASX forced most of the tech companies in that period to release quarterly cash flow statements. All other companies are required to report their earnings and cash flows only twice a year. For a company to get off the quarterly reporting treadmill, they had to post three positive quarterly cash flow statements in succession. For an investor this was priceless. We could look at Reckon's cash flow each quarter to make sure it wasn't running down the cash sitting on its balance sheet that had been cleverly raised during the boom in the late 1990s.

We discovered that not only was Reckon not eating into its cash reserves but, under the new manager, Clive Rabie, it was producing solid cash flows each quarter. We had three catalysts on our hands—a scorched earth valuation, a change in management and a duopoly industry structure. Those three catalysts managed to keep us in the stock for five years, watching not only the earnings grow but also the price to earnings ratio expand from less than 4 to about 12. The company's share price moved 1500 per cent higher between 2003 to 2008.

While this all sounds good, Reckon suffered from being MYOB's poor cousin. MYOB developed and owned its software, giving the investment community good reason to put the stock on a PE ratio of around 20. Reckon, which licensed its Quicken Software from US giant Intuit, was seen as inferior and the market slapped a lowly PE ratio of 12 on the stock. In 2008 MYOB was taken over by a hungry private equity group, leaving Reckon as the only listed accounting software provider. At the time we did not really put much credence in the argument that investors would now take their profits from the MYOB takeover and plough them into Reckon. Sure enough, though, it happened. Reckon's share price rocketed by more than 80 per cent over the next two years as its PE jumped from around 12 to 17. The joys of rising earnings and an expanding PE can be significant.

To identify this catalyst you would need to have a good working knowledge of the industry structure, a thorough understanding of Reckon's favourable licence with Intuit and the quality of Clive Rabie and his management team. As for fully comprehending the business, well that is Clive's job.

Clear vision

In 2002 Geoff was about to jump on a plane when he made a last minute call into the office to try to sell me on the merits of optometry group OPSM. The company had appointed Jonathon Pinshaw as its new managing director, following a sustained period of underperformance. Pinshaw had endeared himself to the investment community as managing director of Freedom Furniture some years earlier. Geoff believed Pinshaw was a winner and we should buy some OPSM shares at around $2 each. He also thought we should book in a company visit and decide whether to build a position in the stock. I didn't have such a high opinion of Pinshaw. My recollection of Freedom Furniture was that as soon as Pinshaw left the building things had started to unravel. I thought he was a great salesman, but that there wasn't much substance lying beneath. Geoff replied, 'Fair enough, but I've bought some stock already, so we better book in a visit and see what he has planned for the company'.

OPSM turned out to be a highly profitable trade. Under the previous management, the company had diversified away from its extremely profitable core retail eyewear business. Peter Lynch, in his book *One Up On Wall Street* had labelled this kind of behaviour diworsification, because the two new businesses failed to make anywhere near the returns of the original core business. OPSM was effectively using a business that was making close to 30 per cent return on equity to pump funds into two other businesses that were struggling to break even. Pinshaw was circumspect about revealing too much to the investment community, except to say he would not have taken on the job unless he thought he could improve things in both the near and long term.

Within a matter of months Pinshaw had sold one of the new businesses for a price that surprised even the most avid supporter. The stock began to re-rate. He then put up for sale the second new business, and once again surprised on the upside. Suddenly we had a single-purpose business capable of engineering significant returns, with a balance sheet as strong as 10 men. The stock was climbing towards $3 a share and I was put back in my box. I had totally missed the catalyst for the stock to re-rate, even though after about six meetings in as many months, I had warmed to Pinshaw, who also was not an optometry expert but understood that good money was chasing bad and he needed to do something about it to get the stock price heading in the right direction.

In the end OSPM was taken over by a large Italian eyewear group in 2004 for $3.80 a share, delivering a 90 per cent return to those shareholders who had jumped on board with Pinshaw only two years before.

Not selective enough

A catalyst can also be crucial for selling a stock. For the vast majority of people, the emotion associated with losing money on a stock seems to far outweigh the jubilation of making money from an investment. So it's dangerous to ignore a negative catalyst.

For years we held an investment in almond farm manager, Select Harvest. We had always been hesitant to invest in stocks that depended heavily on external factors, such as agricultural stocks. Agricultural commodity prices can fall for a variety of reasons, including over supply, drought, flood or disease. We knew very little about agriculture, but history told us many things could go wrong and at some stage it usually did.

To me, Select Harvest was different. It owned some almond farms directly, but its main business was (and still is) the management of almond farms for other people. Select got a fee for planting the crop, a fee for growing the crop and a fee for marketing the crop for sale. Management agreements were generally for the lifetime of a producing almond tree, which was a staggering 25 years. Select had pitched most of its contracts on the volume of the crops, taking out the volatile nature of price. This was a model too good to be true. Almond sales around the world were heading higher and higher on the back of the belief that eating nuts was healthy, and the main supplier of nuts to the globe — California — had many older almond trees whose production was starting to flag.

The stock price went on a streak, climbing from under $2.00 a share in 2001 to $14.90 over a four-year period that included the tech wreck bear market. Earnings were gaining momentum each half as more and more almonds were produced and more fees generated. It was easy to generate a valuation for the company of between $30 and $40 a share, and, given the low capital intensity, the business was going to spew out so much cash it would surpass the current market cap of the stock within five years.

The stock had eased from its lofty heights above $14 a share as talk spread that the federal government was reviewing the eligibility of managed investment schemes (MIS), which would affect the company because its major customer was totally reliant on them. The MIS effectively allowed investors to claim tax deductions on the costs of planting an agricultural crop or a timber crop upfront, even though they would not receive an income from the scheme for many years to come. People from the major capital cities were pouring money into MIS as a means of reducing the amount of tax they were paying from year to year. The federal government, which had been lobbied by genuine farmers and the ATO (Australian Tax Office), decided to review the whole system. This should have sent alarm bells ringing for Select investors. While Select did not sell MIS schemes directly, its biggest customer, Timbercorp, did.

Before the government could conclude its review of MIS schemes, the ATO sent out a ruling that would see all MIS schemes for horticultural products scrapped. Timbercorp's share price fell like a stone, while Select was affected only mildly. After all, the returns on almonds were high enough that there was no need for a tax incentive to invest in them. This may have been true, but it was a naive view of how the real world worked. Timbercorp was the responsible entity for all of its almond farms and before long that company was broke, and the Select share price was sitting back at around $3 (see figure 17.2). A catalyst had stared investors in the face for some time, but when you are long a stock you only see the blue sky and ignore the dark clouds on the horizon.

Figure 17.2: looking for a catalyst — Select Harvest's share price from January 2002 to June 2011

Source: IRESS

Conclusion

Experience tells me that many professional investors convince themselves — and their customers — that they fully understand every business they are investing in. This is patently wrong, given how many company announcements catch investors offguard. The usual response from investors is to blame management for not being forthright with the market. However, professional investors should take more responsibility for their own shortcomings. The more realistic approach is to acknowledge that you will only ever have a rudimentary knowledge of the pivotal factors that make a company more profitable. Instead, investors should concentrate on their job of working out whether a share price is going to move higher or lower. My recommendation is that you stick to the numbers and try to find that catalyst that will change the view of the stock in the market's eyes.

Chapter 18

Old and past it

Experience is perceived as a valuable asset when it comes to managing money. The consensus view is that investing is a serious business that can get tricky, requiring a safe pair of hands and a cool head, especially when the market hits a rough patch: 'You can't buy experience'. And, from what I have seen over the years, you don't want to pay a premium for longevity or excessive experience. Unlike other parts of life where humans edit out the bad memories, sharemarket recollections are littered with errors of judgement or unfortunate circumstances.

Ask any old timer about his or her experiences in the market and he or she will quickly re-tell stories of the bear market of the 1970s, the crash of 1987 and the bursting of the tech bubble in 2000. Rarely does the person reminisce about the stunning performance of the market from 1992 to 2000 or the equally strong bull run from 2003 to 2007. If these exceptional periods do get some air time, then they are usually dismissed as periods of foolish optimism. Irish playwright and author Oscar Wilde possibly best captures the notion of sharemarket experience as the 'name we give our mistakes'.

Respected Australian fund manager Peter Morgan tells a story about when he was an inexperienced fund manager at Perpetual

Trustees in the early 1990s, when he was constantly questioned by financial planners about his junior status. According to Morgan the planners would say, 'You guys are young. You've never been through a recession. How are you going to cope with one?'

Morgan reflected, 'It was the worst thing anyone could have said because the worst had already happened. The market had collapsed and they wanted you to be more pessimistic than you were. In hindsight, we were just entering the greatest bull market of all time'.

From personal experience I would argue that Morgan's take on the early 1990s is not peculiar to that period. In the tech boom that grew out of the 1990s, there were many prophets of doom right from the start, arguing the technology revolution, based on the emergence of the internet, was a passing phase. Many of the market darlings of the era were loss makers that never lived up to the expectations of the ballooning market valuations. It was a re-run of the 1987 experience, when it took the Australian sharemarket eight years to recover from that crash.

Come March 2000, the tech bubble did burst. However, if you had got on board when Morgan suggested in the early 1990s and stuck with it all the way through the tech boom, you would have enjoyed a rise about 200 per cent in the Australian sharemarket. Even if you held on to your investments right through the tech bust that unfolded from 2000 to 2002, you would still have managed to finish at least 100 per cent ahead of when you had started a decade earlier.

I am not suggesting that you needed to load up purely on technology companies and roll the dice. In fact, when I joined Wilson Asset Management we were at the back end of the tech bubble, the blow-off stage inspired by the millennium bug. Our view was that the market had risen for many years and valuations were becoming ridiculous, particularly in the sectors of technology, media and telecommunications. There is one certainty when it comes to sharemarkets—all booms end and more often than not they end with a thud. The great uncertainty is the ultimate timing of the apocalypse. No-one can tell you. In these situations you don't waste your energy telling everyone that stocks are overvalued and it is going to be a slaughterhouse at some stage. Instead, you should keep your head, keep an eye on valuations and prepare for the end by moving into cash or moving into stocks that have fallen out of favour and look like great value.

A similar story could be told about the Australian mining boom that kicked off in 2003, gained attention in 2004 and ran right through until mid 2008. The party suddenly ended in July 2008 when investors realised the impending recession in the United States, triggered by the GFC, would affect the great commodity consumers, such as China. From 1 January 2003 until July 2008 the Australian All Materials index rose about 350 per cent, compared with a gain of 150 per cent in the overall market.

For many people like me, who had undertaken our investing apprenticeship in the 1990s, this was a sobering experience. In the 1990s, resources and precious metals were the pariahs of the market, because of global oversupply and soft demand. It was drummed into our heads that mining companies were highly volatile and, over the course of any cycle, failed to deliver the same returns as their industrial counterparts. Mining company valuations all depended on changes in supply and demand, and management had very little control over the outcome. The key message was stay away from mining stocks if you wanted to avoid a risky situation. Come 2003 and 2004 this advice was next to useless. The professional investors that started to outperform were those who had spent their career working as mining analysts or younger investors and had never experienced the 1990s. The young brigade in the market simply saw rising commodity prices, bulging earnings and cheap stocks. They got on board while people like me cautioned everybody about the risks associated with mining stocks. Even if we extrapolate their performance until today, post the GFC, the All Materials index is still up 250 per cent from 2003, while their industrial rivals are down close to 20 per cent. To borrow a line from Lebanese-American writer Khalil Gibran, 'A little knowledge that acts is worth infinitely more than much knowledge that is idle'.

Zombies

When the Australian sharemarket went into overdrive during 2006 and 2007, the consensus among commentators and market participants was that, when the music stopped playing, it would be young people who had never experienced a market crash or an economic recession who would find it hardest to cope. Generation Y had only experienced an era free of economic recession. Conventional wisdom was that they were self-centred, lazy and ill-prepared for the big downturn. In contrast, the people who had seen the 1987 crash and the severe recession of the early 1990s would be more resilient.

When the market started to cave in during January 2008 the speed of the decline was so swift it was hard to tell who was coping. However, by August with the Lehman Brothers collapse in the United States and markets on high alert, I noticed a few surprising things. Young people, in our office and elsewhere, seemed to be taking the crash in their stride. They were concerned, but they did not fret at any stage about their future or say the end of the world was on our doorstep. In contrast, older and more experienced people in the market were struggling. I will never forget walking along a street in Sydney and running into one of Australia's most revered and experienced investors. He looked more like a white sheet than a man in his fifties. He mumbled a few incoherent words of doom and the end is nigh, before shuffling off along the street. He was not handling the market collapse at all well. Perhaps he was too well connected and actually knew that conditions were worse than the rest of us had been led to believe. Regardless, I could never have contemplated giving him my money to manage in the sharemarket after that short chance meeting. He had taken the GFC personally and just couldn't see through to the other side.

I met many elder statesman of the market during that period who became virtually impotent. They found it hard to come to work and face the daily share price declines and the negative headlines. I gathered that many of them had a lot of their money in the sharemarket and, given their age, could not comprehend how they would recoup that wealth in the twilight of their working lives. They were staggering around the city like zombies. One incredibly wealthy individual who had been around markets for the best part of two decades virtually disappeared from his office for the best part of three months, only to return, some 20 kilograms heavier, when the market started to bounce.

In contrast the younger players were concerned but interested, and were not overcome by their personal situations. They kept cool under pressure. Many of these younger people lost their jobs during that period, but took the opportunity to travel abroad and enjoy themselves, buying time until the sharemarket regained a sense of composure. They were pragmatic about the whole debacle and viewed it as an experience rather than terminal. These observations are obviously generalisations, but I will never forget how unexpectedly people responded to those uncertain times.

For those who have been fortunate to go snow skiing or surfing, they will understand the increasing reluctance to fall as they grow older. As the years pass the fall seems further and hurts more than when you were a youngster. This fear of falling was endemic among sharemarket participants in 2008.

Where credit is due

On a stock level, experience can be a major handbrake. As I mentioned earlier, a stroll through the sharemarket tables reveals a graveyard scene with many stocks that were once market darlings now languishing without an exciting future. At some stage many of these fallen angels were part of our portfolio of stocks and obviously in the portfolios of many others. We watched them rise and then fall, resulting in severe battle scars and a high degree of caution. Instead of remaining optimistic and supremely confident, we would find ourselves dwelling on what could go wrong with a stock. This kind of experience means you may never go broke, but it also means you may never take the necessary risk to gain the full benefits of stock picking. It might also cloud your views, even when extreme valuations are appearing right before your eyes.

One such example of this was debt ledger group Credit Corp (see chapter 17). We weren't so much burned as charred by the crumbling share price from November 2007 to February 2009, which saw 97 per cent disappear off the stock's value. The stock bottomed out at 39 cents, with the market believing its billowing debt levels would see an administrator appointed soon. However, a fresh board breathed new life into the business, instigating a plan that staved off the banks and saw the share price begin to appreciate. At Wilson Asset Management, three of us discussed the future of the stock and whether it was worthwhile investing in again. The youngest and least experienced said it looked very exciting, and that we should buy some shares and keep a very close eye on the company's progress. Of the more experienced members, one was willing to buy the stock as long as it was below the net asset backing, but the other wasn't interested, saying it was a faulty business that had unusual accounting methods. Luckily youth won the day. The stock not only soared through its original asset backing of $1.60 a share, it posted several profit upgrades, and within two years had hit $6.00 a share. If you picked the bottom of 39 cents you were now boasting to your friends of a 1500 per cent gain. Experience blinded two people from the real story that was unfolding.

It would be inaccurate to claim that experience is a total waste of time. In fact there is nothing wrong with some experience, especially in volatile markets. However, people who have seen it all over many years seem to grow overly pessimistic and fear starts to gobble them up. It is not unlike sportspeople who find it harder as they get older because they know what can go wrong and become paralysed by the thought of failure. A younger, less experienced person, seasoned enough to identify an opportunity, but not hampered by ghosts of years past, is in the sweet spot. It is one of the main reasons that I decided to give the professional game away. The younger operators in the office were kicking goals and I was spending most of my time telling them what could go wrong. Occasionally it did go wrong, but that is part of being in the sharemarket. As humorist Don Marquis once said, 'An optimist is a guy that has never had much experience'.

Chapter 19

Smart money—bad results

A trusted sales technique employed by stockbrokers over the years to panic investors into buying or selling has been the smart money drill. It goes something like this: 'I can't say too much about what is going on, but suffice to say there has been some very smart money buying the stock in the last few days'. The natural conclusion for investors is that if the smart money is buying, then it must be a good sign and it is time to jump in. Alternatively, if the smart money is bailing out of a stock, you should follow suit. I can guarantee you that if you hang around the market long enough you will get hit with the sales line about the smart money. Every time I have asked who this smart money was, I have been met by a bland response that makes me feel silly for being so naive about who operates in the market.

So who is this mysterious smart money? Is there a small group of seriously intelligent, super rich people who hang around the market and get every call correct? Are they the billionaires who get access to all the good information ahead of anyone else and trade on it with stunning success? Or are they insiders who know exactly what is going on in a stock and your stockbroker is doing you a favour by bringing you inside the tent? This is all still a mystery to me.

You can safely assume that there is only one conclusion—there is no genuinely smart money in the market. Not one person has a strike rate of 100 per cent. There are so many stocks and so much information swirling around the market that it is virtually impossible for an individual to have sufficient information to make fully informed decisions at all times. Sure, every company has its insiders, who have a very clear line of sight, but this knowledge rarely goes beyond individual stocks. The fact is that these people are insiders and are probably loaded with information that is not generally available to the market and so should not be acted upon. I will leave that decision to those people.

> There is no genuinely smart money in the market.

I can think of many examples over the years when seriously rich individuals, perceived as smart money by the general market, have waded into a share only to watch it fall by the wayside as things start to turn sour for one reason or another.

Taking a punt

Highly successful Brisbane-based property developer Kevin Seymour comes to mind. Seymour proved to be a savvy sharemarket player, especially when he emerged as one of the major shareholders in the privatised Queensland TAB (UNiTAB). Under the management of Dick McIlwain, the stock proved to be a major success, with a significant cost reduction program and a well-priced takeover of the South Australian TAB, making millions and millions of dollars for Seymour. His fortune, which had been generated by developing property in south-east Queensland, was being overshadowed by his investment in UNiTAB. In the end, the company was taken over by Melbourne-based gaming group Tatts Group and McIlwain was invited to be CEO of the merged group, while Seymour snared a board seat. Tatts enjoyed a duopoly ownership of the highly profitable poker machine industry in Victoria and now it owned the stable Queensland and South Australian betting operations.

News that McIlwain would be at the helm of the merged group saw the share price spike higher, with Seymour's holding soaring towards $200 million. The ultra-conservative Victorian gaming group became an aggressive acquirer under McIlwain, with a string of deals, including a joint venture with Macquarie Bank into the exotic European gaming market. Seymour joined the share-buying party, spending just over $20 million acquiring 4.15 million shares at an average price of $5.04 in April 2007. At this stage Tatts' PE ratio had broken new territory skipping to over 20. Not bad for a mature business that needed to make high-risk offshore acquisitions to generate better than anaemic growth. As the overall market headed towards its multi-year peak, Seymour spent another $2.15 million on buying 500 000 shares in September 2007. This time he bought stock at $4.31 a share. As fellow shareholders of the Tatts, we cheered on Seymour's buying, thinking it was a sign that Tatts was travelling extremely well. I was now convinced Tatts was a tremendous investment, so much so that I went one step further by investing funds into a geared vehicle that held Tatts shares. For some reason I decided that I would follow the smart money and ignore the fact the company was trading at historically expensive levels and charting on a risky strategy.

As the market started to head south at a rate of knots in March 2008, Seymour turned seller, offloading 4.5 million shares at an average price of $3.70 a share. This seemed strange, given he had been so bullish only a few months earlier and had been prepared to pay up to 38 per cent more for his stock. On 10 April 2008 the Victorian government announced it was stripping Tatts and Tabcorp of their poker machine duopoly in the state from 2012. The share prices of both companies dived relentlessly. Tatts share price eventually settled just north of $2.00 a share. By mid 2011 the stock trades at $2.34, some 53 per cent below where Seymour was buying in 2007 (see figure 19.1, overleaf).

What can we deduce from the slick investor and board member Seymour? His purchases in 2007 were aggressive, but not fully informed. The real value in the company sat with the government's licensing discretion and not with management's ability to grow a global gaming business. Luckily, he decided to take a more conservative approach by offloading the stock he purchased for a loss of around $6 million. It could have been worse if he had held on. For us, our judgement had been misplaced and we recorded a major loss on our geared investment.

Figure 19.1: smart decisions—Tatts Group's share price from June 2006 to January 2009

Source: IRESS

A king's ransom

Another example of smart money not finding the mark was John Kinghorn's purchase of shares in 2008 of financial leasing group Allco. For many years Kinghorn had kept himself out of the public spotlight by avoiding investing in listed companies. He changed all that when he floated his RAMS Home Loans business in July 2007, selling 80 per cent of his holding to the public for the handy sum of $650 million. He retained his position as the largest shareholder in the group and installed himself as chair. The decline of RAMS is well documented, with the stock falling from its listed price of $2.50 to just 4.6 cents in June 2009 as the full effects of the GFC took hold.

The rapid decline of RAMS failed to dissuade Kinghorn from using some of his hard-earned dollars buying shares in Allco Financial Partners in late 2007 and early 2008. Allco, valued at more than $4 billion by the market in early 2007, was a high-flying company that specialised in financial engineering. The company had hit the headlines when it led a consortium of investors in making a takeover bid for Australia's number one airline, Qantas, in 2006. The takeover was struck at $5.60 a share and valued Qantas at a record price of $11 billion. The bid ultimately failed because of institutional shareholder resistance. Today Qantas shares are trading at just above $2.00 a share (see chapter 15).

When nervous investors started to flee all the financial engineering companies in early 2008, Allco's share price fell faster than a base jumper. Virtually all of the companies that fell into administration during that period firmly pointed the finger at evil short-selling investors for their problems, happily ignoring the truckloads of debt they had tipped into their businesses in the boom years from 2004 to 2007. Allco's executive chairman, David Coe, was possibly the most vocal of these critics of short selling.

As the Allco price tumbled from its high of more than $12.00 a share in late 2006 to just over $3.00 a share in early 2008, Kinghorn waded into the market, snapping up 25 million shares to take a hefty 6.8 per cent in the company. To the outside world Kinghorn was the smart money. He had originally formed Allco and had hired Coe as a young lawyer back in the early 1980s. Coe also sat on the board of Kinghorn's RAMS. In March 2008, Kinghorn stepped into the market again, buying more than 11 million shares to take his personal holding in Allco to just under 10 per cent. In total the Allco investment had cost Kinghorn close to $100 million. As the GFC unfolded, his investment sunk to zero with the administrators called in to the company in November 2008. There is no evidence that Kinghorn managed to offload any of his shares before the company received its death knock.

At the 'hart' of the matter

New Zealand businessman Graeme Hart has a remarkable track record of buying into companies, turning them around and then selling them off for enormous profits. From humble beginnings he has amassed a multi-billion dollar fortune, and there are no doubts that when it comes to business smarts, Hart has very few peers. However, this does not mean that he is immune from making mistakes.

In June 1997 Hart took a significant gamble in buying into the Australian conglomerate Burns Philp, which had narrowed its operations down over the years and become a branded global herbs and spices group. Hart grabbed 20 per cent of the company's shares at $2.50 a piece. By September that year Burns Philp announced a $700 million write down of its herbs and spices division and its debt covenants were on the verge of being breached. The company was forced to undertake a major capital raising, which Hart underwrote in a bid to average down his cost price into the group. By 1999 the Burns Philp share price had found a bottom at 4 cents. Hart had experienced a loss on his original investment of just over 98 per cent — enough to be his undoing.

To his enormous credit, Hart found a way to recapitalise Burns Philp, and with his trusty deputy, Tom Degnan, built the business up again into an attractive asset. Eventually, Hart engineered a profit from his original investment and has since parlayed this into other turnarounds, and his net worth is now estimated to be in excess of $6 billion. The outcome would have seemed like a pipe dream when the company was dissolving before his eyes only a few years before.

Investors who took Hart's original foray into Burns Philp as a green light to start buying the stock must be accused of being lazy and not looking at the finances carefully. If you had snapped up shares at $2.50 you would most likely have bailed out when the stock was heading south, unwilling to back the man again. Even with the company's recapitalisation, it would have been next to impossible to recoup your original investment given that the capital raising was offered in a limited version to the general public. The time to back Hart was not when he made his first foray into Burns Philp, but when things had fallen into a heap and the future was looking hopeless. As Degnan said in 1999 (when we went to see him on a company visit), we were the first people from the market to visit him in close to a year. The market had given up on a stock at a time when Hart and his team were putting in place a structure that would serve as the platform for a major run in the years to come.

There are others examples, such as billionaire Kerry Stokes buying into West Australian Newspapers Holdings only to be hit with a nasty capital loss. The famed Packer family has also suffered its share of losses in the form of telco groups One Tel and the unlisted Comindico. No-one avoids losses, no matter how smart or how informed they are.

Forget being smart, just keep your eyes open

Sure, there are always people who are aware what is going on in certain stocks. You only have to watch the price action of companies in the lead up to a major announcement, whether they be positive or negative. If bad news is about to hit the wires, then the insiders normally stop buying and the share price will slump. If good news, like an upgrade or a takeover is brewing, then someone, somewhere will know and the share price will jump higher.

This is a mug's game and is usually based on inside information. Besides being illegal, it is a lazy approach and it bears little if any fruit. It is impossible to regularly garner such accurate information about a company's activities. My experience tells me that if I am happy to buy a stock when I'm told the smart money is getting on board, then I am a soft target for a stockbroker to fill my boots when he or she has another client looking to get out of a stock. It is a lazy approach to investing and there are many alternatives that will deliver superior returns over time.

There are endless situations when you don't need to be labelled as smart to make money from the sharemarket. There are occasions where you cannot believe what is unfolding before your eyes. One such occasion was in 2008 in one of our funds—WAM Capital (see figure 19.2, overleaf). During the worst days of the GFC in February 2009, we had taken most of our bets off the table, where we planned to keep them until we thought the world had settled down and it was safe to go back into the market. Our average cash level over the years has been a weighty 29 per cent, but in late 2008 we cranked it up to a record 70 per cent. With maximum pessimism in the market and people being forced to offload shares because of margin calls from their lenders, WAM's share price slumped to trade at a 40 per cent discount to its asset backing. Effectively, this meant investors willing to buy into WAM were getting all of the stocks held in the fund plus 10 per cent of the cash for free.

There was absolutely no risk of losing your money, but if memory serves me correctly, only one major client called up to check he wasn't dreaming about the situation. He then started to buy WAM and managed to nearly double his money. I suppose it is easy to recognise an opportunity like this in hindsight, but a level head rather than smart money came out in front on that occasion. Sometimes even when these extreme valuation scenarios present themselves, the share price may still go down for some time, but patience and a belief in reading the financials will ultimately deliver a healthy profit.

Figure 19.2: stocks for free — WAM Capital's share price from January 2007 to January 2010

Source: IRESS

Chapter 20

Other myths

A whole book could be dedicated to debunking stockmarket myths. There are so many accepted sayings that just don't make sense and, moreover, sidetrack you from the ultimate goal—making a decent return on your capital. In this chapter I try to cover some of the more common myths and explain why you should try to ignore them when you are investing in companies.

Timing

There is a pet saying among long-term investors that goes 'it is time in the market and not market timing that matters'. In other words, you shouldn't waste your time trying to pick the eyes out of market tops and bottoms because of their uncertain nature. Instead, you should try to buy a portfolio of quality stocks, sticking with them through thick and thin and, over an extended period, be rest assured you will achieve superior returns as the market moves higher.

While this philosophy works in bull markets, it is patently untrue at other times. An American investor who purchased stocks in the middle of 1929 would have had to wait until 1954 to recoup his capital value. When inflation is taken into account it wasn't until 1960 before the investor achieved a real return. That would be of little consequence if the investor had dived into the market with borrowed money when he was 60 years of age. Similarly, if an investor got caught up in the magic of the sharemarket in 1966, he or she would have had to wait for 16 years to break even. That is long-term investing at its most patient. Finally, those who thought the only way was up for the Australian sharemarket in 2007 must be kicking themselves four years later, with the market still around 30 per cent off its highs. This painful lesson was felt by a large group of investors who raced to throw money into the market after the Australian federal government relaxed taxation laws for superannuation investors back in 2007. Those same people may have been nearing retirement and now sit on a loss that has kept them in the workforce well beyond their original intentions.

The best stock pickers on Earth are going to struggle to deliver a better return than a novice if they dive into the market at the wrong time. For example, a genius stock picker who ploughed funds into the Australian sharemarket in September 1987 would have had to wait at least 15 years to start cranking out returns superior to those of an investor who simply bought an index fund that replicated the top 50 stocks in mid 1992.

The reality sometimes is that timing is everything. There are no guarantees—not even if you buy a conservative portfolio of shares and then sit and wait. Earlier, I made the assertion that there is no easier game on Earth than playing the sharemarket, based upon the fact that you can be continuously wrong in your stock picking and still be able to come out in front. This comment is correct, but it does require some support from the number one ingredient of a great investor—common sense. If a market has risen above the long-term average for many years or has risen sharply over only a few years, investors must show some caution. If a market has been on its knees for an extended period then the chances of its crashing are significantly reduced. What is wrong with steering your investments to cash if you believe the market is overvalued? There will always be a time to re-enter the market, but at least you won't go broke holding on and gritting your teeth.

Warren Buffett says, 'If [investors] insist on trying to time their participation in equities, they should try to be fearful when others are greedy and greedy when others are fearful'. This is a statement that many contrarian investors (investors who always try to do the opposite to the overall market) and Buffett-philes love to roll out, because it makes a tremendous amount of sense. The problem for the average investor, however, is working out when others are being greedy and when they are being fearful. If you believed that investors were being greedy and you sold your entire portfolio of shares in 1996 when US Federal Reserve Bank chairman Alan Greenspan said that sentiment had reached 'irrational exuberance', then you would have missed out on one of the greatest ever three and half year runs by the US sharemarket. If you believed that people were being fearful in March 2008 when Bear Sterns was rescued by the US government, then you would have been wrong, as the GFC was just getting started. The saying about market timing is correct in the sense that you will never be able to pick those tops and bottoms, but there is no evidence that the best course of action is to ameliorate the situation by sitting and suffering. Use your common sense and if you miss the last surges of a bull market or the first leg of a bounce, then so be it. If anyone asked me what one skill gives Warren Buffett his investment edge, I would not say his superior intelligence or his grasp of numbers. Instead I would say it his unique ability to sum up a situation, distil it to its key points and then apply immense common sense. This is the same common sense judgement he uses to select the best managers to run his businesses. In other words his judgement is superior to others because he is able to stay calm and consider the bigger picture. He won't always get it right but, unless his approach changes some time soon, he will never go broke by borrowing enormous amounts of money to buy into a market that looks and is expensive. When it comes to market timing, it would be wise to use some of this judgement to ensure you don't wade into the market only to go backwards for up to decades. In the final section of the book we will discuss how markets have historically behaved, which will hopefully give you some perspective.

Headlines are always wrong

Sharemarket professionals love to stick the boot into the media. I'm not exactly sure why — perhaps it is to make themselves feel better or because these investors love to find contrarian signs so they can tell people it is the right time to buy or sell stocks. Some investors and stockbrokers actually place ill-timed newspaper headlines on the front of their promotional documents in a bid to show how clever and contrarian you need to be to make money out of the sharemarket. I believe the reality is different. Newspaper journalists and financial reporters on television, like all other participants in the equity market, get some of their predictions wrong and get some of them right. A close analysis is most likely to reveal a 50 per cent success ratio — no different from a reasonable investor. Unfortunately, there is no empirical evidence to back up my view.

Some contrarians like to pull out magazine covers from the 1970s that declared capitalism was dead, following a protracted bear market and an economy in recession. We all now know that capitalism survived and prospered, but you must remember that it took until another major recession in the early 1980s to clean up the system and get capitalism back on its feet. Those who went the contrarian tack back in the mid 1970s when the headlines blared, would have experienced a rocky ride for five or six years before any money could be made. In fact the US stockmarket had five separate falls of more than 18 per cent or more during the period from 1976 to 1982. Maybe the headlines were an exaggeration, but they proved slightly more accurate in terms of summing up the situation than some investors would like us to believe.

Another unfortunate call came from *The Economist* magazine in March 1999, which forecast that crude oil might fall to $US5 a barrel. At the time, oil was in the doldrums trading at a generational low of just $US12 a barrel. *The Economists*'s call proved to be the bottom for the oil price, which was reached in late 1999, though it eventually climbed to $US147 a barrel in 2008. Sometimes the press, like everyone else, manages to make a bad call, and no-one is exempt. I have clear memories of occasions when I have bought shares in companies at the peak of their price and sold them when they were hitting their bottom. Any investor who has been in the game more than a few months would be lying if they denied the same experience. I also clearly remember that when the price of oil surged towards its 2008 record, US stockbroker Goldman Sachs went around the globe calling the commodity up to $US200 a barrel. Instead it turned south, before hitting support at just $US30 a barrel.

The press was very early to alert the investing public of the looming tech bubble that was forming in the late 1990s. Endless newspaper columns were dedicated to this call in the late 1990s. The newspapers were also quick to pounce upon the housing problem in the United States in 2007 when low-paid people across America were readily lent money from investment banks when they had little to no chance of paying the money back. This developed into the subprime crisis, which triggered the GFC some 18 months later. Despite the media's constant warnings, the market snoozed through the subprime debacle all the way through 2007, as investors pushed stocks higher.

It would be reckless to base your investment decisions on a contrarian view to the media. Once again this is an indolent approach that will deliver you no edge whatsoever over the market. Instead I would spend my time concentrating on the fundamentals, such as the overall market PE ratio and the yield being generated. If the market is trading outside its historical range of PEs, then start to get interested in either selling or buying.

Market wisdom

Professional investors and sharemarket commentators commonly describe the sharemarket as a discounting mechanism. What exactly does this mean? It is industry jargon for the market's unique ability to look forward, and price in good or bad news today, rather than waiting for it to actually happen in the real world. This is what is affectionately known as collective market wisdom. There is little room to argue the market does attempt at all times to predict the future, as individual investors desperately get a head start on their competition. History shows the market has been able to predict economic recoveries over the years, following a tried and true approach of buying shares when the central bank cuts rates. Conversely, investors have generally picked economic slow downs ahead of time, with the sharemarket heading lower a year or so ahead of the general economy working its way through a recession.

On other occasions the sharemarket has got it shockingly wrong. The lead up to the 1987 crash in Australia was a classic example, where investors simply ignored excessive valuations and, pumped up on debt, bought any story that sounded interesting or exciting. This all came to an end in October 1987, when the market fell 25 per cent in one day and a total of 49 per cent in about four months. It took the Australian sharemarket eight years to reclaim the highs it had reached in 1987.

Prophets of doom were lining up to tell everyone during the late 1990s that the tech bubble was about to burst in a similar fashion to the tulip bubble in Holland of 400 years earlier. The market simply ignored the warnings and the American S&P 500 sharemarket index rose to its most expensive valuation in history in early 2000. The average PE ratio paid by investors rose higher than 25, which was 75 per cent higher than the long-term average. The tech-laden Nasdaq got so expensive in early 2000 that, 11 years on, it is still only about half that value. It could take 20 to 25 years for the Nasdaq to reclaim its record high.

In these examples it is not so much collective market wisdom as collective market stupidity at work. As mentioned earlier, if a market or stock looks expensive and you cannot justify holding it because of the low yield, then don't fight the momentum, just sell it and move to the sidelines until the market catches up and realises it has been foolish. This might take some time, even years, to eventuate. Don't panic, because there are plenty of other opportunities and you will never go broke selling early.

> You will never go broke selling early.

Judgement is not a myth

If I was to leave investors with a message from this section of the book, it is to exercise sound judgement. When brokers and other participants provide esoteric reasons for buying a company's shares, or even the overall market, make sure you do more than accept the suggestion at face value. Go back and do some hard work on the numbers and some background checking on the management team. If a stock has been rising at a rapid rate for some time on the back of moderate earnings growth, make sure that you work out the valuation the market is attributing to it. Don't simply buy because it has a good feel and you have received a tip from someone who already owns the stock. Take on board the tip, do your own work and then trust your own judgement. Be confident and if you get it wrong move onto the next opportunity that presents itself.

Part V
Are professionals better?

Over the last 30 years the growth of Australia's superannuation pool—now surging past the trillion dollar mark—has created a significant industry of well-heeled money managers. Despite a relatively small local economy, the Australian savings industry is the fourth largest in the world and a hot bed for management fees. Are professionals worth their fees and can individuals outperform them? In this section we will attempt to answer these questions.

Chapter 21

Professional versus punter

In my thousands of conversations with investors over the years, two primary reasons have been put forward as to why they have entrusted their money to professional managers. The first is that they simply don't have the time to dedicate to analysing stocks to make informed decisions. The second is that they find the market confusing and are worried about stepping on those wretched landmines that professional investors like to tell everyone about. In other words, they have swallowed the view that the market is a dangerous place and you need to be careful.

In regards to time limitations, this is a personal choice. If you are busy with a full-time job, family or other interests, then it would be foolish to think you can regularly pick stocks successfully without having to spend some time working them out. My personal view is that you don't have to knock yourself out with endless hours of research, but finding adequate time is necessary. For those who are constantly squeezed for investment time, it is worth your while trying to find the right fund manager.

The second reason is, for the most part, a furphy. Everything in life can be categorised as dangerous if it is spun a certain way. Driving a car is terribly dangerous, but a long list of road rules, the need for a drivers licence and a quotient of common sense limit the number of accidents and fatalities. The sharemarket is no different, so don't be afraid of the market and make sure that you set yourself up to ensure you don't fail.

So who has the advantage — the professionals or the ordinary person on the street? Legendary US fund manager Peter Lynch dedicates two entire books to the philosophy that the man on the street can outsmart and outperform the professional on Wall Street. While this is a great story, I think it is exaggerated. I believe the race is neck and neck, with both groups having distinct advantages and disadvantages. If pushed to make a decision I would fall down on Lynch's side when he argues that the person on the street should come out ahead if they can allocate enough time to the job and implement the right approach.

Professionals in straightjackets

History shows that professional investors have found it difficult to add value by beating the sharemarket over an extended period. If a manager does a phenomenal job and beats the market over many years, as value investing legend Robert Maple-Brown has, then it is usually by only 1 or 2 per cent per year. Most other operators have stunning periods, only to trip at some stage, resulting in a failure to outperform over the long haul. In addition, returns to investors delivered by professionals are diluted by fees and other costs that would not be incurred by an individual. When you consider the small capitalisation funds, the results look somewhat rosier, but the volatility among this group is, for the most part, higher, owing to the risky nature of these companies. I love this end of the market, and I invite eager investors to prowl around at this end of town.

It is important here to understand that I am referring to the most common type of professional investor or fund manager — the long-only institution. These are institutional managers who have to stay fully invested and cannot short sell securities. Other management styles have emerged in recent years, following a trend in the northern hemisphere, but for the most part long-only institutions still dominate the investment landscape in Australia.

While professional managers have proven it is tremendously difficult to outperform the overall market over protracted periods, I am not a believer in the efficient market hypothesis (EMH). In summary, this theory states that it is impossible to beat the market because stockmarket efficiency causes existing share prices to incorporate and reflect all relevant information. The theory proposes that stocks always trade at fair value, making it impossible for investors to either purchase undervalued stocks or sell stocks for inflated prices.

The reason investors fail to outperform has nothing to do with the perfect dissemination of information. How else can you explain stocks that are trading below their cash backing, such as WAM Capital did in early 2009, or stocks trading at 80 times forecast future earnings, as Cisco Systems did back in 1999? Underperformance squarely rests with barriers the investors put in front of themselves, such as the size of the funds and the individual stock weightings. Alternatively, underperformance springs from the fact that we are all human and we are prone to make mistakes and wander off course occasionally.

So what makes it so hard for professional investors to generate significant outperformance? Essentially most funds are set up to equal the market, not beat it. Fund managers who garner their funds from large piles of the general public's superannuation have their hands tied from the outset by a set of rules and restrictions that are foisted upon them. No-one wants to take a scintilla of risk when it comes to super.

> Most funds are set up to equal the market, not beat it.

Cashless

For a start, most superannuation management mandates require the money to be invested in the market, even if a manager is nervous about the market, he or she cannot sell stocks and raise cash that could be used to buy stocks when a downturn comes. Instead, they have to have 90 per cent, or even 95 per cent, of their funds invested at all times. I know from personal experience that this restriction can save you from a poor decision by moving into cash just as the market starts to head north. We felt the full brunt of this in 2004 when we thought the Australian sharemarket looked expensive and was due for a pullback. Laden with cash we watched the market march higher for the next three years.

However, the fund manager's inability to move out of the market is a key limitation. During the GFC, for example, a fund that had to be invested to a high level in shares and could not short stocks (long only fund) had virtually no form of protection for its capital, apart from moving out of riskier stocks into defensive ones. This proved to be of only limited use when the markets around the globe hit the skids. Investors had no option but to watch their savings drain away.

Index handbrake

The other straightjacket professionals have to wear comes in the form of indexing—an institutional fund manager has to match their portfolio with the index they are following. For example, a manager who is following the ASX S&P 100 index must attempt to copy that index in terms of names and weightings. The manager attempts to outperform the index by going overweight or underweight certain stocks. For example, if BHP forms 15 per cent of the index, but the manager feels that BHP is a poor investment at the time due to overvaluation or worsening industry conditions, he or she might go underweight BHP and only invest 13 per cent of the fund in the mining giant. This sets up the strange situation where a manager might prefer not to be invested in a stock, for a reason such as valuation, management or macro-economic conditions, but still has to own it. In the BHP example, the manager's holding would still make it the biggest stock in the portfolio. A survey of the top managers would reveal that indexing is the greatest hindrance to their performance and the most despised aspect of professional investing. It makes it difficult for them to outperform by any decent margin. It is analogous to restricting Formula 1 drivers to driving at just 100 kilometres per hour.

Indexing can also force a manager to own a stock that is incredibly expensive. A company may have grown at a staggering rate and now trades on a PE ratio of more than 20, compared with its long-term average of 12. Because the company would then have an increased market capitalisation, the manager is forced to buy more of its shares, because of the restrictions of indexing. Similarly, a stock may have fallen on difficult times, and because its share price has declined it starts to look interesting. A long only fund that is handcuffed to the index will be forced to sell this stock down because of lower capitalisation, rather than buy it because the valuation is now attractive.

A manager who strays too far from his or her benchmark index will be viewed as taking on excessive risk. This will upset many of those people who decide which manager is allocated superannuation funds to manage. Consequently, if the manager starts to underperform for any period, money will start to flow out the door. Consultants have an aversion to risk.

Individual investors do not have these problems. A middle-aged couple I know who love the market embark on a two- to four-month trip each year. They like caravanning to remote places around Australia. For the rest of the year, while at home in Queensland, they actively follow the market by reading, researching, talking to people and following certain fund managers. Over the years they have pumped out returns that would make any professional investor blush. While they are away on the road they either put all their money in cash investments, or sink their money into a fund run by managers they like. They have great flexibility. They also took great delight in telling me every six months when we visited them in Brisbane how they had outperformed our funds over the course of the year. A fact that shows the small guy can easily match it with the professionals. More importantly, the couple are not hamstrung by a set of rules that force them to invest in the market and hold a certain weight in individual stocks.

Bigger is worse

The funds management industry, for the most part, is about getting bigger. A manager—whether owned by a bank, insurance company or an individual—aims to grow the size of their funds under management to increase the fees it generates. The vast majority of funds managers strike their fees as a percentage of the money they have under management. So the game is about getting more funds under management and not necessarily performing for the investors. Generally, investor performance will lead to money inflows and more fees, but eventually every successful manager is hampered by size, especially in a market as small as Australia's.

Why is size a problem? If you are the elephant in the room everyone can see you coming and going. For a large fund manager to make a meaningful addition to its overall fund size it has to take significantly larger positions in a stock than a manager that has fewer funds. This creates several difficulties. First, when the elephant decides to buy a stock it has to buy a hell of a lot of it. It starts buying and continues to do so for extended periods, supporting the share price and, on many occasions, forcing the price upwards until the day it stops buying. As the stock moves higher because of the elephant's buying, many smaller players in the market take the opportunity to sell their shares.

Once the elephant has completed buying a stock, the second possible problem comes into play—how to sell the investment without crushing the share price. For example, if you own 15 per cent of a company whose shares are relatively illiquid, it could take months for you to offload the stock completely. The weight of this selling could result in the share price being forced lower over time. I have lost count of the amount of times we participated in a sell down from a large shareholder in a stock at a discount to the prevailing share price, only to see it pop higher when the line was cleared.

There are some fund managers, such as Perpetual in Australia, that have overcome many of their size problems, but for most investors size is a restriction that ensures the manager can't regularly outperform its designated index. As an individual you don't have to worry about being the elephant in the room. If you do happen to be the elephant, then maybe you have made enough money already and you should start spending it.

Wilson Asset Management, as a small fund manager, actively sought out stocks that had fallen on hard times and had been deserted by institutional investors. If there were signs the company was turning around, then we could jump on board and, over time, enjoy the share price appreciation as the bigger investment managers waded back into the stock. Conversely, the squeeze play of being in a small stock with an elephant who wanted to get out could be painful and detrimental to performance. So when you are planning to invest in a stock at the small end of the market, ask your stockbroker to work out who the top 20 investors are so you can consider that in your decision–making process.

The fee structure that rewards size of capital invested also has the detrimental effect of forcing managers to spend large slices of their time marketing to new and existing investors. This is not ideal and it has led to the rising importance of marketing teams in the larger institutions around the country. I am yet to meet a money manager who loves to hang out with a member of their marketing team, and vice versa. They have different objectives and neither understands the other's job. This is not an ideal scenario and can cause a significant distraction for investing professionals. The private investor does not have to think about marketing his or her product, because they do not receive a fee for managing their own money. Fundamentally, a private investor can concentrate on getting the best possible return for the amount of risk they are prepared to take on. In other words they are focused on what they should be focused on — which is ironic, given that professional investors are supposed to have more time at their disposal to pick the eyes out of the market.

Professionals go boom when the market goes bust

The structure that professional investors operate in is also suspect when it comes to market extremes. In a bull market that has lasted for many years, such 1992 to 2007, the general public start to get wind of the party that is happening. Money floods into funds that have performed strongly in the preceding years. Given that most funds have to be invested to a certain percentage, this money must be put to work in the sharemarket, buying stocks, even though they are significantly more expensive than they were a few years earlier—when no-one was that interested in buying. The fund manager is forced to buy more of the same stocks it already owns, at a time when valuations are stretched and when normally it would be contemplating selling. Eventually the market has a bad year and the people who rushed into the mature bull market end up with egg on their faces and significant losses, and the manager carries the can, producing some unsatisfactory performance numbers.

At the other end of the scale, money has a habit of leaking out of funds when the market has fallen over an extended period. In the initial stages of a bear market, investors can stomach the declines. However, as the bear market continues, the patience evaporates. Investors start to redeem their money, forcing the manager to sell stocks to fund the withdrawals just at a time when the prices of companies are the cheapest they have been in many years, and the chance to go bargain hunting disappears. This happened during the second half of 2008 and in early 2009 as the market came crashing down with the GFC.

More often than not these inflows and outflows are detrimental to the performance of fund managers. This is not a hurdle that an individual investor has to jump over.

What you miss out on

The large fund manager, though, is not at a complete disadvantage to the person on the street. In fact he or she holds a few aces that a smaller player just can't match. The first of these, and the most obvious, is that a professional manager is paid to turn up to work every day of the week to assess the market and its stocks. In comparison, the retail investor does not get paid to spend all day, every day looking at stocks. Only a small percentage of private investors are privileged enough to have enough wealth to have a clear slate to investigate the sharemarket full time. Finally, when a deal that will deliver a sure fire profit is on, the first call will go to the person who hands out the most in brokerage fees, and that will always be the professional who trades a billion dollar fund every day of the week. This is highly profitable in terms of stock placements and the sale of block lines of stock.

Speaking to the people that matter

Without doubt the single most crucial decision an investor has to make when picking stocks is a judgement call on company management. A brilliant manager or management team can make the world of difference to the performance of a company, while a poor management team can do untold damage and destroy shareholder wealth. It never fails to amaze me how destructive a management team can be in what seems like a perfectly good business.

A prime example of management disparity over the years has been in the supermarket industry, where Woolworths consistently beats its main rival, Coles. Both have a massive footprint across the nation, both have phenomenal purchasing power and both have ample capital to implement their plans, but Woolworths has delivered superior returns to its shareholders from 1995 to 2008. Most analysts have attributed the gulf in performance to the quality of the management teams. Since 2008, however, Coles has been taken over by Western Australian conglomerate Wesfarmers, and sweeping changes have been implemented, the most obvious of which has been an overhaul of senior management and an improvement in the culture. Coles is now beginning to close the gap on Woolworths and Wesfarmers investors have enjoyed an improving share price.

Management is a mystery to everyone

How do we assess management of a company? This is the $64 million question that many investors find incredibly difficult. If I was to pinpoint the single most significant shortfall of the fund manager, it is his or her ability to rate management effectively (see chapter 15). The fund manager struggles with this concept because he or she is not trained, and does not have the innate ability, to judge other people's management skills and characteristics. The professional investor is trained to analyse numbers and to second guess the sentiment of the overall sharemarket. Australian fund managers generally rely on financial results to rate management.

Rarely if ever does a fund manager ask a company manager about the culture of the company, the values they hold or who the company manager considers to be the most important stakeholders in the organisation. All of these topics are pivotal to forming a view on management and the future prospects of the company. To concentrate solely on the numbers is dangerous because numbers never tell the complete story. An unreliable or shrewd manager can make the numbers sing for quite a time, but eventually, if there are flaws in the individual, then they will affect the company and the shareholders will suffer — especially in large companies, where underperformance can take years to surface in the accounts.

The company visit

Despite their inability to judge management properly, professional investors have the colossal advantage over the person on the street of being able to regularly meet management at various levels. When trying to determine whether to invest in a company, a big driver in the decision-making process is the interview of the management team. The interview is not about garnering inside information: it's about assessing the capabilities of the men and women paid to run the company that you have invested in, or are considering an investment in. While sitting across the table from management you will be able to get a fix on whether they can answer questions competently about the strategic and financial fundamentals of the company. You will also be able to see their body language. Do they look stressed? Do they fail to make eye contact when asked a difficult question? Do they cross their arms and avoid answering certain questions? Do they behave arrogantly? All of these factors are crucial to a company's fortunes and for the person in the street the lack of an interview is a major liability.

Peter Lynch, legendary American fund manager and author of *One Up On Wall Street*, has suggested that a retail investor could interview the company if they so desired by simply calling the head office and asking to see the investor relations person. Our former croupier Peter Proksa has done exactly that, but he sits in the privileged position of having enough capital to be a full-time sharemarket investor. For the rest of us, do not give up; instead, attempt to conduct your own interviews. The reality, however, is the professional will always get a better hearing.

Unforgettable visits

My best guess is that between 1998 and 2011, I attended about 3000 one-on-one meetings or group presentations with companies. Some were non-events; many helped to solidify a view; and a percentage were so clear cut that I didn't need to even bother with the financials and made up my mind on the spot. Let's review some of the latter.

Motorcycles are not for me

On a trip to Perth in 2009, Chris Stott and I dropped in to see a company called V-Moto. The business was unique in that it was the only listed motor scooter manufacturer in Australia. When a Sydney stockbroker suggested that we visit the company I was sceptical, because I was suspicious the company needed to raise money. As a rule, though, we always went into meetings with an open mind, especially when we had never visited the company before.

V-Moto's head office was on St Georges Terrace, the central business street in Perth. We went up in the lift, rang the buzzer and were greeted by the CEO, who seemed quite genial. He ushered us into the modern premises, which had traditional offices divided by glass to the left and a large door to the right. We turned right through the door into a large, open-plan room, big enough to kick a football in. The first sight that struck us was a stunning view of the

Swan River. Standing in front of the view was a life-sized cardboard cut-out of model Megan Gale in a bikini. We all sat down in the comfortable plush leather lounge feeling anything but relaxed, with Gale staring down on us. The CEO waxed lyrical about the prospects of the company and the enormous market they were going to tap into. We listened intently. We soon realised there were other smaller pictures pinned up around the room of another scantily clad female draped over one of the company's scooters. The CEO explained that she was the marketing manager and had put herself into the promotional material to save money! The room could only be compared to a cross between a US college fraternity house and an Aussie mechanic's garage. To this day I have been baffled as to why the company had the cut-out figure of supermodel Gale in the room, on display for investors.

Both Chris and I soon knew that we would never invest in V-Moto (see figure 21.1). In addition to the shock we received when we toured the office, the company was in an early phase of its development and had failed to make any meaningful profits. It needed money to put its business plan into operation and from our point of view it was a company that had listed far too early in its development. V-Moto did raise $6 million at 20 cents a share a few months after our visit. Today it trades at just 2 cents a share.

Figure 21.1: free-wheeling — V-Moto's share price from January 2009 to June 2011

Source: IRESS

Cash on the coast

The boom market of 2003–07 went just long enough to produce a bunch of highly questionable entrepreneurial companies that had managed to capture the imagination of the sharemarket. Representing the glamorous sandy strip of the Gold Coast was MFS Limited. MFS started out life as McLaughlin Financial Services, a lender of debt to property developers in south-east Queensland. A couple of switched-on lawyers realised they could advertise for money, paying 8 per cent to investors, pool the funds raised and lend it to property developers, who were happy to borrow at 11 or even 12 per cent. MFS would take the margin. A nice business, especially on the Gold Coast, where a long list of property developers found it difficult to get all their funding from conservative retail banks.

When we first met MFS in late 2003, Philip Adams was the front person. Phil usually attended meetings in a shiny silver suit with an open neck shirt and pointy shoes, looking the part of a Gold Coast businessman. He was a likeable guy who did his best to answer all our questions. Our first meeting came about because the company wanted to raise fresh capital by getting us and other professional investors to commit to buying their listed options and then exercising these options to raise fresh capital. We had never really made any money out of underwriting company options, so we shied away from the deal. MFS's share price was hovering between $1.20 and $1.50 at the time.

We met Phil again on several occasions as MFS rapidly expanded its business and its profile. In addition to its burgeoning financial services business, the company had splashed out on a series of tourism assets, which it planned to aggregate before re-selling them to a third party with a management contract attached. MFS was to be the manager and would collect the fees. It became known as Queensland's mini Macquarie Group. The company was aggressive and had caught the eye of some major stockbrokers, who saw an opportunity to raise money for the group as it went on a buying spree.

In 2005 I turned up at a group presentation to find that Philip Adams had disappeared and had been replaced by his partner,

Michael King. Adams had been shipped off to run the group's new but booming operations in Dubai. Anyone who was anyone in the business world was racing to get a toe hold in Dubai. I thought this was strange, because we had always been told that King had never enjoyed the spotlight of the sharemarket and its pesky investors. Obviously he had changed his mind. It struck me that King was much more aggressive than Phil and by the end of the meeting I had realised it was King who had been driving the bus all this time.

In early 2006, I attended MFS's profit presentation, hosted by a large stockbroking firm. The room was packed with fund managers intrigued by the mushrooming company whose share price had risen a hefty 200 per cent in just a bit over two years. Michael King was firmly in charge now and the group had bought into a string of travel agents and accommodation-letting outfits.

The profit result for the period was about in line with market expectations at $25 million. However, the operating cash flow told a different story, sitting at less than $1 million. King opened the presentation by concentrating on the prepared material, only to be interrupted by some questions about the sickly looking cash flow. He responded in the most curious fashion, saying that he had briefed the host stockbroker's analyst about the cash flow statement before the meeting and any questions on the issue should be directed to him. This led to a 10-minute conversation about why King couldn't answer the question for himself, given there were shareholders in the room. I have never attended a presentation where a company has told shareholders to ask a broker about the key numbers in the report. As the questions then came thick and fast, King stuck firmly to his original answer. There was now tension in the room but eventually King shrugged off the annoying cash flow questions and hurriedly moved back to the prepared material.

Just as he got started again, a fund manager, Karl Siegling from Cadence Capital, running late walked into the room, sat down and immediately interrupted King with a question about the cash flow. Heads dropped around the room in embarrassment and you could almost see the steam coming out of King's ears. He raised his voice, telling the fund manager in no uncertain terms that he needed to talk to the analyst about the cash flow and he would not field any further questions about the issue. Siegling seemed miffed by the incident and rightly so.

From that presentation onwards I, and probably many others in that room, decided we would not invest in MFS. King's deflection of a question about a fundamental element of the business and the anger in his voice sent warning signals to anyone who wanted to pay attention. In my mind you didn't need to do any further research.

Later in 2006, with the sharemarket boom hitting top gear and striding towards its inevitable climax, the market had forgiven King and had rejoined the MFS party. The share price had shrugged off its previous slump and was heading towards $5.00. King, hungry for more acquisitions, pushed the button to raise fresh equity. The money came flooding in and the company raised a healthy $120 million at a share price of $4.55.

Out of curiosity, I attended a presentation given while the company was raising the money. King no longer looked angry. Instead his new approach was to totally dismiss investors and he made it clear he was unwilling to answer any questions about the financials. The written presentation again raised issues about the cash flow, but King just said in a flippant manner to the audience that we could read about the numbers ourselves and come to our own conclusions. He made it clear that he wasn't going to bother with them here. He was more interested in getting the money in the door to keep on building his Gold Coast–based empire.

In early 2008, MFS was one of the first victims of the emerging GFC. It was virtually here one day and gone the next. In a bizarre period of about two weeks, the company made a string of announcements that included plans to de-merge and a possible sale of its tourism business, followed by the sale of its financial assets. The market was completely bemused by what was happening. Eventually the company went into trading halt. It re-listed two days later, with King fronting an investor conference call that outlined a de-merger and the raising of $500 million. Irate Queensland stockbroker Charlie Green tore strips off King about blind-siding the market by the capital raising. King responded with interest. During the conference call the stock plummeted from around $3.60 to just 71 cents a share. It was a massive destruction of value in such a short space of time. The stock should have been suspended during the call but investors took advantage of the oversight and dumped their shares quick smart. Soon after, MFS's shares were suspended again and have never reappeared. The company was then placed in administration and the management team was forced to step aside.

Our own Gordon Gekko

In the heady days of 1998 and 1999 the Australian sharemarket got a small taste of the technology boom that had gripped the United States for the best part of a decade. Suddenly Australia had technology, telecommunications and media companies taking off. It was an exciting time, and a surfeit of new floats appeared as investors rushed to get a piece of the action.

Among the highest profile names of that period was telecommunications group Davnet (see figure 21.2). The company was based in Melbourne and specialised in providing telecommunications products to companies in the city using microwave signals through line of sight. Revenue had started to trickle in but the company had made no real profits to speak of. There were big plans to move beyond the southern capital to the Sydney market and then the more lucrative market of Hong Kong. We had participated in several of Davnet's early capital raisings, enjoying a profit on each occasion as the market got carried away with any story associated with technology. Davnet's share price began to rocket higher as the century moved towards a close. As the share price headed north we decided the company was far too expensive to buy shares in and the market was becoming too volatile to play with any safety.

Even though we had left the share register some time earlier, Davnet managing director Stephen Moignard was kind enough to drop in and give us an update on how the company was going when he was in Sydney. He wore a pin-striped suit and sported a slicked-back hair style, and when he took off his coat revealed a pink shirt, gold cufflinks and a pair of wide braces. He started to outline the company's ambitious plans to take its technology into Asia, with

Hong Kong the first stop on a world domination tour. He talked energetically, pausing only to ask if I minded him smoking, at which point he pulled out a long, fat cigar, lit up and took a deep draw, throwing his head back and puffing the billowing smoke into the air. I sat there, without uttering a word, thinking that I was talking to Gordon Gekko, straight out of the movie *Wall Street*. The tech boom was reaching its peak and it was time to be very careful.

Davnet's fortunes turned sour once the tech bubble burst in 2000. By 2001 Moignard had departed and not long afterwards Davnet ceased to exist, with the core of the business being picked up by Geoff Lord's technology service business, UXC.

Figure 21.2: Gordon Gekko in Australia — Davnet's share price from January 1999 to December 2001

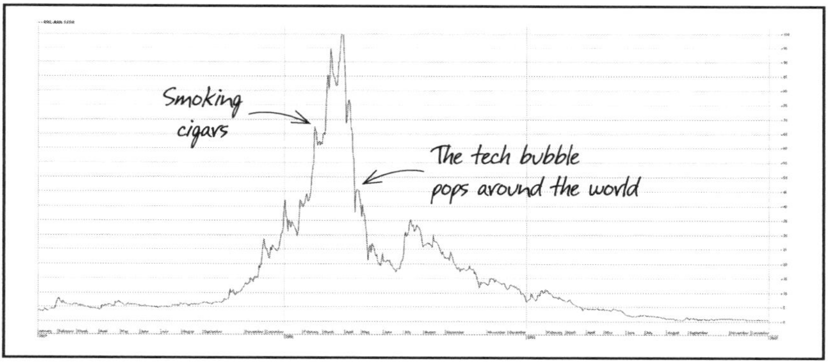

Source: IRESS

Getting the right message face to face

I can recall hundreds of meetings over the years that made immediate impressions on me. On many occasions the managing director of a company would get aggressive in response to benign questions. One time I was accused of not being good enough to conduct the interview: I was underprepared and that wasn't acceptable to the managing director. That company survived but it has underperformed dramatically in recent years. Another managing director accused me of ambushing him when I brought a colleague along to the meeting.

That company went into administration. A high-profile CEO spent a large part of our meeting striding around and around the table we were sitting at, or at least we were supposed to be sitting at. This felt strange, and it made us dizzy. Sure enough, the company has fallen on difficult times of late, requiring shareholders to bail it out of debt problems.

Don't forget to dress up

The company interview also allows professional investors to assess a manager's dress sense. Some people would argue that stock picking is not a fashion parade. I would counter that by saying every bit of information that you collect about management and managers can influence your investment decision, including what clothes, jewellery and hairstyle a manager is sporting. I have always believed that a manager who wears excessive rings or a silk hanky in the top pocket of his jacket should be viewed with caution. These are common traits of an entrepreneur who will prosper in bull market conditions only to watch things unravel when times get tough. Hairstyle is another sign that should always be taken into account. While it might be considered excessively conservative to judge a person by his or her hairstyle, in the world of business most people are shockingly conservative and certain standards are expected. I can only recall the shoulder-length hair that Eddie Groves of ABC Learning Centres and the goatee Wayne Boss from Sausage Software paraded in their early days. Both companies fell on difficult times when the market started to become pessimistic rather than optimistic.

If there is one part of the investment process where professional investors can display their judgement, it is when they interview a managing director or a management team. A strong character at the top of an organisation can affect the whole culture of the company, so it is paramount that the people at the top behave in a manner that shows they have poise, wherewithal and their own sound judgement. Without doubt, it is the company interview that I will miss most as a private investor.

And the winner is ...

So who has the best environment to play the sharemarket — the person on the street or the professional holed up in a city office tower? I would be foolish to claim that all individuals can outperform their professional competitors, but I do believe there are considerable advantages for the person on the street. The sheer flexibility the individual has available cannot be underestimated. In addition, the average individual does not have the albatross of being too big hanging around his or her neck. Trying to manage big chunks of money, which sometimes measure in the billions, can be debilitating. Eventually size will blunt the performance of every investor on the Earth.

In contrast, the individual investor simply does not have access to the same company information that a professional investor has. In particular, the retail investor has only limited exposure to management teams and slim hope of conducting a one-on-one interview. This liability can be mitigated to some degree but it cannot be fully compensated for. For me the loss of the ability to talk regularly to management teams will be tremendously difficult to overcome. In contrast, it can be strongly argued that many professional investors' capability of judging a management team is so poor that a one on one interview can be a negative and not a positive, as you would think it should be.

On this basis I would plump for the individual having the greatest ability to outperform the market as a whole, provided the individual has not set themselves up to fail. Prepare yourself correctly and over time you should be able to match or even beat the market without having to pay fees for other people to do it for you.

Chapter 22

Money managers, money makers

There are plenty of rich fund managers in Australia, but not many rich clients. I'm not picking on anyone in particular when I make this comment, but the reality is that fund managers generally get paid considerable sums for the wealth they create for other people. There are some notable exceptions, but the trend for money managers to charge a fee based on the percentage of funds under management follows US practice, where seven-figure salaries and bonuses for money managers are commonplace. As in any other human pursuit, there is a select bunch of great money managers, a small number of poor ones and a large pool in the middle. The elite group who consistently outperform the market deserve to be well compensated, while the people at the bottom of the list will undoubtedly be found out over time.

The manager does not get paid for his or her time like a lawyer, doctor or accountant; instead he or she receives a set percentage of the money they manage. Occasionally the manager, depending on his or her employment contract, also gets a performance fee for beating a pre-determined benchmark return. This means they get paid all day, every day, on weekends and even while they sleep. Meanwhile, investors cop the ups and downs of the sharemarket, hopefully earning an average return of 10.5 per cent once the advisory and management costs are stripped out. This is a more than healthy return, but there is a mismatch between the manager and the investor. Personally, I would be happy to pay managers well if they show they can perform, but perennial underperformance should not be rewarded.

With this in mind I would always argue that an individual, if they have sufficient time, should invest their own money in the market instead of using a professional to do it for them. However, if the time and confidence are not available, then you have to look at what is on offer from the professional ranks.

Did we mention perfect?

The business of managing money is almost perfect. Essentially, if you are good enough, you can get rich on other people's money (OPM). In most businesses, a person has to borrow from a bank or another financial institution to access capital they need to get established and to fund ongoing requirements. Of course, financial institutions will charge an interest rate on this money and at some stage expect to get their money back. When it comes to funds management and OPM, no interest is charged and, for the most part, there is no need to pay the money back at a pre-determined date. It is a fabulous business for the manager.

In addition, the fund manager has negligible upfront costs if he or she wants to put out the shingle and start a business. Essentially, the only items he or she genuinely needs to fund before opening for business are some computer screens and furniture to sit on. Add in some legal expenses to obtain a licence and you are ready to manage billions of dollars. The remaining costs (such as employees, rent, telecommunications and technical systems) are operating costs that should be matched with the revenue being generated. In funds management the biggest hurdle is not financial—the trick is convincing investors you are talented enough to make money for them and extracting it from their bank accounts and into your newly established fund. If the manager can achieve this, the returns are enormous, making it close to the ideal business.

In Barton Biggs's interesting book *Hedgehogging*, he describes at length the difficulties of setting up a hedge fund and making it work. He quotes the statistics that in 2004 about 1000 hedge funds in the United States went out of business, most of them unable to get sufficient funds through the door to support their inflated overheads. Many of these people trying to set up hedge funds had cut their teeth working for a large institution, getting paid a king's ransom. No doubt many of these people involved in failed ventures believed they could maintain their existing lavish lifestyle despite having to start from scratch.

What Biggs fails to point out is that something like 90 per cent of all start-up businesses fail within the first three years. Fund managers are not special. The only real difference between the money manager and the rest of the world is that the money manager has the ability to earn ridiculous amounts of money if they do survive.

A hedge fund is a special type of fund manager that is more common in the United States than in Australia, but these funds are starting to gain traction as investment managers from around the country see just how much money they can make from a hedge fund. There are thousands of different varieties of hedge funds in the United States, but most aim to achieve a positive return rather than being content with just beating the benchmark index they may be following, by having maximum flexibility to go long and short or hold high levels of cash. Most of the time a hedge fund adds a considerable amount of debt to the investor funds in a bid to gross up the returns being achieved. It is simple maths—if you can borrow money at 6 per cent and you achieve an 8 per cent return then you are making a return on those funds, improving the overall performance of the fund. Finally, a hedge fund will charge a management fee of around 1.5 per cent and a performance fee of 20 per cent of any gains over a certain benchmark. So if you are able to build a fund of $1 billion then you will receive an annual fee of $15 million. In addition, if you are able to beat the designated benchmark by just 5 per cent then another $10 million gets added to the investor's bill. So total revenue comes in at a hefty $25 million. With costs of say $15 million, including staff payments and bonuses, the boss can walk away with $10 million for the year. Not bad in anybody's language, especially when start-up costs are negligible. The key for hedge fund managers is to print a good performance in the first year or two, and then market the hell out of the fund. Poor performance in these formative years is likely to be the killer and it is in this period that funds need to have very low overheads (such as rent, staff and the owner's pay packets) to make sure they get through. Those who manage to consistently outperform their benchmark index get paid well and there is a strong argument to say their pay is well deserved—performance should always be rewarded.

The Australian funds management landscape at this stage of maturation is vastly different to that in the United States. Most money managers in Australian work for long-only institutions (see chapter 21), such as Colonial First State, Perpetual Trustees and BT Australia. These people generally manage superannuation fund or retail money collected through financial planners, who are dotted around the nation. The long-only funds tend to rely on management fees rather than an attractive performance fee, which means they get paid more if they manage a larger amount of money. This results in many institutions managing billions and billions of dollars in Australia's relatively small market. Size is normally a handicap that is close to insurmountable for most managers. Portfolio managers at these organisations can enjoy seven-figure salaries and their analysts are probably not far behind in earnings.

Over the last 25 years many high-profile individuals have left their institutional jobs to kick off their own investment shops. Pioneering the cause was Robert Maple-Brown and Kerr Neilson. Neilson made a name for himself at Bankers Trust (now BT Australia) in the 1980s before leaving and setting up Platinum Asset Management, which floated on the Australian sharemarket in 2007. When the company was listed, Neilson's personal wealth soared to more than $2 billion. Other people—such as David Paradice from Paradice Asset Management, Tim Ryan from Orion Asset Management, Chris Mackay from Magellan Financial Group and Peter Morgan from 452 Capital—have followed Neilson's lead and charted their own course. In the main these people have been able to prove themselves as tremendous performers.

So who do you pick?

For most Australians, the closest they get to the sharemarket is through their superannuation, which is automatically funnelled into a fund of their own choice. The administrators of the super fund then allocate member funds to various money managers around the country. The growth of self managed super funds in recent years has changed, and will continue to change, this landscape and, as the baby boomers reach retirement age, this trend is likely to accelerate rather than slow down. On top of this there is a great swell of people, like our croupier Peter Proksa, who will always manage their own money because they enjoy the market and believe they can deliver superior results.

The upshot of this trend is that more people will need to either pick their own stocks or choose a manager who has the ability to increase the value of their money. Before you pick anyone to manage your money, you must have made the decisions we talked about earlier. First up, what type of investor are you and what risk do you enjoy taking? Once this process is complete and you decide not to manage your own money because of time constraints or a lack of confidence, then you have to pick a manager.

If, for example, you are a risk-averse investor, who wants to be sure their money is in safe hands, then a long-only manager (see chapter 21) who concentrates on the top 50 Australian stocks is probably your best bet. While you will still suffer the slings and arrows of outrageous fortune during a bear market, you will not wake up one morning and see that your money has disappeared without a trace. I would also recommend that you seriously consider bypassing an active manager in these circumstances and simply pick an index fund, such as Vanguard, the biggest fund manager in the world. Index funds track the index and charge minimal fees. Effectively, by taking this route, you are eliminating the risk of a manager performing poorly over a period due to unfortunate stock choices—a problem usually accentuated during bear markets, such as in 2008. You will also avoid seeing a slice of your wealth being siphoned off each year in fees.

If you do decide to choose an active manager because you believe they can deliver superior returns after the deduction of fees, then there are some other considerations. First, the manager should have some form of track record and investment style that you can study. As mentioned earlier, I am not a fan of picking ,the most experienced manager, because of the historical baggage they carry, but it is crucial that they have been in operation for a few years so you can assess whether their actions are consistent with their marketing statements. While past performance is no guide to the future, it is really all we have to work with and it must be taken into consideration. If a manager has been able to achieve superior performance by playing the hot sector, say tech stocks from 1998 to 2000, it would be wise to steer clear. So there must be a quality filter in your decision making. The track record also gives you some protection against fly-by-night operations that sprang up in the bull market, such as financial planning and funds management group Storm Financial, which left thousands of people stranded when its model turned pear-shaped around the time of the GFC.

I would also strongly recommend that you scrutinise the fees being charged. If, for example, the manager is simply providing a long-only fund that concentrates on the top 50 stocks and charges fees of 1 per cent or more, then I would start to question why, when it seems very little value is being added and there are cheaper alternatives. Or, as in Storm Financial's case, every time an investor put money into the sharemarket, Storm charged a massive one-off fee of 6 per cent. You have to do your homework.

As for recent inventions, such as exchange traded funds (ETFs), I am yet to work out whether they are safe options. An ETF allows you to trade an index or sector in one security listed on the sharemarket. You can trade a benchmark index, sectors like gold or virtually anything that takes your fancy. I will not go into the complexities of ETF structures, but investors should be aware that ETFs are derivative products and many of them are highly geared with debt. If an event such as the crash of 1987 was repeated, where the market opened for the first trade in the morning some 20 per cent below the previous night's close, then I believe many ETFs would be battling to stay intact.

In the bowels of the market

If your risk appetite is far greater and you want to venture into the wild jungles of the market outside the top 50, the story starts to change. An abundance of managers in Australia specialise in funds investing in small to medium-sized listed companies. These managers have more recently been able to introduce a performance fee in addition to their management fee. The argument for this double dipping is that stock picking becomes more critical as you start to go off the beaten track and into the bowels of the market. It is here that the efficient market hypothesis (EMH) starts to fall by the wayside and is a weak phenomenon. The EMH pre-supposes that investors cannot outperform the overall market because the market is so efficient that all available information is reflected into the share price at all times. If you can choose the right stocks then you will deliver outperformance and you should be rewarded for this skill. It is also argued that performance fees are an incentive not to grow your funds too large, mitigating the recurring problem of becoming too big to perform.

Over the years, groups such as Paradice Investment Management, Adam Smith Asset Management, Hunter Hall Investment Management, Watermark Funds Management, Regal Funds Management and Cadence Capital have delivered outstanding results in this area, proving themselves to be fabulous stock pickers. This type of stock picking has resulted in these funds beating the relevant benchmark indexes hands down over several years.

However, there is a very real risk that a manager won't deliver superior returns once fees are taken into account, so always be careful to check what you are actually paying. You will find these types of managers through a financial planner or stockbroker, or through the press, where many professionals regularly comment on the market.

Be bold and knock on the door

The problem with simply jumping on board with one of these managers is that past performance is no guarantee to future success. However, past performance is about all we have to go with. Retail investors looking for exposure to this part of the market generally have to rely on the fund's historical performance or the guidance of a financial adviser. I would argue that neither of these is acceptable and you will need to do more.

If you are considering putting your money with a certain manager or a series of managers, start by reading as much about them as you possibly can. Most managers will have their own website, which will show performance, style and personnel. While this may be informative, you must remember it is a marketing tool that should be read with a healthy dose of scepticism. Once you have picked over the marketing material then you should take the bold step of calling the manager and ask for an interview. Generally the manager will hate this, because they see themselves as money managers and not a call centre. If they fail to take your call or refuse a face-to-face meeting, then reject them. It is absurd to think that you would give anyone a percentage of your wealth without meeting the person to assess their skills and personality. It is hard enough to pick stocks without having the luxury of meeting the management team, let alone selecting a fund manager to look after your life savings.

If the manager does happen to take your meeting, then prepare a list of questions that include how the manager invests, who makes the decisions, do they have more than one fund, what fees do they charge, how they discover companies and how they decide to sell them. Attempt to ascertain what motivates them and never forget to ask about their daily routine. Also ask them to explain how they achieved their performance over the years, running through each 12 months over a five-year period. Many retail investors would be shocked to learn how some fund managers have taken their foot off the pedal, especially those who have enjoyed previous success and have been handsomely rewarded. I have always held the belief that, while it might be tempting to give your money to an experienced money manager, the better bet is to bypass the grey hair and plump for the younger person who has started to hit his straps after a handful of years of experience and is still hungry to reach the top. It doesn't take long to work out if the person is still hungry; you can normally see it by the energy they exude in an interview. By the time the interview is finished, hopefully you will have a clearer view of whether the person on the other end of the conversation is the right one to manage your money. It all sounds a little like dating and that's because it is.

A comforting feature of using a professional manager to look after your money is that on most occasions there is little chance of being totally wiped out. The reality is that most fund managers are risk averse and will hug the index they follow. If they do outperform then it will be only marginally and if they underperform it is unlikely to be a train wreck. So, if your first choice of manager is wrong, then don't panic. Withdraw your money and start your search again.

Do-it-yourself handyman

If you can find the time, I firmly believe that you should invest your own money before you consider handing the family fortune over to a third party. If you approach the market correctly, along the lines discussed in the previous chapters, there is no reason why you cannot match the performance dished out by professional managers. A challenge made easier by the fact you don't have to pay yourself fees. Hopefully the story of Peter Proksa provides some inspiration for people thinking about going solo.

A smart approach that many investors have used over the years is to take one or more positions in listed investment companies (LICs), such as AFIC and Argo, which are listed and traded on the sharemarket. An LIC starts by raising money from the market through selling shares to retail investors. The LIC managers invest the money from the capital raising into other listed companies. The LIC charges low management fees, pays robust fully franked dividends and gives you an exposure to the market. Another advantage is that they announce their performance each month and reveal many of their major shareholdings. In addition, because the LIC is a listed company, it must hold an annual general meeting for its shareholders. This gives you a chance to go along and meet the manager and discuss any stock ideas that you might have. My former employer, Wilson Asset Mangement, managed three separate LICs targeting at picking small and medium cap stocks.

A great investment opportunity can also arise from studying the LIC market. For some absurd reason an LIC's share price can trade above the net asset backing—the total value of the companies they own—and at other times it can trade at a discount. This should be easy enough to work out because the ASX requires each LIC to announce its NTA within two weeks of the end of the previous month. You can rummage through the NTA announcements released to the ASX and displayed on its website to see if the company's share price is trading above or below this number. I would never recommend that an investor purchase an LIC if its share price is at or above its NTA. In the simplest terms, you would never give someone $1.10 in return for $1.00. However, a marvellous opportunity can appear if an LIC is trading at a discount to its assets, and this happens on a regular basis. For one reason or another, LICs can trade at up to 30 per cent discount to their asset backing and in times of great panic, such as the market collapse of 2008, the discount can blow out further. If you could pay someone 70 cents and they gave you $1.00, then you would try and do this every day of the week for the rest of your life. If the manager's performance has been sound, his or her portfolio of stocks looks acceptable and the share price is trading at a 30 or even 40 per cent discount, then you must seriously consider making an investment in this company. Over the years at Wilson Asset Management, we have invested in many LICs trading at major discounts to their asset backing and this practice has delivered handsome returns. Before jumping in, though, remember to work out the fee structure charged by the manager, which is always an important consideration.

Ideally, you could place a portion of your capital with one, two or maybe three LICs while the rest of your money could be invested directly into the market. This gives you greater information flows and is a way of tapping into a broader investment community. As we mentioned earlier, investing in isolation is a guaranteed way to fail when it comes to the sharemarket.

Looking for a planner

A hefty proportion of older investors who look after their own investing will do so with the help of a financial planner. For those of you who are confused about the difference between a financial planner and a fund manager don't think you are alone, because it is confusing. Fundamentally, a financial planner helps an individual work out how to structure their investments based on their individual circumstances and who the individual should place their money with. A fund manager is usually a recipient of these funds, which they invest in the market.

The financial planner plays the role of measuring the right amount of risk you should be taking on and limiting the tax you will have to pay. I've lost count of the times people have asked me if I know a good financial planner. It took me about 10 years to find one, and I have been quick to recommend him to all and sundry.

The simple questions to guide your choice of a financial planner should be:

- Do they take, or at least return, your phone calls?
- Are they charging exorbitant fees to give you advice? This will require some benchmarking by surveying other planners.
- Have they reduced your tax burden?
- Do you feel comfortable with them when discussing money?

The key is not to stick with someone if they don't tick all of these boxes. Keep looking, because there are hundreds of planners out there and a good one is worth their weight in gold. Obviously, once you have been using a financial planner you have to monitor the amount of money you are making on the back of their decisions.

Many low-quality investment opportunities, such as MIS schemes and high-yielding property development funds, have been highly successful for the financial planning community over the years, while thousands of small-time investors have seen their money vanish into a black hole and legal actions have been launched as a result. Essentially, these problem products were able to see the light of day because of a flawed system. The product manufacturers—the people who come up with the idea for an investment and launch it into the market—work hard to get a recommendation from a certified research house. This recommendation gives financial planners around the country the green light to start selling the product to their clients. To encourage planners to sell the investment scheme, the product manufacturers offer them a generous fee. In a handful of cases planners are hypnotised by the amount of fees they can generate by recommending the product, instead of concentrating on the quality of what they are peddling. This was seen at its most aggressive in the 1990s and early 2000s when financial planners were paid hefty fees to promote tax-effective agricultural managed investment schemes (MISs).

Hopefully, the federal government's decision in 2011 to change the way financial planners are paid from commissions to a fee-for-service model will help eradicate many of these problems. Only time will tell.

Part VI
When does a bull become a bear?

To the chagrin of the investing public, the US and Australian sharemarkets have found it difficult to deliver a positive return in recent years. The investing public, commentators and market experts have warned we must get used to lower returns in the future. After long and arduous research, I have concluded that the best guide to the future is the past. In this final section of the book I look closely at the nature of bull and bear markets and how previous market periods could provide the answers we are looking for. Fortunately, neither bulls nor bears control the fort forever.

Chapter 23

Is this a bull or a bear?

In my final few weeks working as a fund manager, I spent a lot of time doing what all financial types do—going to lunch. It was flattering that many brokers and colleagues wanted to toast my new beginning, but it was one conversation on this farewell tour that stuck in my head more than all the others. I casually commented to stockbroker James Gordon that it would remain tough to make money while ever we were working our way through the bear market. James shot back at me, 'We're not in a bear market. The index is up about 50 per cent from the bottom in March 2009—that can't be a bear market.' I left the lunch thinking I needed to get to the bottom of the issue and resolve what constitutes a bear market and what constitutes a bull market. I had been under the impression that we were still suffering from a bear market, but I could not argue against what James was saying.

My research was extremely fruitful and revealed that it was crucial to know what environment we were operating in. Put simply, when you are in a bull market you should always stay bullish, no matter the circumstances, and when you are in a bear market you have to learn to swing from being a bear to a bull and back to a bear. My experience also told me that very few people have the ability or the willingness to apply the flexible approach required when they are traversing a bear market. Fortunately, sharemarkets tend to go up a lot more than they go down.

Is there a bear in there?

The standard definition of a bear market is a fall of 20 per cent in the index from its top. In the last 110 years, the Dow Jones index in the United States has fallen by 20 per cent or more 15 times, with the average decline a teeth-clenching 39.3 per cent. On average a new bear market starts about every seven years and lasts for about 20 months. I have used the US market instead of the Australian because the local market had very little depth in the period before World War II, and until 1987 it was run through state-based exchanges instead of a national one headquartered in Sydney. In other words, I have used the United States as a proxy for the local situation.

Standard or secular

A fall of 20 per cent is the simple part of understanding a bear market. But this standard definition is inadequate for describing a market that gives nothing back to investors over a longer period. Old timers in the market say that from the late 1960s to the early 1980s the market delivered next to no overall return, making it almost impossible to generate a sufficient return to live on, while sapping the confidence from participants. In the 16 years from 1966 to 1982 the US market recorded five drops of 20 per cent or more — a frequency of one almost every three years; twice as often as the long-term average. This type of bear market — one that generates no returns for decades — is not your standard bear market but a different creature, which is called a secular bear market.

Now this is where it starts to get a bit tricky. In a secular bear market there can be a series of rallies of more than 20 per cent by the index, suggesting that a bull market is back in place. However, the longer term trend is down, because the rallies are short lived and always fail. The secular bear market cannot be officially said to have finished until a sustained rally occurs and the index rises until it eclipses the previous record high. In the 1970s secular bear market in the United States, it wasn't until 1983 that the Dow Jones and the benchmark S&P 500 index marched past their old highs and kept on rising until the end of the tech wreck in April 2000, some 17 years later.

This takes us back to my conversation with James Gordon, and the start of my trying to work out whether we are in a bull or bear market currently. The answer is we could both be right. James's comment that the market is up 50 per cent since March 2009 could well represent the first stage of a new bull market, but until the Australian market surpasses its previous high in November 2007, we won't be able to declare a bull market. Alternatively, I could be correct and the market could experience another decline of 20 per cent or more before starting a new bull market era. If my scenario pans out, the benchmark All Ordinaries index would have to climb more than 70 per cent to move past the high it set way back in November 2007. We can't be certain of the existence of a secular bear market and, unfortunately, only time will tell. But more on that in chapter 25.

In the United States, the stockmarket has only experienced three secular bear markets over the last 110 years. The first was from October 1929 to early 1942, when the index fell 75 per cent, reaching its ultimate low in 1932. The market eventually surpassed its 1929 high in 1954, some 25 years after the whole horrible process began. If inflation is added to the equation, you are looking at well over 30 years before you would have achieved a profit if you were unfortunate enough to have invested near the sharemarket peak in early 1929.

The second secular bear market started in 1966 and bottomed eight years later in 1974, posting a decline of 41.9 per cent. The old high wasn't clearly passed until 1983, 17 years after the fall started. If you take into account inflation, then an investor who entered the market right at the peak in 1966 didn't make a real return until around 1986, or about 20 years. As you can appreciate from these numbers, market timing is a much under-valued aspect of the investment decision-making process.

The third and final secular bear market started in April 2000 and is still with us. We cannot review the statistics of this secular bear market yet because it is not officially over. In fact, the period from late 2002 to late 2007 saw the US market rise close to 100 per cent, but eventually it failed and never posted a clear new high. As it currently stands, the bear market started in April 2000 with the broad-based S&P 500 index falling about 52 per cent to a secular bear market low in March 2009. By August 2011 the index was still sitting 27 per cent below the March 2000 high, more than 11 years after it all started. An end to this secular bear market will only be declared when the S&P 500 index manages to eclipse the 2000 high of 1527 by a comfortable margin.

Bulls are harder to find than bears

Unlike the bear market, the bull market does not have a precise definition. It could well be that when a market rises 20 per cent following an official bear market, the pundits can claim it is a new bull market. This is the criterion that James Gordon was using when he commented that we could no longer be a bear market in early 2011. And he could well be right. However, people do not seem to want to measure a bull market with the same precision they use to define a bear market. One possible method is to declare that bull markets exist whenever we are not in a secular bear market because markets go up over time.

Secular bulls are the key

With that in mind, it is probably worthwhile concentrating on defining a secular bull market. This is a market that delivers enormous returns over an extended period. Importantly, a secular bull market can include a series of standard bear markets, but the longer term trend is up. A classic was the great US secular bull market from 1983 to 2000. This included the 1987 sharemarket crash, when the US market fell 22 per cent in just one day, notching up the quickest technical bear market in history. However, this did not result in a long-term decline in the market, but rather was a speed hump in a secular bull market. It is crucial to understand this—primarily because when a market does correct 20 per cent or more in a secular bull market, it is imperative that you do not sell your portfolio of shares, but instead buy more shares to take advantage of the next climb higher. The trick is identifying whether you are in a secular bull or secular bear market, a task that most experts have found next to impossible. Don't lose heart, though; the more study you undertake of previous secular bull and bear markets the closer you will get to beating the experts.

Possibly the only reasonable technique of identifying what type of market we are in is time. If a secular bull market has started—in other words the market has surged to a new historic high and it is only five years or less old—then you can safely say that a 20 per cent decline is only a correction and not a new secular bear market. I say this because secular bull markets tend to last for extended periods of more than a decade. In the case of the 1987 crash, the US market had been heading higher and notching up record highs for only about four years and history shows the secular bull market lasted for a further 13 prosperous years.

In the last 110 years, the Dow Jones has posted three secular bull markets. On average they have lasted close to 23 years and posted a return of 1172 per cent. The first kicked off in 1903 and went right through to Black Friday in October 1929. In that 26-year period, the Dow Jones clocked up a return of 1136 per cent, despite experiencing two declines of more than 20 per cent.

The second great secular bull market in the United States was born in the improbable year of 1942, just after the United States entered the Second World War. The market stormed higher for 24 years, recording a gain of 971.2 per cent in a relatively calm period, with only one correction of more than 20 per cent in 1961.

The third secular bull market had its origins in late 1982, when unemployment in the United States was hovering around 10 per cent and talk of the death of capitalism was all the rage. This secular bull market ran for only 18 years, but it managed to outshine its predecessors when the index rose an astonishing 1409 per cent.

So now that we know what bull and bear markets are, we can get on with trying to work out where we sit in 2011.

Chapter 24

History has the answers

In October 2007 Geoff Wilson and I sat down to discuss the best way to handle a 30 per cent fall in the sharemarket. We were both anxious that something awful was about to unfold, but we just didn't know when.

The Australian market had found a bottom of 2800 after the tech wreck in March 2003, and in the four and half years since then it had risen a whopping 150 per cent. The rally for the most part had been built on the solid foundations of tremendous earnings per share growth but in the last 12 months of the run the rise in share prices was simply the expansion of company PEs. In other words, stocks were rapidly getting expensive—a phenomenon associated with behaviour towards the end of major bull market runs.

The market threw everyone a dummy in July 2007, when it fell 17 per cent in a matter of weeks, only to pick itself off the deck and climb to a record high of 6873 by the end of October. Drunk with optimism on the basis of previous wins and unwilling to face the prospect of a bear market, most market participants used that July fall as evidence that nothing could derail a bull market that had been built on the back of a resources boom inspired by China's ongoing industrialisation. It was a case of buy the dip.

Like all other fund managers in October 2007, we were close to being fully invested. We couldn't afford to be anything else, given that the market was in the process of clocking up its fifth successive year of 20 per cent plus gains. In previous market rallies we had been roundly criticised for holding too much cash and underperforming the market—which had made us gun shy. Despite these concerns we decided to bite the bullet and move the fund to a cash level of 30 per cent by Christmas. In the meantime Geoff was going to investigate how much it would cost to buy some protection for our portfolio against a major market tumble. We believed the best way to do this was by entering the options market. The idea was that we had the option to sell the value of our portfolio if the market fell to a certain level.

Geoff moved with alacrity and within 24 hours we had concluded that option protection would only kick in if the market fell 14 per cent and, because we were stock pickers and not index huggers, protection against the overall Australian sharemarket falling was not a perfect hedge for our portfolio. In other words, we couldn't make it add up, and so we decided to ignore the option strategy and protect ourselves by increasing our cash position through selling stocks we owned.

We started to ease out of our stocks and, with a late rush on the verge of Christmas, managed to get to 30 per cent cash. I spent a week over the New Year holiday in New Zealand with the family and felt sick as I watched the market rally three days in succession.

I see red, I see red, I see red

I arrived back at the office in the first few days of January 2008, and found myself alone in the office with everyone else still on holidays. Over the course of the next 12 trading days the market nose-dived a breathtaking 21 per cent; almost the equivalent of the sharemarket crash in October 1987. The simmering concerns about a subprime debt crisis in the United States had started to rise to the surface and the biggest equity market in the world had got the wobbles. The Australian market, which was relatively expensive compared with its international peers, did not take time to ask questions, with investors all trying to squeeze out the small exit door at the one time.

By January 21 we all knew the bull market was over and the bear had entered the room, ready to tear investors apart swipe by swipe. It was a sudden change, and for most market participants it spoiled a relaxing summer holiday, paid for by bulging bonuses from the previous year.

I would rate that two-week period in January 2008 as the most unproductive period of my tenure at Wilson Asset Management. Every day I watched a screen emblazoned with red names and numbers, marking falling shares, hoping we would get a relief bounce to sell some of our stocks. For the most part I just sat and watched as every stock we owned lurched lower and lower. The fact that most of them had little to no debt on their balance sheets was irrelevant, because in those early days of the new bear market there was no discrimination. We could not luxuriate in the comfort of our 30 per cent cash holding, because the small companies that dominated our portfolio were torched as liquidity dried up. By lunchtime on most days I was exhausted from doing nothing except staring at the screen. I would walk outside at lunchtime and wonder why people were so calm — didn't they understand the market had collapsed and the world was about to change? By 21 January I had become so absorbed by my dire thoughts that I couldn't understand why people weren't begging for food in Macquarie Street.

With the benefit of hindsight, we all now know the Australian sharemarket acted in lock-step with its American contemporary, falling 55 per cent over a 16-month period. It was the second largest continuous decline in Australian sharemarket history, just behind the 59 per cent drop during 1973 and 1974. That period was also categorised by global turmoil and the deflating of a resources bubble that had developed during the late 1960s and early 1970s.

The emperor had no clothes

During the 16 months of cascading share prices that started in November 2007 and the subsequent 2009 rally, I learned many things about the sharemarket and its participants. The first and most telling was that most market experts just had no answers for what was happening. When the initial shock of the market collapse had passed, most stockbrokers and strategists, like me, idiotically thought the rout was exactly what was needed and we could get back on with the business of picking stocks in a bull market.

When the US government decided to bail out the troubled trading bank Bear Stearns in March 2008, I agreed with everyone that a line had been drawn in the sand, and the worst was behind us. The market found its feet for a few months, but then the selling came again in waves.

If I had had any long-term perspective, I would have realised that, after a 15-year bull market, born in 1992, we had entered a new bear phase that would not go away any time soon. By about July 2008, I was starting to wake up to what was going on and decided to keep on selling any stocks we owned, in a bid to raise as much cash as possible. Geoff, haunted by the ghosts of the 1987 crash, was also keen to liquidate what we owned.

It was also at about this time that I started to realise that many people that I thought were good judges when it came to picking stocks and market direction were way behind the eight ball. The fact was that the market had entered a bear phase and most market participants, especially those who relied heavily on fundamentals, such as profits and dividends, were living in fairy land. The general message about the market was that we needed to start buying stocks across the board because they were ridiculously cheap. The pundits couldn't have been more wrong.

> After a 15-year bull market, born in 1992, we had entered a new bear phase that would not go away any time soon.

As the GFC unfolded towards the end of 2008 and into the early parts of 2009, most professional players in Sydney and Melbourne finally gave up on their buy calls and started to yell 'Sell!' Company analysts became so disillusioned with events that they ditched their traditional discounted cash flow valuation methods, simply because they were absurdly higher than the actual share prices. They were being laughed out of the room by professional investors.

Enter the historians

In my desperation to get some clear answers about the way forward, I stumbled across two market historians, a rare breed in Australia. At about that time two market historians, Craig Scheef and Andrew McCauley, visited our offices within days of each other. Craig was a former professional fund manager who had left Sydney for the calmer environs of the mid north coast of New South Wales. After a two-year break he had started investing again and was happy to discuss his views with a select group of people. Andrew, a veteran stockbroker, worked just down the road in Macquarie Street. Both men had discovered, like me, that the best answers to the future tend to lie in what has happened in the past. Initially, both men were negative, but come the start of 2009 they simultaneously started thumping the table about buying the market, which they said was going to reverse sharply and drive higher at a rapid pace. I thought these guys were mad.

McCauley's argument was based on his extensive study of quarterly performance of the Australian market. He said the local market had never notched up seven quarterly declines in a row and the March 2009 quarter was the sixth one in succession. He reasoned that unless history was about to be made, the market would bottom and start to rally. To me this was not overly convincing, given that I had supposedly seen history being made several times in 2008.

Scheef came at the problem from a totally different direction. To the outside world, he would be considered a market technician through his extensive study of charts and the use of time series based on multiples of 30 days to gauge human behaviour. To me, though, he is a market historian, and understanding history is a fabulous way to understand more fully how people react in varying circumstances. Scheef became passionate about the market ending its dive in February 2009 and would say that to anyone who would listen.

History tells us both men were correct, and in March 2009 the market turned and started to head higher. As with most aspects of Australian life, the sharemarket's history is virtually ignored, and few or no records kept. The study of history is a powerfully instructive force that many people could do well to indulge in. It took me the best part of a decade to realise this.

A third person worth mentioning at this time is Credit Suisse analyst Atul Lele. While not a pure historian, Lele has proven to be accurate with his calls, which are based upon global liquidity factors and his own fear ratio. In other words he has been able to conjure up a financial ratio that effectively measures excessive fear and excessive optimism. In early 2009 he also believed the fear and liquidity ratios were all pointing towards a rally. His behavioural approach to markets may be scoffed at by many fundamentalists, but from my point of view I would prefer accurate predictions rather than an approved textbook view.

Scheef's and McCauley's correct market calls got me intensely interested in market behaviour and market history. In particular I thought it should be compulsory to study the secular bull and bear markets over the last 100 years, attempting to work out how long they lasted and if there were any repeating features. So far my research, from late 2007 to mid 2011, has been far more enlightening than virtually any other method of understanding the market, giving me a better idea of what is happening now than the hapless predictions of many highly paid market strategists, who seem to be six months behind what is actually happening. If you understand which way the market is heading you can then knuckle down to the task of picking the stocks that will perform in that environment.

I would like to now look at three secular bear markets — one in Australia and two in the United States. I believe the behavioural patterns exhibited in these periods reveal a great deal of what is going on in 2011. While some people will argue this is too small a sample size to come to any decisive conclusions, I would counter with the fact the two US bear markets cover 40 years from a total of about 82 years. While the Australian secular bear market accounts for eight of the past 24 years.

I also believe it is folly to discuss the current secular bear market with the one currently running in Japan, which has been in progress for 21 years. The Japanese market is 75 per cent below its peak of 1990. The Japanese market and culture are substantially different from those in the United States and Australia. I will not elaborate at this point, but it is fair to say there is not a core capitalist belief in Japan that requires companies to generate sufficient returns to power the sharemarket higher. In the main the Japanese are more concerned with employment and saving face than maximising corporate profits. This is a more rounded and holistic view of life, but it does not drive big secular bull markets.

The crash and the growling bear

The first of these secular bear markets occurred during an eight-year period in Australia from September 1987 to 1995 (see figure 24.1). This was the last true secular bear market in Australia even though it was in the middle of a secular bull market in the United States. How could this be, you ask? Well let's have a look.

Figure 24.1: after the crash—the Australian All Ordinaries index from September 1987 to December 1995

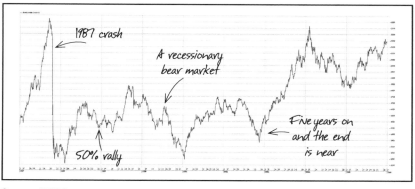

Source: IRESS

The Australian sharemarket had experienced a fabulous 13-year run from its bottom of 220 in September 1974 to its historical peak in September 1987, posting a gain of more than 1200 per cent. The market peaked at 2450 in September 1987, before it started to head south for about four weeks. The bull market, though, was officially declared over a month later in October, when the local market crashed 25 per cent in one session the day after a similar drop was recorded in the United States. This was the single biggest session decline both markets had ever recorded. While the US market managed to bounce back rapidly, the Australian market kept falling for another four months until it hit bottom at 1250 in February 1988. The total decline from the peak was 49 per cent, a feat never previously achieved in a five-month period in Australia.

The amount of the local market's decline could be explained away by the excessive nature of the bull market, sent into hyper-drive by the government's decision in 1985 to de-regulate the banking system and symbolised by a string of entrepreneurs who had borrowed truck loads of money. These entrepreneurs included Christopher Skase, John Spalvins, Alan Bond and John Elliot. Just before the crash, the ASX thought it prudent to introduce the Entrepreneurs Sector of the All Ordinaries index in recognition of the size and importance of this part of the market. After the crash the Entrepreneurs Sector disappeared without a whimper, as many companies went broke when banks put the kybosh on providing any more credit.

After the crash

For our purposes, though, the important part of this slice of history is what happened after the dust had settled in February 1988. The All Ordinaries index actually started to rally strongly. Over the space of the next 17 months the market rose 50 per cent, back up to 1800, inspired by low interest rates and a piping-hot residential property market. The Reserve Bank of Australia (RBA) believed it had to increase monetary access following the sharemarket crash, but all this did was to create a bubble in the residential property market. Investors had fled the sharemarket when it crashed and parlayed many of their bull market winnings into residential property, cheered along by the availability of cheap money and leaping prices. Residential property prices rocketed higher all around the country, but the big moves were savoured for the top end of the market where individual records were set. But this was all short lived. Inevitably, top end real estate is the last to boom and one of the first to bust, and this time was no exception.

The RBA, after cutting official interest rates to avoid a liquidity trap and an economic recession following the sharemarket crash, realised they had overreacted, with inflation flaring and asset prices leaping higher. About half way through 1989, the RBA started to lift official interest rates and continued to aggressively do so for the best part of a year. This induced one of the most crippling recessions in Australian economic history, with unemployment kissing 11 per cent a few years later in 1992.

The RBA's decision to lift rates had an immediate impact on investors and the new bull market that had kicked off in February 1988 ended abruptly in mid 1989. Over the course of the next 18 months the All Ordinaries index fell just over 30 per cent, as interest rates climbed and company earnings slumped on the back of a faltering economy. By the beginning of 1991, the All Ordinaries index had fallen all the way back down to where it had landed after the crash three years earlier, at just above 1200 points. At this point the market rallied again, rising all the way back up to 1800, before fading more than 20 per cent to just 1400 points in 1992. The net result was that the Australian sharemarket, five years on from the crash, was still more than 41 per cent below its peak in September 1987. To equal this fall in today's context, the All Ordinaries would have to fall to 4050 between mid 2011 and late 2012, a further decline of almost 15 per cent.

No-one in Australia, in a time of deep recession, knew it in late 1992, but the bear market that had sucked the life out of all investors was coming to a close, and a new bull market was set to begin. The crash had erased the leveraged cowboys and the tumultuous times of the next five or so years had convinced most investors to give up, in the belief that the sharemarket's glory days would never return. There was no-one left to sell. Over the course of the next 15 years the market clocked up a robust capital return of 385 per cent, representing growth of slightly more than 11 per cent a year, compared with economic growth of around 3.5 per cent. In the same period, the All Ordinaries Accumulation index, which includes dividends paid, racked up a gain of more than 700 per cent.

Those awful '70s

The 1970s has long been considered the lost decade for US stocks. While the 45 per cent free fall from early 1973 to late 1974 captures the lion's share of headlines, the Dow Jones was wallowing in a secular bear market for nearly 17 years, from early 1966 to the end of 1982. In that period the index actually declined from 995 to 777, a fall of almost 22 per cent in absolute terms and closer to 50 per cent once inflation is taken into account. If a period could destroy the optimism of a sharemarket investor that would have just about done the trick. Throughout the 1970s, headlines blared that capitalism was dead and that the United States needed to look towards industrialising Japan to see how to conduct business in the new era.

It would be a superficial analysis of the US market during that period to simply pick the start and finish dates and record the demise. Five times in that period the Dow Jones fell by more than 20 per cent. The worst fall was over the period during 1973 and 1974. The market also managed to rally five times by more than 20 per cent during the same stretch, which included the staggering gain of 66 per cent from mid 1970 to early 1973, and 75 per cent over two years from 1974 to 1976 (see figure 24.2). As you can appreciate, volatility was extreme.

Figure 24.2: the 1970s secular bear market—the Dow Jones index from 1966 to 1986

Source: IRESS

The reasons for such volatility over such a long period were numerous. The first cause, as with other secular bear markets, was the extreme valuation that stocks had reached in 1966 after a 24-year bull market forged from the Great Depression and the Second World War. These historically high valuations persisted right through until early 1973, with the emergence of the Nifty Fifty stocks that represented the first US companies to discover the business world outside of the United States. Many of the Nifty Fifty, including McDonalds and Xerox, traded on PEs of more than 50—investors thought earnings would grow at an elevated level for many years to come.

As we rolled into the mid 1970s the world and US economies did not, however, oblige investors. The first oil price spike of 1973 triggered the unknown concepts of very little economic growth and high inflation, resulting in the term 'stagflation' being coined. Inflation became the enemy of capitalism, and investors lost all confidence.

Secular flexibility

The key to our analysis, though, is the rough ride investors experienced, particularly after the big bear market that ran from early 1973 to late 1974. In secular bear markets, you have to learn to switch from being bearish to bullish and back to bearish frequently (see chapter 23)—a task near impossible for the average investor. For two years after the great decline, from early 1973 to September 1974, the Dow Jones rose at a furious rate, gaining a total of 75 per cent and almost touching the high of just over 1000 set in 1973. Professional investors would have been crucified by their clients if they didn't get a piece of that action, despite having all their optimism sucked out of them just a few months before.

Just when things looked settled again, the Dow Jones fell 27 per cent over a 15-month period from late 1976 to early 1978. Even a strong rally in 1980, which saw the Dow Jones back over 1000 for the third time in eight years, failed when another fall of 25 per cent followed. It was at about this stage that unemployment in the United States reached more than 10 per cent, the highest level since the Great Depression some 50 years before. The Federal Reserve, led by its new chairman Paul Volcker, raised interest rates in order to kill the demon of inflation once and for all. Surprisingly this heavy dose of medicine, which crippled the real economy, was the impetus the sharemarket required to at last break the shackles of the past 17 years.

The Dow Jones started to rally in late 1982, and didn't have another correction of 20 per cent or more until the crash in October 1987. In that period the Dow Jones rose 250 per cent, from 777 to 2722, well above the previous high of 1051 set in early 1973. The secular bear market had at long last come to an end. Even the crash of 1987 only took the Dow Jones down to 1738, which was still 70 per cent above the 1973 mark.

Like the 1987 to 1995 secular bear market in Australia, the US experience in the 1970s shows that after a downward movement by the market, there will be several bounces and probably several 20 per cent plus falls in the proceeding years. You are not served well by the buy and hold philosophy in these periods, and the only winners are those market participants who are devoid of emotion and pragmatic enough to switch from being bearish to bullish and back to bearish to consistently make money. For many of us, this is simply too hard and it would be better to wait until the next secular bull market starts.

Great in name only

The bear market pundits love to compare our current woes with the 1929 crash that triggered the Great Depression of the 1930s (see figure 24.3). This period in US history is possibly the only time that masses of people living in the richest nation on Earth endured the economic conditions normally associated with developing nations. While this bear market is instructive, writing this book would be a fruitless exercise if our current predicament delivered a similar outcome. Given the devastating destruction in value and the time it took to play out, we can only hope that it was a once in a millennium event. With that in mind, the key aspect of discussion should be the behaviour of investors rather than the numbers associated with the event.

From 1914 to 1929, the US stockmarket enjoyed a magnificent uninterrupted bull run, rising some 628 per cent. The first great crash took place in October 1929, when the S&P 500 index fell 15 per cent in one day. Despite some short, sharp rebounds, the market continued to slide for the best part of two and half years, eventually recording a bottom in mid 1932 some 89 per cent lower than the high set in October 1929. No market decline has ever come near matching the devastation of this 27-month period. It is said the dumb investors went broke in 1929, the smart investors went broke in 1930 and the really smart guys went broke in 1931. To put the collapse in perspective, at the absolute bottom in 1932 the market needed to rise more than 800 per cent just to get back to where it had peaked in 1929.

In the midst of the Great Depression, with unemployment galloping towards 20 per cent, the market found a bottom and proceeded to climb 370 per cent in a period of almost five years from 1932 to 1937. That equates to a stunning gain of about 40 per cent a year. Given the size of the initial fall, it is difficult to comprehend that there would be enough money around in the 1930s to mount such a rally. By the beginning of 1937 the market had managed to recapture nearly half the losses of the 1929–32 wipe out.

Figure 24.3: the Great Depression — the S&P 500 index from 1929 to 1955

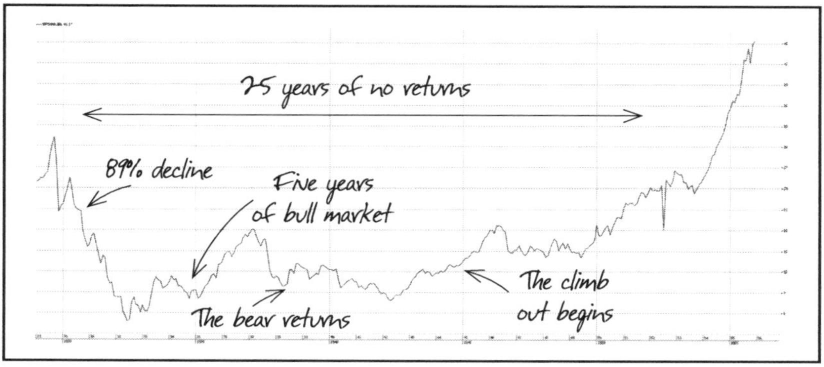

Source: IRESS

Unfortunately, that was not the end of this secular bear market. With the Depression proving almost impossible to shake and the emergence of war in Europe and the Pacific, the S&P 500 index lost another crippling 50 per cent over a five-year period from 1937 to 1942. The market was by then sitting more than 75 per cent below the peak it had reached 13 years earlier, before the crash. To put this into perspective, the Australian benchmark index, the All Ordinaries, would have to fall about 63 per cent from the mid 2011 level of about 4500 points over the next nine years to match the effect of the US market between 1929 to 1942. Starting to feel depressed?

But in the United States, just when all seemed helpless, with war raging across the globe and the Japanese and German aggressors looking like probable winners, the market started to rally again. From 1942 to 1966 the sharemarket gained 971.2 per cent, pausing only once in 1961 for a sharp fall of 27 per cent to punctuate the rise.

The message

While I am not advocating that we are about to feel the pain of 1929 to 1942, there are several salient points to be extracted from this segment of sharemarket history. Like the other secular bear markets we have discussed, the initial dramatic drop that captured all the headlines was not the end of the pain. Secular bear markets take many years to play out.

Taking the current situation, the Australian and US markets may never surpass the low hit in early 2009, but it will take many years, possibly a decade, to reclaim a record high. In between, there can be some tremendous rallies, such as we saw in 1932 to 1937 and again from 1974 to 1976, but in the end they will fail and a second or possibly third bear market will appear to zap our last bit of hope. That is exactly what a secular bear market does. Only the most pragmatic and impervious individuals have the ability to navigate this seesawing behaviour. Significantly, very few people have these supreme qualities. The grind of a secular bear market over many years will eventually claim so many victims that most investors will firmly believe that the market will never deliver a decent return ever again. The secular bear market is soul destroying and only the strongest manage to survive.

Even our croupier, Peter Proksa, now has eyes for history. He recently decided that to avoid another downturn in the market he needed to take some bets off the table and put the cash in the bank. Proksa has learned the hard way from previous market collapses and believes that we might just have one more major soft period before he starts looking for those one cent pearls again.

With this fresh in our thoughts, we should now turn to see where we sit in 2011.

Chapter 25

Where are we in 2011?

We live in most unusual times in 2011. A secular bear market coexists in the United States and Australia, a scenario that has not played out since 1969–74, some 36 years ago. Importantly for Australia, this time around we were late to the funeral and, as chapter 24 revealed, many would argue the GFC-inspired bear market is already behind us and that a big bull strode into town back in March 2009. After much reflection and poring over historical data I do not believe this to be the case: I believe the bear is still with us and will inflict more pain before relief arrives.

We will come back to the Australian market after we analyse the US market, which, despite its detractors, is still the largest and most influential stockmarket in the world, as graphically displayed by the crash of 2008. The US sharemarket accounts for about 30 per cent of world equity markets, while the US economy is just under 20 per cent of the global economy.

The United States—a long way down the track

The US stockmarket entered its third secular bear market of the last 82 years in April 2000. The initial stage of the decline was branded the tech wreck, when the inflated prices of technology, telecommunication and media companies deflated to the point where most of the air had been sucked out of the room. This was a slow and arduous affair that took the best part of two and half years, punctuated by the terrorist attacks of 11 September 2001. As the tech wreck unfolded, the occasional murmurings that a much more protracted and painful bear market had taken grip and would dominate proceedings for the next decade, but most investors were blissfully unaware of the roller coaster ride that was to come.

The top of the market in March 2000 saw the broad–based S&P 500 index hit 1527 points, only for it to decline by 46 per cent over the course of the next 30 months, falling all the way back down to 820 points. In October 2002, as the United States prepared to go to war in Iraq, the sharemarket started to rally. At first the rally came in fits and starts, but eventually, encouraged by generational low interest rates, the market began to move higher at a swift rate and the tech wreck became a distant memory. By October 2007, just five years later, the S&P 500 index had risen 95 per cent to 1576, recouping all of the tech wreck losses. It was a delightful period to be in the market, with so much money sloshing around.

But in October 2007 the S&P 500 index literally went into free fall over the next 17 months as many financial institutions went to the wall on the back of the subprime housing loan bubble bursting. This decline was considerably more speedy and brutal than the tech wreck, with the S&P 500 index falling 56 per cent, all the way back down to the devil's number of 666 by 6 March 2009. This was a torrid time for all market participants, with large financial institutions collapsing or, if deemed important enough, nationalised in a bid to avoid a total collapse of the system. This was a financial crisis not experienced by investors since 1929 and most market participants found it difficult to respond with any confidence.

Like all market bottoms, it came without warning or fanfare. Between March 2009 and mid August 2011 the S&P 500 index has managed to rise 76 per cent, a performance that virtually no-one predicted when the GFC was raging. The financial crisis spilled over into one of the most severe and protracted recessions in US economic history, but the sharemarket has merrily danced higher in the expectation of a brighter future. The reasons for the market's tremendous resilience have been well documented, with the Federal Reserve's (FED) decision to keep official interest rates close to zero and spend trillions of dollars buying US bonds' capturing most of the attention. The experts consider the FED buying of bonds is akin to printing money. This highly accommodative policy has pumped trillions of dollars into the hands of corporations and investors, which has in turn been used to buy shares and commodities. The FED's actions have also been supported by an expanding government fiscal policy. The US government's debt has surged past the record level of $14 trillion dollars. This ballooning debt level caused much anxiety among investors during July and August of 2011.

The question we now have to answer is this: what happens next? Predicting the future is always fraught with danger and is invariably inaccurate. With this in mind I can only turn to history to find answers.

The pain is not over

If the benchmark S&P 500 index continues on its upward path and in the next 12 months powers through its previous record highs, then the secular bear market would be declared over. To achieve this outcome, the index would have to rally a further 33 per from its current level in August 2011, a distinct possibility given the momentum of the last two years. It is also quite feasible if you focus purely on the stunning earnings corporate America has been able to produce despite the moribund economic climate. In other words, the US market is not expensive trading on a forward PE of about 13.5, compared with the long-term average of between 14 and 15.

The good

History tells us, though, this scenario is highly unlikely. To blast past the previous high in 2012, or even 2013, would, at 13 years of age, make it the shortest and least painful secular bear market the United States has experienced in the last 82 years. In the past two secular bear markets, it took 26 years and 18 years respectively for the market to comfortably reclaim the index record. Given the severity of the economic malaise and the enormous secular bull market leading up to April 2000, it would seem the current secular bear market has to be long and painful. After all, the S&P 500 index in early 2000 was trading at a record high PE ratio of more than 25. At the end of secular bear markets, PE ratios and earnings are traditionally low, setting investors up for a long and rewarding run as the economy slowly recovers. During the 1970s the average PE for S&P 500 index companies was less than 10 times future earnings.

> Given the severity of the economic malaise and the enormous secular bull market leading up to April 2000, it would seem the current secular bear market has to be long and painful.

The bad

A far more probable outcome is for the US market to experience another fall of 20 per cent or more over the course of 2011 and 2012 before the long climb out of the bear and into a new bull starts. Assuming this fall would be 25 per cent, the S&P 500 index would bottom out at just above 1000, some 30 per cent below the bottom of March 2000 before the tech wreck started the secular bear rot. From this point, history shows the market would spike strongly and it might only take another two years to reach the old record high. This takes us to late 2014 or possibly early 2015. Even this scenario is letting investors off lightly compared with the pain inflicted from previous bear markets.

The ugly

A third outcome, and the one I personally believe will happen, is that another major bear market will emerge as the final act of the secular bear market (see figure 25.1). This would involve a decline of close to 35 per cent over 18 months to two years. Under this scenario the S&P 500 index would slump back to around 850 in the first half of calendar year 2013. From here it would take a rally of around 100 per cent over about three years to finish the bear market. It is quite possible that the final 35 per cent decline in this secular bear market may have already started, but only time will tell us that. Ideally, investors would jump back into the market in 2013, but most people will be so defeated by the length of the current secular bear that they will only rediscover equities some years after the new secular bull has kicked off. Prices will no longer be compelling by then, but the underlying economic environment will have sufficiently improved to get people excited about the future.

While it sounds depressing we must remember that even under the worst case scenario, the US is 11 years into what I believe will turn out to be a 13-year destruction of value. That leaves just less than two years before the rally that ends the pain starts to take shape.

Figure 25.1: today's secular bear market—the S&P 500 index from January 1999 to July 2011

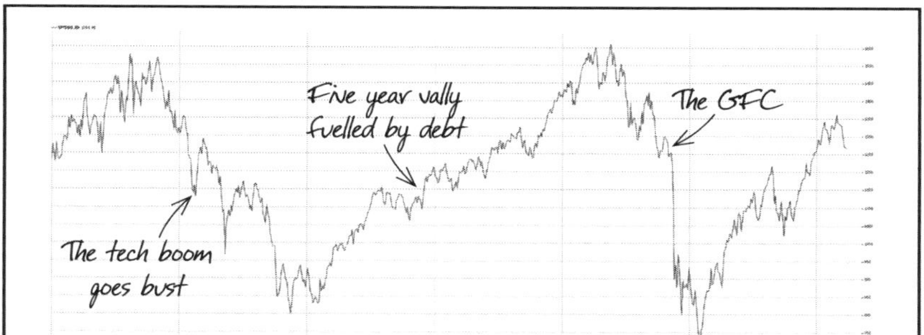

Source: IRESS

The fundamentals

Many readers will not accept this analysis at face value. The perennial bulls need more than history to be convinced that the US market could be brought to its knees again only a few years after almost self-destructing. They will need fundamentals, despite fundamentals proving to be a dismal predictor of the future at any time in the past 11 years. Just to appease this portion of the financial community, I will attempt to construct a case based on deteriorating fundamentals.

Let's start with the US economy. The health of the US economy is still the number one driver of share prices in the United States, and probably globally. While company earnings are a close second, the way the market perceives the state of the US economy seems to be the key consideration for investors trying to predict the future.

There are three main parts to the US economy — corporations, households and governments. During the period from the recession of the early 1990s to 2007, a small group of financial corporations, households and individuals, and to a lesser extent governments, took on too much debt. The main culprits in this debt binge were a handful of financial corporations that levered their balance sheets to levels never experienced before. For every dollar of equity provided, these companies were regularly borrowing $20 or even $40. In turn they were lending this money out to individuals to buy houses around the country. Many of the people borrowing the money were seduced into the loans by low upfront interest rates but had virtually no chance of paying this debt back when the interest rates charged reverted to a more normal level. As individual households began to default on their debts, the financial corporations were forced to write down the value of their loans. As is well documented, this financial company debt brought the global economy to its knees in 2008 and early 2009, forcing the government to bail out company after company. As normal credit lines dried up, the rest of corporate America was also forced to slash costs, propelling unemployment to 10 per cent. Two years on, US unemployment remains stubbornly high at 9.1 per cent and there are no signs of a hiring frenzy breaking out any time soon, with most industries experiencing lacklustre revenue growth.

The catalyst for the financial demise of corporate America was ordinary Americans who had borrowed unsustainable amounts to buy real estate and started to default on their mortgage commitments. Easy credit tightened up and in the space of only a few years, Americans realised they had built three million too many homes. This triggered the greatest residential slump since the Great Depression, with housing starts falling from a high of 2 million per year in 2006 to just one quarter of that by 2009. The lasting impact of this catastrophe was a psychological change across the country. With credit evaporating, people started to save and they haven't really stopped. Economists have described this as households repairing their balance sheets. In other words, instead of taking on more debt, as people had done for the 40 years leading up to 2007, individuals were saving and paying down their liabilities in fear of another GFC crippling them completely. From all accounts the savings fad is going to continue for at least two more years as the excess supply of housing works it way through the system.

The Federal Reserve's unprecedented attempts to get everyone borrowing and spending again to boost the economy have largely failed. Zero official interest rates have not encouraged banks to lend, and individuals have simply pulled down the shutters on the American dream of buying the best and biggest of everything. Given the US consumer accounts for close to 70 per cent of the country's GDP, household spending needs to fire again before the traditional revenue growth for corporations of 5 to 10 per cent can resume. While consumer spending is not likely to get worse, it is unlikely over the next two years to provide the impetus for national growth, as it had previously.

Shuffling the deck chairs

Unfortunately for the United States, its debt problems remain. The US federal government has been forced to raise its debt ceiling, with the principal amount rocketing through the $14 trillion mark for the first time in history. This money is owed to lenders around the globe, and with the US economy languishing, the government is finding it difficult to pay the interest bill, let alone reduce the principal amount. The situation has reached the point where ratings agency Standard & Poor's cut the US federal government debt rating from AAA to AA+. Large amounts of this debt came as a direct result of the need to bail out corporate America in 2008 and 2009, ensuring the entire global financial system did not fail. Another part of this debt has come from the need to spend—to stimulate the economy as the private sector cowers in the wake of the GFC. A final part of this debt was the result of overspending and running deficits in the lead up to 2008, an affliction that has affected many other countries, including Japan and most European countries. The result of all these actions has seen the public percentage of the US economy balloon to 25 per cent, up from the traditional 19 to 20 per cent.

Governments across the United States must now somehow reduce their debt load. They will also have to diminish their overall contribution to the economy over the next two, three or possibly ten years. The most prominent part of this will be the US Federal Reserve withdrawing the stimulus it has provided since 2008 by printing money to the tune of trillions of dollars. This change will be a major drag on the $15 trillion economy that corporates and individuals are not yet ready to replace. The United States should slip back into a recession, with unemployment edging higher or at best remaining stubbornly high. If government bodies such as the Federal Reserve continue to pump prime the economy for fear of an economic malaise, then the inevitable debt problem will magnify and the pain will only be deferred and not solved. In recent times this has been described as kicking the can down the road.

Unfortunately, the US economy and its participants committed one of the seven deadly sins—greed—and the punishment is severe and enduring.

Only time will tell whether this view is right, and some answers may have been provided by the time many people read this. However, I believe the US sharemarket will continue to decline over the course of late 2011 and through 2012—it is just a matter of by how much. When the pain is most acute the sharemarket will jolt back into life in preparation for the next chapter of its history.

Down under—for some time to come

The Australian sharemarket did not enjoy the outrageous bull market the United States celebrated in the 1990s tech boom. Sure, the local market rose gradually during the decade, but the local situation was more about the plodding recovery from the vicious recession of the early 1990s that saw unemployment grow to 11 per cent. The technology boom came late down under, and did not encroach upon the mainstream market in the way it did in the United States. The net result in Australia was not so much a tech wreck bear market, but a pause before things started to really swing into gear.

Australia's market was dancing to a different drum beat than that of its big brother in the northern hemisphere. The new bull market had started only in late 1992, while the US market had, despite the hiccup of the 1987 crash, been motoring higher since 1983. Effectively, by the time the tech wreck hit Australia, the local bull run was still immature and not ready to fall over just yet. Instead, it quickly claimed a record high in 2004 and set out to double in less than four years. The petrol on the bull market fire was an unprecedented boom in the resources sector, as commodity prices hurtled to record highs as a result of the insatiable demand from industrialising China. The benchmark All Ordinaries index peaked on 1 November 2007 at 6873, a gain of 374 per cent in about 15 years. It was at this point that the Australian market started a new secular bear market, some seven and a half years after the US market had begun its pain.

Australian sharemarket history informs us that it should take roughly five years to ride out the bear market before a new secular bull market germinates. After the bear market struck in 1969, it wasn't until September 1974 that the market actually hit bottom at 220, and it was another five years before the previous high water mark was surpassed. Then in 1987 the market crashed 49 per cent. A series of rallies all failed over the next five years, before a spluttering rally eventually saw the old record of October 1987 eclipsed in 1995, reaching 2500.

If these two previous secular bear markets are any guide to the current rout, then the All Ordinaries index will not enjoy a sustainable rally until late 2012 or even early 2013, about 18 months after I wrote this chapter. The last stages of a secular bear market can also be agonising, with a 20 per cent plus decline likely to completely kill off investment sentiment. If this were to happen, you could expect the Australian market to slide 25 to 30 per cent from its 2011 high of around 5000, taking the index down to about 3750. If this happened, the Australian market would need to rise between

71 and 83 per cent to get back to the previous high mark of late 2007. I would imagine this stunning rise would take place by early 2016, a bit more than eight years after the whole calamity began.

Perfect timing

I would make two observations about this. First, the shape of the current secular bear market (see figure 25.2), now three and half years old, is eerily like the one that unfolded after the 1987 crash. In that instance the ultimate bottom was actually reached less than four months after the crash. Then a rally over an 18-month period recouped 50 per cent of the losses, before it failed, taking the market back down close to the previous low.

I would imagine the ultimate bottom of the current bear market will be the one touched in March 2009, at just below 3200. Interestingly, the rally since March 2009 has also been approximately 50 per cent. But I would expect the current rally to fail and the market to head lower, as it did in 1990 and 1991.

Second, if these forecasts are accurate, the Australian and US sharemarkets should be concluding their respective secular bear markets at around the same time. This means we would be in lock step again, as we set out on the next secular bull market, which we will discuss in the next chapter.

Figure 25.2: the secular bear market at home—the All Ordinaries index from January 2007 to July 2011

Source: IRESS

Fundamentally Australian

What are the drivers that are going to take the Australian sharemarket lower over the course of the next 12 months? There is a distinct possibility that Australia will slump into its first economic recession since the early 1990s. This recession may already have kicked off in 2011, and it could possibly stretch right through 2012. I would argue that three economic drivers will bring about this economic contraction, placing ongoing pressure on corporate earnings and share prices:

* a reduction in household debt
* consumers curtailing their spending
* the end of the resources boom.

A reduction in household debt

Australia has one of the most expensive residential property markets in the world. There are various ways of measuring how expensive houses are in Australia. Experts believe that, by mid 2011, houses in Australia were on average 20 to 25 per cent too expensive compared with the long-term average. This type of situation has only presented itself twice in the last 25 years: the late 1980s, before the crippling early 1990s recession, and on the eve of the GFC in 2007. As we have seen in the United States and United Kingdom, falling home values is a sadistic economic plight that severely curtails the consumer's spending habits.

We have been hoodwinked into believing that Australia's housing landscape is structurally different to that in the United States, where owners can simply give back their house to the lender and not be liable for any excess debt associated with the original mortgage. Unsurprisingly, very few commentators mention that the UK housing market is very similar to Australia's, but it too has felt the pain of falling valuations. Credit growth, much of which heads straight into housing, bubbled along at somewhere between 8 and 20 per cent from 1970 to 2007, while the general economy has only managed to eke out an overall growth rate of just over 3 per cent. An unsustainable debt binge has taken place over many years.

The process of realigning Australian home valuations to an acceptable long-term level that Australians can afford seems to have started, with reports around the country of soft and even declining house prices. To get the ratio back in line, wages have to rocket higher, interest rates collapse or house prices continue to decline. I would imagine the decline will be a long and drawn-out process, with all three of these elements contributing to the realignment.

Consumers curtailing their spending

Australian consumers were just as, if not more, indulgent than their American and European counterparts in the lead up to 2007. In fact, Australian households achieved the remarkable feat of spending more than they earned over 2002–05, a record the Americans cannot boast of. Instead of paying off their home loans Australians were using their homes as ATM machines, continually increasing the size of their mortgages as home prices leapt higher. Households used the funds raised this way to dramatically ramp up their standard of living, buying overseas holidays, new cars, a range of electronic products and a raft of other goods from around the globe. With the consumer representing around 60 per cent of the Australian economy, this was an almighty fillip to the economic growth of the country. But since the onset of the GFC in 2008, this trend has abruptly reversed and households have become miserly, saving at a rate not witnessed for more than two decades. This is a tremendous trend reversal that would need to be in place for at least two to three more years to get household debt levels down to an acceptable long-term level. That means the consumer should be on strike for some time to come, particularly if house prices continue to decline. Fortuitously, the combination of deflating residential real estate prices and a frugal consumer has been in place for a period now and the Australian economy has still been able to side step its first recession in 20 years. That takes us to the almighty resources market.

The end of the resources boom

Australia is enjoying its greatest commodities boom in living memory. The emergence of China since it began liberalising its economy in 1979 has been dramatic, and since about 2003 the Chinese appetite has swung the dial in terms of global demand for a range of raw materials. China, and to a lesser extent India, have had an insatiable appetite for bulk commodities, such as coking coal and iron ore; minerals, such as copper, nickel and zinc; and, more recently, soft commodities, such as wheat, rice and sugar. All of these products, especially bulk commodities, are produced at the highest quality and in significant quantities in Australia. The net result has been that demand has outstripped supply, pushing commodity prices up to levels never seen before. While commodity-based industries only employ about 5 per cent of Australians and account for 14 per cent of gross domestic product, the impact has been dramatic. The multiplier effect of the mining industry has been spectacular since 2003, with tax receipts from burgeoning company profits allowing the Howard and Rudd governments to deliver tax cuts to many ordinary Australians. This has been parlayed into a spending spree that only petered out with the onset of the GFC.

Critically, the GFC only briefly derailed Chinese economic growth and demand for commodities, allowing the mining industry to re-draft its gargantuan plans for expansion. After many delays these expansion plans—which include multi-billion dollar projects in coal seam natural gas in Queensland, and gas and iron ore expansion in Western Australia—are about to get under way. This is great news for economic activity and the income we generate from shipping our goods offshore. And it is a primary reason why it is unlikely that the Reserve Bank will cut interest rates to help most Australians, who do not work in the mining industry, to pay down their large debt burdens built up over many years from buying real estate.

But here is the thing about mining. Commodities are priced according to supply and demand fundamentals. In recent years demand has outstripped supply by a clear margin, as the Chinese finally industrialise their economy, hundreds of years after the English started the process. Supply, which has long lead times, has not been able to keep up with the surprising acceleration in demand. The GFC and the federal government mining tax has further delayed supply coming on stream, extending the price boom. However, supply will eventually come on stream and the dynamics will change. It always surprises me in the commodity game that, just as the industry achieves high prices and stunning profit margins, it races out to build more mines, which eventually crucify those lovely high prices. Alas, it is happening again and prices will fall. The best estimate for these events taking place is over 2013 and 2014, even though previous forecasts have been more optimistic.

Australia's current commodities boom is probably the biggest in history, but it is not necessarily special. Booms of this nature have happened before and will probably happen again, but they always come to an end, because of their cyclical nature. They are not the permanent fixtures that commodity bulls would like us to think, and prices will not stay high forever.

When gold was discovered in Victoria and New South Wales in the 1850s, the colonies of the yet to be formed Australia enjoyed an economic boom that made it one of the most prosperous places on Earth, easily outstripping the industrialising United States. This boom effectively lasted for 40 years. But from the mid 1890s until the Second World War, commodity prices floundered and the standard of living in Australia stalled. Luckily, since the Second World War the commodities boom flared again as countries rebuilt their damaged economies and Japan became a global powerhouse. This started to unravel in the 1970s, and a recovery did not begin until China emerged in 2003.

Just another economy

We have to remember that Australia does not have an economy characterised by depth. We are a well-educated country that is heavily dependent on the cyclical nature of commodities and housing. Real long-term economic prosperity comes not from digging products out of the ground and loading them on a boat for other people to produce products and sell them back to us. Real wealth is created by intellectual property that drives productivity. Commodity price appreciation is transitory and it is matter of when, and not if, prices turn down and a slump is on us. If this slump arrives while Australian consumers are attempting to get their balance sheets in order it could be a recipe for a major recession. Hopefully, the boom can last for many more years and China can keep on paying record prices for as far as the eye can see.

Significantly, the sharemarket will not wait until the mining boom is over. It will try to predict the end of the boom and it has a 50 per cent chance of getting it right. So a predicted downturn in commodity prices in 2013 could be reflected in share prices 12 to 18 months earlier. If this scenario does unfold it would fit neatly with our forecast of a weaker sharemarket through the course of 2012. Time will tell.

Chapter 26

Get ready to touch the sky

Can you imagine the All Ordinaries index rising 400 per cent and hitting 15 000 points in the foreseeable future? Is it possible for the Dow Jones, the barometer of economic well-being in the crumbling American empire, to power towards 100 000 points? What about the broad-based S&P 500 index trading at 10 000 points? As I sit here in mid 2011 enduring a painful bear market, it feels like these predictions have as much chance of coming true as peace in the Middle East or Tony Abbott becoming a Republican. However, when it comes to the sharemarket you should always expect the unexpected, especially when we consider the instinctive abilities of human beings to re-create and improve themselves.

When the current secular bear market finally runs out of steam, the US and Australian sharemarkets will enter a new secular bull market. There will be no transition period and stock prices will start to rise, despite most commentators and market participants being in total denial. The bear will be dominant just long enough for virtually everyone to proclaim that it is different this time and the sharemarket will never reclaim its golden days. Once the bottom has been hit and the sharemarket begins to rise, it will take a minimum of three years, and possibly up to seven, for the previous index highs to be surpassed. When the Australian and US sharemarkets hit new record highs the first recruits to the new bull market will become vocal.

With this prediction, investors who have shied away from shares in the tumultuous period since the GFC should seriously consider re-entering the game over the next 12 to 18 months. Think carefully about your approach, get to know your investment personality and implement a plan. In 10 years time you will be pleasantly surprised by how much wealth you have created.

Why can I be so confident of this outcome? The answer lies in history and how markets have behaved when secular bear markets have eventually run their course.

With this in mind we should take a close look at three of the great bull runs that have played out in the United States and Australia over the last 80 years:

- the end of the Great Depression—1942 to 1966
- the era of Bill Gates and the PC—1982 to 2000
- the Australian Economic Revolution 1992 to 2007.

This review will reveal that the US market will again post a 1000 per cent gain over a 20-year period and Australia will enjoy an extended period of above average gains—possibly for 15 years.

The end of the Great Depression

Americans had only just recovered from the pain of the Great Depression when they entered the Second World War on 7 December 1941, in response to the Japanese bombing of Pearl Harbor in Hawaii. In the early years of the war, the United States had remained in splendid isolation, preferring to profiteer from the war in Europe than commit troops to the fight. But Pearl Harbor left no other option but a call to arms.

The US sharemarket had not fared well with war erupting in Europe. The rise of Nazi Germany and Imperial Japan had been primary considerations in a major sharemarket sell off that saw the Dow Jones and broad-based S&P 500 index fall more than 50 per cent between early 1937 and early 1942. At that stage the Nazis and the Japanese both looked like they had strong chances of winning their respective battles. History shows that 1942 was the darkest hour and it was exactly then that stock prices in the United States started to rally. By the time the Second World War ended in 1945, the Dow Jones had risen a miraculous 128 per cent in just four years. The French saying, 'Buy on the cannons, sell on the trumpets', proved to be prophetic again.

Inspired by Allied victories in Europe and the Pacific, the US sharemarket paused for a few years following the war before continuing to power higher. The postwar period was a prosperous one that combined the need to rebuild whole countries ripped apart by war, and the introduction of products, such as plastics and chemicals, on a broad scale that drove productivity to new levels. From 1942 to 1966 the S&P 500 index notched up a capital gain of 971 per cent, excluding dividends (see figure 26.1). In that period of 24 years the US market experienced only one decline of more than 20 per cent as it hurtled towards highs that seemed unimaginable when American troops were sent to fight the Japanese. That was the second secular bull market of the twentieth century and the people of the developed world enjoyed stunning increases in their standards of living.

Figure 26.1: the S&P 500 index from 1942 to 1966

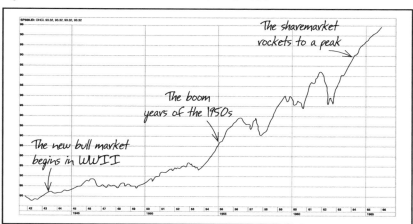

Source: IRESS

Bill Gates and IBM

The 1970s was a dismal period for Americans. The dreaded combination of high inflation and low economic growth, described as stagflation by economists, proved to be lethal for sharemarket investors. The post–Second World War party concluded with an expensive war in Vietnam and a sudden spike in the oil price. Americans had become reliant on imported oil and the decision by the OPEC countries to curtail production resulted in a sudden jump in oil prices around the globe. The price for many products that used oil or oil byproducts rose sharply producing an insidious combination of low economic growth and high inflation. Investors ran for the hills, dramatically reducing the average PE of stocks across the board. Headlines heralded the end of capitalism, and manufacturing was shipped offshore to the cheaper and more efficient Japanese. Nothing seemed to be going right, and the United States looked like losing its status as the number one country on the globe. The sharemarket, like a barometer of well-being, reflected this gloom by falling into a secular bear market that delivered negative returns from 1966 to 1982.

The election of former actor Ronald Reagan to the US presidency in late 1980 was the first step towards a new era of optimism. As Reagan settled into the White House, several other decisive events took place that would reshape both the US and the world economy over the next two decades. New FED Chairman Paul Volcker declared war on inflation by raising interest rates and forcing the country back into recession, even though it had never really recovering from the oil price spike–induced inflation of the 1970s. Unemployment soared above 10 per cent, its highest level since the 1930s, and the average American worker felt like they would never enjoy the standard of living experienced by their parents in the 1950s and 1960s. Volcker's medicine worked, though: it killed the disease of inflation and destroyed the excesses that had hampered the economy over the past decade.

Simultaneously, technology companies like IBM were successfully reducing the size of the average computer, to where eventually it would sit on every employee's desk. This permanently changed how people in the Western world worked with information and records that could be transferred between individuals and stored in the most efficient fashion ever experienced. The United States and many other Western economies were rapidly becoming service-based economies, rather than the manufacturing powerhouses of the previous decades. Soon after the arrival of the personal computer in the workplace, Bill Gates and his team at Microsoft delivered the software that not only fitted perfectly with the personal computer, but also changed forever the way humans would conduct their business.

In late 1982, the stockmarket stopped heading south and produced a stunning 65.7 per cent rally in the space of a little more than 12 months (see figure 26.2, overleaf). Most investors, jaded by the 16-year bear market, didn't see the changes that were happening and missed the first sharp leg of the upward move. A slight pull back in 1984 allowed them to get set and ride the new bull market for a 150 per cent gain over the next three and half years, before stocks were crunched by the October 1987 crash. To pinpoint a reason for the sudden collapse of share prices has been difficult, but the most likely cause was probably that share prices rose too high, too fast. In the space of just two months the Dow Jones dropped 36 per cent—but this proved to be a temporary pause in an upward march that gained stunning momentum in the late 1980s and ran all the way through to March 2000. Sure, there was a mild economic recession in the early 1990s, but this was hardly a blip on the powerful wave of optimism that took hold of the sharemarket.

The 18-year period from 1982 to 2000 delivered a capital return on the Dow Jones of 1409 per cent. This was the greatest continuous gain by the Dow Jones in the past 100 years, and that number does not include the dividends investors received. The broader S&P 500 index rose 2350 per cent over 26 years from the bottom in 1974 to the peak in March 2000. This equates to about 13 per cent per year, or about 70 per cent better than the long-term average. Both of these gains, though, were dwarfed by the colossal performance of the tech-laden Nasdaq. From the bottom of 293 after the 1987 crash to a peak of 5048 in April 2000, the Nasdaq rose 1600 per cent or about 24 per cent a year.

By the start of the new millennium, many Americans had become rich by simply playing the sharemarket, and millions of new participants entered the fray just to get a piece of the action. Of course by the time we entered the new century the party was on the brink of ending, and all those new mum and dad investors who had never experienced a bear market were in for the shock of their lives as stock prices headed down. In the case of the Nasdaq, it was a meltdown: 11 years on the index was at 2507, some 50 per cent below the peak of April 2000.

Figure 26.2: the S&P 500 index from 1982 to 2000

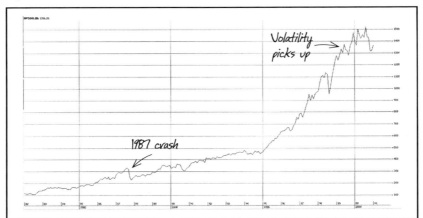

Source: IRESS

Drunk on a bug

The tremendous bull market that closed out the century went through many stages, but a consistent theme that propelled it along was a technological revolution that started with the personal computer and ended with the emergence of the internet. Productivity, the elixir of the sharemarket, made stunning gains during this 18-year period. Unfortunately, what started out as a sound and logical reason for share prices to run higher, ended with outlandish optimism and a hoax called the Y2K bug, which resulted in virtually every corporation around the globe spending excessive amounts on their systems preparing for our computers and electronic calendars to tick over into the 2000s.

Company valuations reached unprecedented levels. The average share price for the benchmark S&P 500 index rose to over 25 times prospective earnings for the first time since records were kept, and about 10 PE points higher than the long-term average. In hindsight there was only one way for stock prices to move—but somehow it caught millions of investors by surprise. Those final stages of the bull market will always be remembered by Federal Reserve chairman Alan Greenspan's comments on the market's irrational exuberance way back in 1996. At the time investors entered a short reflective period before piling in again, pushing stock prices higher for three and half more years. Eventually the bubble burst and the popping noise was heard around the globe as the United States entered the current secular bear market.

The Australian economic revolution

The seeds for the Australian bull market of 1992 to 2007 were planted in the previous decade, with the 1980s proving to be a seminal period for the Australian economy. Myriad changes took place, both domestically and abroad, which created the environment for an era of prosperity not experienced since the gold rush days of the second half of the nineteenth century. It also formed the backdrop for a secular bull market that lasted right through to November 2007.

A reformist Labor government from 1983 to 1991 turned the local economy upside down with a raft of changes that induced a productivity boom. At the core of these reforms was the introduction of a competition policy, the re-balancing of the tax base with the introduction of a capital gains tax, and the reduction of income taxes. Inflation was whipped, several years after the Americans had achieved it, by striking a wages accord with the powerful union movement, and the Australian dollar was floated to assist the country's global competitiveness.

Finally, in 1983 a national savings scheme called superannuation was put in place, which would result in millions of Australian's having some exposure to the sharemarket for the first time in their lives.

Before this, the sharemarket had been populated by people living in the well-heeled suburbs of Sydney, Melbourne and Perth.

This reformist agenda was continued into the late 1990s by the Coalition government under John Howard, whose workplace reforms drove productivity and prosperity to new levels in Australia.

Offshore, the death of Chairman Mao in China in 1976 paved the way for economic liberalisation in that country, which accelerated through the 1980s. China was effectively opening up its economy and its 1.3 billion people to the rest of the world, a move that would change the way business was done in Australia — possibly forever. China started to feverishly buy Australia's abundant natural resources, and by 2005 it was our largest and most influential trading partner.

Too much too soon

All of these measures were a boost for the sharemarket, which had bottomed in 1974 but had been hamstrung by surging inflation and doggedly high unemployment through most of the 1970s. The breaking of the drought in 1983 and the election of a new Labor government proved to be the catalysts for the sharemarket to move into overdrive. Fuel was thrown on the fire with the deregulation of the banking system, allowing foreign banks to enter the country and compete with our four big players for the first time. This provided enormous amounts of capital that had previously been unavailable, and the market raced towards its zenith in 1987. Corporations and individuals gorged on debt provided by willing banks.

The avalanche of changes, while highly beneficial for the longer run, proved too much too quickly for the Australian economy and Australian sharemarket. The October 1987 crash was the beginning of a new secular bear market in Australia (see chapter 25). Put simply, the reforms had been dramatic and sharemarket valuations had become unsustainable. Two of our four major local banks, Westpac and ANZ, got caught up in the lending spree in a bid to stave off their new foreign competitors. By 1992 both needed recapitalisation.

The platform for a new bull market

It is important that we look closely at the economic changes of the 1980s and the repair of the banking system following the early 1990s recession to understand the platform that was built for the new bull market that kicked off in late 1992. At the time Australian unemployment was hovering around 11 per cent and the heady times of the mid to late 1980s had become a distant memory.

The All Ordinaries index had been spluttering through the early part of the new decade, but like all new bull markets, it took off without warning in late 1992, climbing 67 per cent in less than 18 months to 2350. The platform for sustainable economic growth had been put in place nearly a decade before, and interest rates had been slashed in 1992 in a bid to get the economy going. Inflation was no longer the bogey man and productivity levels were surging. These favourable conditions were enhanced under the Howard government. These factors proved to be the spark that beaten-up investors needed to start buying shares again.

A pause in 1994 proved just that, and fears of another bear market were quickly dashed. Investors gathered themselves and charged back into the market, as companies, with reduced costs and resurgent revenues, clocked up impressive earnings growth and major productivity gains. Even the tech wreck that smashed the US sharemarket proved to be no more than a prolonged speed hump in Australia.

As in all good secular bull markets, there seems to be a stage when prices and valuations get out of hand. For Australia this came in the period from 2004 to late 2007, when a booming Chinese economy was the impetus for a rampant commodities market. Mining stocks across the board rocketed higher, and even when the GFC struck in the first half of 2008, it failed to knock investor belief in the Chinese juggernaut. Eventually, though, the whole market deflated like a soufflé when the enormity of the GFC became apparent in the second half of 2008, and the love affair with resources ended in divorce.

> As in all good secular bull markets, there seems to be a stage when prices and valuations get out of hand.

From the start of the bull run in late 1992 until the peak on 1 November 2007, the All Ordinaries index had risen more than

374 per cent. If you included dividends, the return was closer to a highly impressive 700 per cent.

The new bull is just around the corner

If history is an accurate forecasting tool, the current pain tormenting investors will end and a new, prosperous period of our lives will start soon. As we discussed in the previous chapter this is unlikely to happen before the end of 2012 or even the first half of 2013, but it will happen.

The arrival of the new secular bull market will not be heralded by a single pundit in its early stages. In fact, investor faith will have been shattered and a rally will be proclaimed as just another bear trap that needs to be carefully avoided. Forecasters will have become so bearish that people will be focused on how much lower the market can go. This bearish sentiment had not arrived at the beginning of 2011. An *Australian Financial Review* survey of leading stockbroking strategists in January 2011 predicted a bullish average rise of 14 per cent for the calendar year, a sure sign the bear has more time to play before it goes into hibernation. Even when the market had fallen 12 per cent by August 2011, the overall sentiment for the market remained positive with professional investors claiming this was a great buying opportunity.

So what does all this mean? I believe that some time in 2013, the US sharemarket will begin a new secular bull market that should last for somewhere between 15 and 25 years. The gain will be in the range of 500 and 1500 per cent. If we take the average of this wide range, the Dow Jones should almost hit the 100 000 point mark in about 20 years from 2011. In Australia, the new bull market could well kick off around the same time, and the All Ordinaries index should be able to rise fourfold to about 15 000 by 2026. Let's hope Mark Twain's comment that 'history does not repeat itself, but it does rhyme', has proved true again.

The plight of the US sharemarket

All this is exceedingly difficult to see at this point in sharemarket and economic cycles. The US economy is labouring under a mountain of public debt, and its global hegemony is under threat from China, the world's most populous nation. The engine room of world economic growth is switching from North America to Central and South-East Asia at a pace that seemed improbable five or six years ago. So how can the US sharemarket shrug off these issues and resume its upward trajectory, which has been in train for 200 years, despite the odd decade or two of secular bear markets?

The first element that we cannot forget is the continuing dominance of the US sharemarket. While the US economy has fallen from close to 25 per cent of the world economy to around 19 per cent in recent decades, its sharemarket is still close to 30 per cent of the listed world. The rising powers of China and India have relatively immature stockmarkets that are trailing well behind the size of their respective economies. This could change with time but, as we have witnessed, the British sharemarket remains relevant despite that country's diminishing role as an economy. Therefore, a prosperous economic period is more likely to be reflected and measured by the US sharemarket rather than an alternative for some years to come.

Value will emerge

If my prediction of a final downward stumble does eventuate, and the S&P 500 index in the United States sinks below 1000 points again over the next 18 months, the obvious catalyst for a nascent bull market will be extreme value. Companies across America have been frugal in the current economic crises, acting as they always do, concentrating on preserving and enhancing the bottom line rather than considering larger issues, such as employment. This means that, even at current levels, the US sharemarket is not expensive. Extremely low valuation has the ability to drive the sharemarket higher for an extended period, allowing the emerging underlying trends to become apparent. In other words the real drivers of the longer term secular bull market may not be known to the investing public until 2016 or possibly 2017.

Housing

In the five-year period 2012–17, the United States must have worked its way through its housing crisis, which has seen price declines of

33 per cent; a figure not recorded even in the 1930s. With the excess supply of houses not expected to be whittled away until 2014, this is a genuine possibility. As we commented earlier, the consumer still represents more than 65 per cent of US gross domestic product, and a housing recovery could well kick start that part of the economy, which has been shackled since 2006.

Killing the debt burden

By the middle of this decade, the federal government will have to prove it has the ability to amortise its $14 trillion worth of debts. I get the feeling there will be little if any headway on the federal debt until the next presidential election is completed in November 2012. This belief stems from the political stalemate between conservative Republicans and liberal Democrats that failed to resolve the issue before the country's debt was downgraded by ratings agency Standard & Poor's in August 2011. At some stage soon a belligerent program must be implemented that will see the nation's revenue base expanded and costs curtailed. To keep on building the debt mountain just to avoid another recession is a sure way to permanently impair America's standard of living. While all this fiscal austerity is taking place historically, today's loose monetary policy will have to be tightened by the FED, ending years of overspending. The FED has made it clear it is not prepared to take this step until 2013 at the earliest.

Notably, the American household has started its long journey of repairing its own balance sheet. Unlike the federal government, the Federal Reserve and Wall Street, the American consumer has risen to the challenge and clearly understands that it must pay down its debts or face an even tougher future.

At the centre of a new secular bull market will be new inventions that allow productivity to surge. In the past, this has been the railways, the car, the airplane, chemicals, plastics, the personal computer and, more recently, the internet. What will be the invention at the heart of the next leap in economic opulence is virtually impossible to predict, but the lead candidate must be a drive into alternative clean energy, a sector that has much attention and ample capital.

Embracing the new world

Finally, for the US sharemarket to enter a new secular bull market it has to be the barometer for world growth rather than just for the world's biggest economy. At some stage in the next 30 years, the Chinese economy will surpass the United States as the world's largest. If India can keep up its current economic growth rates, it will also eventually overtake the American economy. On the bright side, this will create a much larger economic world, and companies across the United States should enjoy tapping the emergence of middle class people in volumes never experienced before.

Political risk

The greatest risk to the next secular bull market is unlikely to be financial or economic matters. The biggest hurdle to overcome is more likely to be political, as the world enters a new era of two super powers, a situation not seen since the late 1980s when the Soviet Union crumbled under the burden of excessive debts. China is already joining the United States as a second super power, and with India quickly rising, a three way tussle might eventuate over the next 20 to 30 years. History indicates that two super powers find it difficult to coexist peacefully.

With the United States floundering under a truck load of debt it remains highly fragile and susceptible to a challenge that it would not take very kindly to. Let's hope the United States sorts itself out and a period of economic growth and prosperity drowns out the need for individual countries to impose themselves on their regions or around the globe.

Australia and a recession

The Australian sharemarket will probably shake off the secular bear market that began in November 2007 in the traditional way—the Reserve Bank (RBA) cutting official interest rates. In mid 2011, the Australian economy is in a dramatically different part of the economic cycle than the United States. Following the stockmarket crash of 2008 and the GFC, the RBA cut interest rates in a stunning fashion—mostly as insurance against the worst impacts of the GFC infiltrating the Australian banking system. At the time the federal government also felt the need to help out by guaranteeing retail bank deposits and lending its AAA credit rating to anyone with a banking licence. All of these policies proved vital in keeping the local economy out of recession.

However, once it became apparent that Australia would avoid the worst of the GFC, the RBA was swift to lift official interest rates. It was particularly concerned about rising home prices and tightness in the labour market. It was, and it remains, cognisant of the current immense capital expenditure program in the energy and mining sectors, especially in liquefied natural gas and iron ore. More than $100 billion worth of capital projects are expected to be implemented over the next few years, with mining investment forecast to rise from 3 per cent of gross domestic product to 6 per cent by the end of 2012.

It would seem that the RBA is content to keep interest rates at higher levels. Not only is this insurance against the possibility of elevated inflation from the mining boom, but it is also a means of rebalancing the economy. The RBA knows that Australian house prices are high in terms of average incomes and also compared with homes in other Western countries. A gentle multi-year adjustment of house prices would be perfect for the RBA, which has been overjoyed by the events of 2011, in which residential property prices have fallen by about 5 per cent. This would be a major coup for the RBA, because history shows this rarely happens.

Tight economic settings have been enhanced by the federal government's desire to balance its budget. One would expect the government to persist with this rhetoric until close to the next election, or if the economy does start to reverse. For now, though, the aim is to cut spending and produce a fiscal surplus.

Mums and dads saving for the future

Can Australia's policy makers pull it off? I'm betting against it. The average Australian household is behaving in a most peculiar way. Australians are saving a whopping 10 per cent of their incomes—more than their American counterparts—despite not having experienced a recession, let alone a crippling one. This is the highest savings level since the early 1990s, when a brutal economic downturn was taking place. Most experts are flummoxed by the behaviour of Australian households and can only put it down to a combination of conservative banking policies and the fear spread by the popular media about the GFC and the crash of the sharemarket. I believe it is a natural reversion to the mean, as shareholders pay for the spending binge they went on for more than a decade leading up to 2008. The RBA seems content, and so they should be, for households to save their money and repair their balance sheets. In the long term this has to be a positive consequence of the GFC.

The downside to all this economic sobriety is that weak consumer spending has multiplier effects that are just starting to be felt by the broader economy. Companies, always slow to react, will start to pare back their capital expenditure programs and attempt to cut costs. This means unemployment will begin to rise from its current historically low 4.9 per cent. Eventually, a recession will prevail and the RBA will bin its concerns about inflation and aim to stimulate the economy by cutting official interest rates. This is a tool that is still available to the central bank, in a way that it is not for its US counterpart.

Adding to all this woe is a persistently high Australian dollar that is playing a major role in making our exports expensive and less competitive. This is another handbrake on the economy and one the RBA has little say in at the moment, as the United States keeps its currency weak with low interest rates and excessive public spending.

What does all this mean for the Australian sharemarket? The All Ordinaries index, which has struggled to break through the 5000 mark since the GFC, shows that investors are concerned about the state of the economy and the prospects for company earnings growth. The All Ordinaries has underperformed the US and European markets, despite the country having avoided a recession. I would imagine the market will fall further into 2012, making it cheap in historical and relative terms. If at that stage the RBA comes to the party with a decision to cut interest rates, the sharemarket will break its shackles and start to move higher.

Future winners

I am a strong believer that the underperformers of the past decade will be the winners in the decade ahead. At the top of this list would be the industrial component of the sharemarket. This sector — which includes Wesfarmers, Woolworths, Lend Lease, CSR, Fosters and Amcor — has posted a negative return over the last 10 years and is currently trading on generational low PE ratios. With the advent of low interest rates and higher domestic growth, especially from the housing sector, in 2013 and 2014 the friendless industrial stocks should start to gain investor support. Some time following this you should see the banking sector return to higher growth levels, followed by the much maligned property trust index. Importantly, none of these trends should become apparent for several years, well after the sharemarket has bottomed and started to rally simply because stocks are cheap and everyone who wants to sell has sold.

In contrast, the darling of the last decade, the mining sector, faces the possibility of some major headwinds. The All Materials index has posted a gain of more than 250 per cent over the last 10 years, a stunning performance given the deflation of asset prices around the globe. China has been like the fat kid at the party, with an insatiable appetite for raw materials. Chinese growth, despite the best efforts from authorities, will have a major hiccup at some stage and economic growth will ease. Longer term, though, China will need to rebalance its own economy away from one obsessed with spending money on capital items to one in which the consumer plays a larger role. This should take place gradually over the next decade, when the demand for raw materials produced in Australia will ease. Once again this may not be obvious in the next year or so, but it will play out over a longer period and the sharemarket will not wait until it actually happens.

EPILOGUE:
OUR FORMER CROUPIER

It will be interesting to see if Peter Proksa can handle a new bull market. Our former croupier went on a seesawing ride before he eventually conquered many of his investment demons by coming up with a set of ground rules to work within. These rules, or parameters if you prefer, were born out of tough and desperate times. He faced a near-death experience on more than one occasion, steeling him for action. Critically, he realised there was no upside in keeping at risk forever his hard-won gains from a single investment. He eventually concluded the better approach was to protect some of his capital by selling a percentage of a winning investment—at least the dollar value originally outlaid—and then let the rest run until the situation changed. This one strategic change might just stop him from hitting the skids again.

But a bull market is completely different. Because the undercurrent becomes so strong and the winnings so effortless, it is easy to drop your guard and become lazy. I know in the boom days of 2003 to 2007 at Wilson Asset Management we ended up with stocks that nine times out of ten we would not have considered in the past. The idea that you can make money regardless of the quality of the stock at times infiltrates your process. Eventually this lazy approach can catch up with you, making bull markets almost as dangerous as the bear we are currently grinding our way through. When your portfolio is loaded with stocks bought on a whim, a slight downturn in sentiment can wipe out your gains in a matter of months. I can normally tell that I have let my structure and discipline slide when a series of mining exploration, biotech and high PE stocks appear in my portfolio. In the two financial years that the WAM Capital portfolio underperformed the overall market—2004–05 and 2008–09—these types of stocks had become far too prevalent in our portfolio. I had broken my own set of rules because I got carried away with the moment.

Peter's desire to protect some of his capital instead of risking it every day was borne out in his comments that he was suspicious of overall market trends back in May 2011. Hopefully, he listened to his newfound caution and sold down his portfolio to raise some cash, limiting the damage from the 20 per cent decline by the Australian market in July and August.

The bull market also presents other dilemmas for Peter. It may become difficult to find opportunities to buy stocks that trade at 1 cent or less, when most stocks are trading higher in an improved economic environment and investor optimism. The key for Peter is to stick to the rules that he put in place in 2010 following several disasters. These rules should protect the downside, allowing the upside to take care of itself. If Peter—or any of us for that matter—can achieve this goal, the returns will be stunning.

Peter must also stick to what suits his flamboyant personality. When a bull market picks up a head of steam, the opportunities on offer become so enticing that people can start to behave well outside the parameters of their personalities, setting themselves up for a fall. The spruikers Peter discovered back in 1999 when he was working the tables at Crown Casino will reappear. They will try to seduce him with marvellous new stories that seem just too good to pass up. These people and their claims must be viewed with caution, or Peter may find himself stuck with a handful of stocks that are sinking quicker than a stone, just like in 2000 and 2008. These bull market peddlers will be even more dangerous this time around, appearing not just in person but on your internet screen, blogging their uninformed views to hundreds and thousands of readers.

That said, Peter and I, and all those other investors out there, will be cheering in the new era when it eventually arrives. Bring on 2013.

FINAL WORD

The sharemarket is a dynamic and evolving entity. When I completed the manuscript for *Bulls, Bears and a Croupier* in mid-July 2011, the benchmark Australian index, the All Ordinaries, was trading at around 4600 points. As you can glean from the text of the book, I was bearish about the near- to medium-term for the Australian market. To put this into context, I believed that the sharemarket would drift lower over the rest of 2011 and for most of 2012. The most likely outcome was that the index would bottom out at around 3500 points late in 2012 or possibly early 2013. Clearly, I was too cautious. Within the space of three weeks the sharemarket fell a hefty 550 points, or 12 per cent. Since then share prices have bounced but as I write this postscript in September 2011 the market is floundering at 4200, still 9 per cent off its July position and some 16 per cent off the high reached in April 2011.

The catalyst for the latest down draft was threefold — renewed uncertainty about the growth prospects for the US economy, the worsening sovereign debt crises in Europe and a slowing Chinese economy. These three events conspired to panic investors into a selling frenzy during early August that took the sharemarket from the middle of the newspapers to the front page. Unfortunately, none of these issues are close to resolution.

So what now? The overall theme that the sharemarket will head lower is still intact. What has possibly changed is the time in which the market will take to reach its ultimate low. The recent dramatic sell-off potentially means that a bottom and (quite possibly) the end of the secular bear market currently hitting investors may arrive sooner than the end of 2012. I still believe that the low will see the All Ordinaries hit 3500, but the severity of the situation will sting authorities into remedial action.

The European sovereign debt crisis is approaching flashpoint, and there is a strong chance the authorities will need to start printing money to avoid a broad-based banking collapse. This would mimic the actions of the US Federal Reserve after the GFC in 2008. Indeed this measure may have been implemented by the time you read this book.

Just as crucially, the latest stagnation in US growth will almost certainly provoke a policy reaction from the Federal Reserve and Washington. This stimulus may build a bridge for the private sector to jolt out of neutral and into gear in 2013 or, at the latest, 2014. At the centre of this private sector revival will be a renewal of bank lending growth and the start of the long awaited improvement in the housing market.

China is much more problematic. That country is suffering from short-term inflation pressures and the looming crises of too much spending on capital items. It is quite possible that the second biggest economy in the world may be on the precipice of a major economic malaise. Time will tell.

What does all this mean for Australia? The direction of the sharemarket will primarily be decided by the machinations of the northern hemisphere, in particular the US, which still accounts for 30 per cent of the world equity markets. As I have indicated, I would imagine the US sharemarket will head lower over the course of the next six to 12 months punctuated by short sharp rallies that peter out. Economically, the Australia economy will continue to slow in the first half of 2012 and any kickback will heavily depend on when the Reserve Bank of Australia decides to pull the trigger on cutting interest rates. If it waits until early 2012 the economy won't find its legs until late 2012.

This all sounds terribly depressing. However, it is my belief that we are quickly approaching the end of the current secular bear market. My original prediction of late 2012 or early 2013 may have been dragged forward four to six months due to the turmoil of recent months. If the All Ordinaries does sink to somewhere around 3500 then history tells us that it will take around four years for the market to regain its old high of 6873. That still takes us out to 2016. In other words, the market would have nearly doubled in the space of four years, clocking up annual gains of close to 20 per cent for that period. In the current economic and political climate this prediction seems like folly. However, the sharemarket will hit bottom and would have been rising for the best part of 12 months, possibly two years, before the real world economy seemingly rights itself.

I am firmly convinced that once a new high is reached in 2016 or thereabouts the sharemarket will continue to surge higher, as the next great secular bull market grips the investing world. Don't give up, just be prepared.

Matthew Kidman

September 2011

INDEX

Index

Index